iDisorder

iDisorder

UNDERSTANDING OUR OBSESSION
WITH TECHNOLOGY AND
OVERCOMING ITS HOLD ON US

Larry D. Rosen, Ph.D.

WITH

Nancy A. Cheever, Ph.D.

L. Mark Carrier, Ph.D.

palgrave
macmillan

iDISORDER
Copyright © Larry D. Rosen, 2012.
All rights reserved.

First published in hardcover in 2012 by PALGRAVE MACMILLAN® in
the US—a division of St. Martin's Press LLC, 175 Fifth Avenue, New York,
NY 10010.

Where this book is distributed in the UK, Europe and the rest of the world,
this is by Palgrave Macmillan, a division of Macmillan Publishers Limited,
registered in England, company number 785998, of Houndmills, Basingstoke,
Hampshire RG21 6XS.

Palgrave Macmillan is the global academic imprint of the above companies
and has companies and representatives throughout the world.

Palgrave® and Macmillan® are registered trademarks in the United States,
the United Kingdom, Europe and other countries.

ISBN: 978-1-137-27831-9

Library of Congress Cataloging-in-Publication Data

Rosen, Larry D.
   iDisorder : understanding our obsession with technology and overcoming
its hold on us / Larry D. Rosen, Ph.D.
      p.   cm.
   ISBN 978–0–230–11757–0 (hardback)
   1. Information technology—Psychological aspects. 2. Internet addiction.
I. Title.
T58.5.R667   2012
303.48'3—dc23

2011037963

A catalogue record of the book is available from the British Library.

Design by Letra Libre Inc.

First PALGRAVE MACMILLAN paperback edition: August 2013

10 9 8 7 6 5 4 3 2 1

Printed in the United States of America.

Contents

Dedication

[LR]: To my parents, Oscar and Sarah, and to Steve Jobs, a true American legend without whom there would be no little "i."

[NC]: To my parents, for teaching me the value of hard work, independence, and delayed gratification!

[LMC]: To A. and M., for endlessly listening to me talk about "the book." It always seems like it will never be done. (P.S. You're in the book!)

Acknowledgements

I cannot express how important my friendships and working relationships are with Dr. Mark Carrier and Dr. Nancy Cheever. This book is a group effort. We worked together and I know that it is better because we are all different in our approach to writing and research. I am the detail guy who revels in technical writing and in doing statistics. Mark is the big picture guy who asks the tough questions, often coming from a theoretical point of view that I have not thought through. Nancy is the writing wizard who can tell in a snap if something needs to be rewritten. I am proud to call them both my friends.

I am able to research the "psychology of technology" and write books solely because of everybody affiliated with the George Marsh Applied Cognition (GMAC) Laboratory at California State University, Dominguez Hills. Mark, Nancy, and I created this lab several years ago, finding a few dollars here for computers and a few there for supplies. Our campus has been particularly helpful by allowing us to gain incentives from teaching large courses and affording us the time to mentor 10 undergraduate students each year. Thanks in particular to Dean Laura Robles, past dean Chuck Hohm, the McNair Scholar's Program, and the MBRS-RISE Program for making this possible. A special thanks to all of the GMACers past and present (in alphabetical order): Michelle Albertella, Murat Arikan, Jyenny Babcock, Joanne Barba, Sandra Benitez, Vanessa Black, Lyzette Blanco, John Bunce, Norma Castillo, Jennifer Chang, Amber Chavez, Cheyenne Cummings, Lynne Erwin, Julie Felt, Esbeyde Garcia, Izabela Grey, Helen Gutierrez, Tristan Hahn, Mike Kersten, Alex Lim, Roxanne Luna, Scott Mariano, Stephen McGee, Saira Rab, Julia Rifa, B.B. Rush, Alex Spradlin, Brittany Tillman, Erika Torres, Leslie Vasquez, Ludivina Vasquez, Kelly Whaling, and Dr. Cheryl Wolcott.

Amazingly, this is my fifth book and it is only possible because I have an extremely supportive family, including my partner, Vicki Nevins, Ph.D., my parents, Oscar and Sarah Rosen, my sister and brother-in-law, Judy and Michael Heumann, my brother and sister-in-law, Bruce and Liane Rosen, and, of course, my children, Adam Rosen (and his new bride, Farris, who is expecting my second grandchild at the publication date of this book), Farris' daughter Jacqueline (Adam, thanks for marrying Farris and giving me a built-in teenage grandchild in Jacqueline), Arielle Rosen, Chris Weil (and his partner, Tiffany Burke) and Kaylee Weil (who will be graduating from Yale in June). My friends—Bob Indseth, Dr. Sandy Kaler, Dr. Phyllisann Maguire, Wendy Golden—are also always there for me, and I know that I would be less of a person without them. Also, a special thanks to George Walker for inviting me to join his wine-making club.

I cannot say enough about those around me who are dedicated to making my books better. Stacey Glick, my agent at Dystel & Goderich Literary Management, has gone to bat for me more times than I can count. My editor, Laurie Harting, is always there for me even when I ask the same questions over and over again. Alan Bradshaw, who shepherded this book and the previous ones through the production process, is always calm and reassuring and seems to be online at any given time of day to respond to my confusing messages. Thanks also to Jen Simington, who copyedited the manuscript and made it better.

As I was putting the finishing touches on this book, the world lost a legendary genius, Steve Jobs. I was an early geek and started using personal computers when the TRS-80 hit the shelves. But once I got a taste of an Apple IIe and then a Mac, there was no turning back. I was hooked on Apple. Steve Jobs, with his products constructed with the user firmly in mind, is responsible for changing the technology landscape and facilitating dramatic changes in our values and beliefs about what technology should be and what it should do for us. We have gained an "i" in our vocabulary but lost an irreplaceable hero of the people.

ONE

iDisorder

Why Are We All Acting Crazy?

It has become appallingly obvious that our technology has exceeded our humanity.

—Albert Einstein

If it keeps up, man will atrophy all his limbs but the push-button finger.

—Frank Lloyd Wright

Einstein and Wright had some pretty strong thoughts about technology, thoughts that are particularly prescient since they were uttered decades before the invention of the Internet, the smartphone, and the iPad. Consider the following all-too-typical scenario. The other night I went out to dinner and a movie. Dinner was at a popular local restaurant known for its seafood and casual ambiance. As the waitress led us to our table, I couldn't help but notice how nearly every single person had a cell phone lying flat on the table right next to their dinner plate. Literally, it seemed as though most people were eating fish with a side of smartphone. As we ordered and ate I watched diners continuously pick up the phones, tap some keys, and put them back down, only to repeat the same action again and again. Younger people appeared to do this more often, but nearly everyone, young and old, picked up their phone at least once during the meal. It felt a little like I was watching a room full of people engaging in obsessive-compulsive behaviors.

We arrived at the movie early enough to watch the previews, and the theater was packed. During the previews I realized that again nearly everyone had a cell phone in their hand and nearly all were actively engaged with their devices—I could see quite a few glowing screens in front of me displaying text messages, e-mail messages, websites, and other unrecognizable small video images. The final preview screen asked patrons to please turn off their phones and I did so and put my phone away in my pocket. Ten minutes into the movie the woman in front of me pulled out her phone, tapped some keys, and sent a text as a man next to her appeared miffed. After she did it twice more in a matter of a minute, the man tapped her on the shoulder and quietly and politely asked her to please turn off her phone. She looked at him as though he were asking her to do something so horrific that she couldn't comprehend his request. A few rows ahead a young man checked his phone every 30 seconds or so as though waiting for an important message. I would guess that at least one in four people used their phone during the movie, some continuously. When the movie ended nearly every single person immediately pulled out their phone, even before the credits started rolling, and scrolled through whatever it was that they had missed over the last 90 minutes. If I didn't know better I would say that many of the moviegoers were suffering from some form of attention-deficit disorder.

Back in the mid-1990s, when the Internet was just starting to become popular, I wrote a book about fighting *TechnoStress*. I followed that up with a book on how to parent high-tech kids during the MySpace craze and then wrote about how to educate our iGeneration teens and children using Web 2.0 tools. In all this, I started to see a pattern: Every year a bevy of new gadgets, apps, and other technological innovations appears and immediately becomes part of our common language. Look at all those technologies that did not exist a mere five to ten years ago and are now part of our normal everyday lexicon: Twitter, Facebook, iPad, and more. In 2008, the New Oxford American Dictionary's number one new word was *hypermiling* (driving your car to maximize fuel economy) but in the top ten were *tweet, moofer, link baiting,* and *overshare,* all technology-related terms. In 2009, *unfriend* was the number one new word, and four other tech words were in the top ten (*netbook, hashtag, sexting,* and *intexticated*). In 2010, the word of the year was *refudiate,* which came from a Sarah Palin–tweeted shortening of the words *refute* and *repudiate,* followed by *retweet* and *webisode.* The bottom line is that we are seeing more new technologies each year, and we are rapidly making those technologies—and their descriptors—part of contemporary society.[1]

Where does this rapid influx of technology leave us as we cruise into the second decade of the new millennium? Consider the following scenarios:

- A young adult receives a Facebook post that carries a mild put-down and lashes back with a barrage of insults. The exchange carries on for days with escalating nasty posts.
- A college student leaves home and is almost to campus before discovering that she left her cell phone at home. She immediately drives home and back again at the expense of missing her first class.
- A businessman continually checks his BlackBerry at the dinner table, ignoring questions from his wife and children.
- A mom calls her 11-year-old son to dinner a dozen times with no response only to find him firmly planted in front of his Wii, seemingly deaf to her exhortations.
- A young woman watches hours of television shows featuring young, svelte, good-looking actresses and reality television stars, and diets excessively trying to make her body look "perfect."
- A middle-aged man clicks on one of his son's Facebook friends' photos and spends hours jumping from one page to another looking at the pictures.
- An elderly woman wanting information about her continually aching leg muscles joins an online discussion group called "real limb pain" and brings reams of printouts to her doctor to convince him that she has a variety of diseases from gout to cancer.
- A high school student is studying for his final in history and continues to switch his focus with almost no conscious control from reading the textbook to Facebook back to reading a few

sentences and then to an IM conversation, music on his iPod, a reality TV show, and his cell phone.

All of these are familiar scenarios that are repeated across the world. But if we saw two young adults screaming insults at each other or a businessman continually checking work papers at dinner and ignoring his family, you most likely would say that those people had a problem, perhaps even a psychological disorder. Yet these examples are neither uncommon nor are they evidence of a certified diagnostic psychiatric condition. What we are looking at is a new disorder, one that combines elements of many psychiatric maladies and is centered on the way we all relate to technology and media: an iDisorder.

In this groundbreaking book, I, along with my colleagues Dr. Nancy Cheever and Dr. L. Mark Carrier, will take you through some of the more common psychiatric disorders—communication disorders (including aspects of antisocial personality disorder, social phobia, autism, and Asperger's syndrome), attention-deficit hyperactivity disorder, depression, obsessive-compulsive disorder, narcissistic personality disorder, hypochondriasis, schizoaffective and schizotypal disorders, body dysmorphia, voyeurism, and addiction—and provide evidence from up-to-date research in a variety of fields ranging from psychology to neuroscience, from sociology to anthropology, from communication to biology, to show you how we are all manifesting the symptoms of these serious disorders.

I am not anti-technology. Far from it. I have always been an early adopter, starting back in the 1970s, when computer technology began to make inroads into our lives. I have owned at least a dozen computers, from my first TRS-80 to more PCs than I can count. I carry a smartphone and an iPad and spend hours texting my kids and friends.

The argument that I will make is that overreliance on gadgets and websites has created an enmeshed relationship with technology and that this relationship can cause significant problems in our psyche, what I call an iDisorder. I will also argue that we are being compelled to use technologies that are so user friendly that the very use fosters our obsessions, dependence, and stress reactions. I will paint you a picture of a population driven to an iDisorder, and I will show how we all need to be aware of our relationship with technology in order to avoid being pulled into a world of button clicks, finger swipes, and glowing screens.

ARE WE ALL CRAZY?

According to recent statistics from the National Institute of Mental Health,[2] a whopping 46 percent of American adults will suffer from a psychological disorder in their lifetime; an equal percentage of children and adolescents will also experience bouts of anxiety, attention-deficit hyperactivity disorder (ADHD), or some other psychological malady. I am not arguing that we are all crazy and technology is to blame. I find, however, that our actions and behaviors when we use technology make us *appear* out of control. And I have to wonder whether all this technology is actually helping or hurting us.

We can't ignore our phones even as we're driving a car, walking, eating a meal, or talking to a friend. We can't do seemingly simple activities without first consulting the Internet. We can't tear ourselves away from the highly addictive, highly compelling world of cyberspace. As you will see in the following chapters, we are, according to the signs and symptoms in the current American Psychiatric Association's *Diagnostic and Statistical Manual (DSM-IV-TR)*,[3] suffering from several clinical and personality disorders along what are known as Axis I, or mood disorders (e.g., depression, ADHD, schizophrenia), and Axis II, or personality disorders (e.g., antisocial personality disorder, narcissistic personality disorder, obsessive-compulsive personality disorder).

In the next ten chapters I will explore some of the most common psychiatric disorders and show solid research that demonstrates how the technologies that we use daily coerce us to act in ways that may be detrimental to our well-being. I will also show you—through a variety of sound psychological perspectives and theories—why I think that happens. Finally, in each chapter I will provide you with straightforward strategies to reduce and even eliminate the symptoms. I am not proposing that you give up all technology and media, not even for a day. That's not possible. We are way past the point of no return. But it is not too late to recognize the craziness that technology *can* promote and discover new ways to stay sane in a world that encourages—and even promotes—insanity.

MY PERSPECTIVE

One of the strengths of this book is that I come from a psychological perspective that integrates theory surrounding the psychological impact of technology and scientific research demonstrating how specific media and technologies can and do promote mental imbalance. I began my scientific research in the early 1980s as one of the first psychologists to examine reactions to new technologies. I first studied computerphobia in the 1980s, then switched to technophobia in the early 1990s, when our world changed drastically with the introduction of the Internet and, more specifically, the increasing popularity of the World Wide Web in the mid-1990s. As I continued my research I soon realized that what emerged was not a contained, specific phobia like agoraphobia or arachnophobia, but rather an ongoing state of anxiety that I termed *TechnoStress*.[4]

Fast forward to the end of the millennium and we began to see the emergence of mobile technologies, including laptops and cell phones, which would prove to be the root cause of an impending major societal change. No longer did we face most of our technology in the home or the workplace. Now we carried it with us wherever we went and consulted it for a variety of purposes. No longer did technology make us anxious—in fact, quite the opposite. We came to depend on it. We were happily traipsing down the road to an iDisorder.

Don't doubt that many of us suffer from an iDisorder. It is unavoidable, as you will see in this book. It is not fatal and we are not doomed to spend time in a mental institution or a rehab center (although there are hundreds of these designed to treat Internet addiction all over the world). With a few simple strategies we can safely emerge from our TechnoCocoons[5] and rejoin the world of the healthy.

As I prepared to write this book I realized that while we had done a hefty amount of research on issues pertaining to the impact of technology

and media on parenting, education, generational similarities and differences, and cognition, we had not specifically studied psychiatric disorders
and their relationship to our connected behavior in our wired world.[6] So, in
early 2011, using anonymous, online surveys, my colleagues and I administered a well-respected test of psychiatric disorders[7] to survey more than 750
teens and adults and examined the relationship between their psychological status and their use of media and technology.[8] On the technology front
we asked our participants—who ranged in age from young teens to adults
in their seventies—how many hours a day they are: online, on a computer
but not online, texting, making and receiving phone calls, joining instant
message (IM) conversations, watching television, listening to music, sending and receiving e-mail, and playing video games. Given the popularity of
social networks, we also asked how often they used Facebook, MySpace,
and Twitter and, at a more detailed level, how often they read Facebook
postings, posted status updates, and posted photos, and how they felt about
offering self-revelations and gaining social support online. In addition, we
asked our participants about their attitudes toward technology, including:
how often they kept up with new technology; how often they checked in
with their technologies; how much anxiety they had about being away from
their gadgets; how they went about personalizing their phones and computers; and how much they relied on computerized assistance in order to
work effectively. Finally, given the research we have done in the past on
multitasking,[9] we asked about people's preferences for multitasking versus
focusing on a single task at a time.

In all, the 766 participants included 85 Baby Boomers, 118 Gen Xers
(born between 1965 and 1979), 409 members of the Net Generation (1980–
1989), and 154 iGeneration teenagers[10] (1990–1998). The group was well
represented by different ethnic and cultural backgrounds from urban and
suburban Southern California and had a range of education levels, occu-
pations, socioeconomic statuses, and living situations. As with most of our
large-scale survey studies, the sample represented the Southern California
census figures.

The purpose of the study, as I stated earlier, was to determine whether
the level of someone's psychological health might be related to his or her
use of technology. With this in mind, we examined those variables that might

predict poor or good mental health from among a variety of technologies and media as well as attitudes and beliefs. In all analyses we attempted to be fair and reasonable in our conclusions by first eliminating (statistically) any possible confounding variables including gender, age, socioeconomic status, education, living situation, and ethnic or cultural background, all of which can be related to both technology use and mental health.

A SNEAK PREVIEW

Although I will cover data relevant to specific disorders in each chapter, I would like to offer you a sneak preview. Based on our data, certain technologies appear to be related to certain psychological disorders. For example, those people who spend their days sending and receiving e-mail messages demonstrate many of the signs and symptoms of narcissistic personality disorder. Taken alone, this may not tell the whole picture. However, when you add in that narcissists are also more likely to use their cell phones for both talking and texting, spend more time on Facebook uploading more personal photos and updating their page constantly with status posts, are more likely to personalize their technology (e.g., naming their car, talking to their GPS as though it were a real person), and become more anxious and nervous when not able to check texts, phone messages, and Facebook posts, it all begins to paint a complex but understandable picture of how technology is leading many of us to our own personal iDisorder.

Similarly, those people who spend more time on Facebook or video gaming are more likely to develop a major, multi-symptomatic iDisorder than those who spend less time social networking or battling alien enemies on their home gaming system. Other technologies, such as sending and receiving e-mail or watching television, are also related to certain specific disorders.

WHY NOW?

What is it about twenty-first-century technologies that lead to this precipitous condition? In my opinion, it is a complex interplay between the technology and our own human needs that provide the cues for our maladaptive behaviors. For one, you may notice that your interactions with people are no longer face to face or even by telephone; the majority of your interactions are likely now occurring through electronic connections. These e-communications have five very critical features that can compel us to act in ways that we would not contemplate if our conversational partner (or partners, in the case of social networking or other virtual online sharing vehicles) were right there beside us in the flesh:

1.   They are simple and easy to use.
2.   They exploit our senses by drawing us toward their appealing and entrancing brilliant visual displays and crystal clear sounds.
3.   They make us feel as though we are anonymous since nobody can see us.
4.   They exploit the fact that any communication without physical cues allows us to feel unencumbered and unconcerned about the impact we are having on the human being receiving our message.
5.   They are *always* available through many devices.

Each of these is a major factor in empowering technology to march us directly to our own personal iDisorder. Our devices are becoming a transparent part of our world. A cell phone used to be a luxury with complex buttons (who knew ten years ago that to make a call you pressed "send"?) and an expensive calling plan. Now nearly everyone in the world has one,[11] and they have gone from extravagant devices to appendages. As smartphones replace flip cell phones these devices will become even more a part of our 24/7 world. According to a 2011 study of more than 3,500 people from 1,100 large corporations worldwide, 61 percent of those surveyed keep their cell phone in the bedroom and more than four in ten have it within arm's reach while they sleep. If you just look at the Net Generation employees, those figures shoot up to 77 percent and 60 percent, respectively. Those who keep their phone close to the bed are 60 percent more likely than average to wake during the night and check their phones.[12]

On a purely sensory basis, technology is extremely clever in exploiting our human desire for clear visual and auditory information. In my most recent book, *Rewired: Understanding the iGeneration and the Way They Learn,*[13] I presented a model based on the realism of simulated environments to explain why multi-sensory educational tools are superior for engaging students. For example, a classroom lecture can be more engaging than a dry textbook if the teacher is good at delivering the information and uses an array of possible technologies. Add in a YouTube video and students are more engaged. Now provide the same information through a video game and you can exploit an environment that taps into the two major senses as well as the tactile/kinesthetic system incorporating touch and motion. Now graduate to a multi-user virtual environment such as an interactive, immersive online role-playing game or a virtual world such as Second Life and you have added a simulated 3-D effect, making the learning more engaging and more real. The motive behind the recent bevy of 3-D movies is to attract and engage young people and persuade them to leave their world of Facebook and YouTube and get a better experience, a more engaging experience.

WE ARE ALL FEELING ANONYMOUS

You have just stayed in a hotel with dirty floors and a lack of clean towels. You gleefully write a scathing review, give the hotel zero stars, and think nothing of the reaction that the management might have about your experience. Why? Because you are anonymous. They don't know you and can't find you hiding behind your clever username of Softball_guy22 or BeachGirl18. What you say cannot come back to haunt you.

Now consider your behavior when you write an e-mail to someone to complain about their behavior. Perhaps your friend forgot your birthday or your neighbor's dog tore up your roses. Do you feel like you are anonymous even though you can visualize your friend's face and you will see your neighbor leave for work in the morning? It is *disinhibition,* a strange kind of feeling that I described in detail in *Me, MySpace, and I.*[14] When you are sitting behind a screen, whether it is a computer screen, a tablet screen, or even a small smartphone screen, you cannot see the person at the other end. You may actually feel somewhat anonymous even though the person at the other end might be a good friend. It is a phenomenon born of our electronic generation that we are seeing more and more of in our research. A student who is quiet and meek in class e-mails the professor to vociferously complain about her test grade or the confusing lecture, something she would never do face to face during or even after class. The middle manager pens a caustic e-mail to his boss complaining about a policy decision even though he sat mutely through a meeting where that policy was discussed and voted in force. *On the Internet, nobody knows you're a dog,* says a classic comic strip depicting a canine typing online. And behind the safety of the screen you *feel* as though you are free to say whatever you want, however you want, without repercussions. You are classically disinhibited on the Internet, and, as MIT professor Sherry Turkle said in her landmark book *Life on the Screen: Identity in the Age of the Internet,* we are all feeling free to pop off and say things in our "screen life" that we would never say in "real life."[15]

Finally, one additional culprit that is driving us all to our own personal iDisorder is the ubiquitous device that we now carry in our pockets and, from the research quoted earlier, sleep with next to our beds. Each year the number of portable devices that can act as Internet browsers, guidance systems, book readers, and electronic communicators expands exponentially. Laptops weren't portable enough so the netbook was born. Perhaps the netbook will prove to be too big to carry around because you can do the same things with your smartphone. But with all that video that we want to watch on the go we need a larger device so the tablet or e-reader was born. And don't forget the iPod, which was followed by the iPod Touch, coupling the love of music with all things in cyberspace. You can even purchase a special vest[16] with 22 pockets specially designed to fit your entire retinue of traveling technology. There's a pocket for your iPod with built-in clips for those pesky ear buds and their forever-tangled cords. Have an iPad? There is a pocket for that, too. They call it all part of your "Personal Area Network," clearly a play on a LAN (local area network) or WAN (wide area network). The vest screams, "IT'S PORTABLE AND YOU CAN ALWAYS HAVE IT WITHIN REACH." This is our world, and, as you will see over the rest of the book, we are all in peril of contracting an iDisorder.

MY UNIQUE PERSPECTIVE

In each of the next ten chapters I take a particular psychological disorder or set of related disorders and explore how people's relationships to
their various media and technologies give rise to the symptoms and signs
that define that disorder. I will make the point that the way we interact
electronically with the world—including our friends, acquaintances, and
even strangers—tends to produce psychological disorder–like symptoms that are being ignored as we quietly slip into a technology-induced
iDisorder.

My job is threefold. First, I will dissect each disorder into its component parts of signs, symptoms, and manifestations in the real world and
link those behaviors to the internal, virtual worlds that we inhabit many
hours a day. I will argue that if you already have symptoms of a psychological disorder, technology may make it worse. But I will also show you how,
in completely symptom-free adults, those same technologies can create an
iDisorder that can be every bit as serious. Second, I will explain, according
to well-respected theories and up-to-date, cutting-edge research in the behavioral and neurological sciences, why we are compelled to display these
maladaptive, emotionally dangerous thoughts and actions to the (real)
world, behind the safety of many screens, from the forty-two-inch television to the two-inch smartphone. Finally, I will provide you with simple,
effective, down-to-earth strategies to avoid falling into your personal iDisorder and stay sane in this increasingly high-tech, often crazy-making world
we inhabit.

SHOULD YOU GIVE UP YOUR TECHNOLOGY?

I will not argue that you should eschew all technology, become a Luddite,
and refuse to partake in the technological world. I know that is impossible. In our research we asked people of all ages how often they check
in with text messages, phone calls, Facebook, e-mail, and voice mail and
how anxious they feel if they can't access those technologies as often as
they would like. The results were nothing short of astounding, as you can
see in Table 1.1. The top of the table shows the various technologies that

TABLE 1.1. PERCENTAGE OF PEOPLE WHO CHECK IN WITH THEIR TECHNOLOGIES OFTEN AND GET ANXIOUS WHEN THEY CAN'T CHECK THEM

PERCENTAGE WHO CHECK THEIR TECHNOLOGIES EVERY 15 MINUTES OR LESS

Generations	Text Messages	Cell Phone Calls	Facebook	Personal E-Mail	Work E-Mail	Voice Mail
iGeneration	62%	34%	32%	17%	NA	10%
Net Generation	64%	42%	36%	28%	22%	17%
Generation X	42%	36%	17%	21%	21%	16%
Baby Boomers	18%	20%	8%	12%	16%	18%

PERCENTAGE WHO GET MODERATELY OR HIGHLY ANXIOUS WHEN THEY CAN'T CHECK THEIR TECHNOLOGIES AS OFTEN AS THEY WOULD LIKE

Generations	Text Messages	Cell Phone Calls	Facebook	Personal E-Mail	Work E-Mail	Voice Mail
iGeneration	51%	33%	27%	10%	NA	13%
Net Generation	51%	41%	28%	20%	19%	19%
Generation X	27%	31%	10%	20%	17%	34%
Baby Boomers	15%	18%	6%	15%	19%	54%

* Rosen, L. D., Carrier, L. M., Cheever, N. A., Rab, S., Arikan, M., & Whaling, K. (unpublished manuscript). *iDisorder: The relationship between media use and signs and symptoms of psychiatric disorders.*

constantly occupy our thoughts while the side shows the four generations that we studied. The top half of the table reflects the percentage of people who check in with each technology anywhere from every 15 minutes to "all the time." The bottom half of the table shows the percentage of teens and adults who feel highly or moderately anxious if they aren't able to keep track of their techno-worlds as often as they would like.

This table shows a clear picture of how we are keeping track of the technologies that are relevant to our age group or generation.[17] Looking at the top half of the table we can see that our teens are, by and large, checking their phones for text messages very often and social networks less often. They are not as compulsive as their older brothers and sisters in the Net Generation. These college-aged students appear to be, as a group, obsessed with keeping constant tabs on the two most important connection vehicles in their lives—text messages and Facebook—and they do so with a vengeance. Gen Xers, now in their thirties and forties, appear to be less crazed by technology, but we still see that nearly half check their texts constantly. Boomers are the least interested in keeping in constant touch with their phones or social networks. Along the same lines, but even more startling, teens and young adults get anxious if they can't check their texts and, to a lesser extent, their phone calls, while older generations appear to be less burdened by that anxiety. It is a striking trend but it is a clear one: Teens, college-aged adults, and even many middle-aged and older adults are hooked on their connective technologies and need to know who texted and who posted, and they need to know NOW.

As a blogger for the popular magazine *Psychology Today* I write about "how technology influences family life, education, the workplace and every waking moment of our lives."[18] In a post in late 2010,[19] I chronicled two experiments that were performed to see how people could deal without having their technologies available for a period of time. At Harrisburg College in Pennsylvania the administration declared a week without social media on campus while at Lincoln High School in Portland, Oregon, 53 students went even further and eliminated all technology from their lives for one week. Both attempts failed miserably. Only 10 percent to 15 percent of the Harrisburg students adhered, and, according to late-night television host Jimmy Fallon, the reasons were obvious: "Check this out," Fallon said. "A college in Pennsylvania is blocking computer access to social networking sites for an entire week and then requiring students to write an essay about the experience. Yep. The essay will be called, 'We all have smartphones, dumb ass.'" The high school experiment, predictably, went the same way, with one student summing up the experience: "I feel really anxious because I don't know if I'm missing something important. I keep thinking I can't wait for this to end because I need to check my e-mail. How many Facebook notifications am I going to have after this?"

You can be sure that the constant dependence on technology is not limited to high school and college students. At a recent education conference the speaker asked the 500 or so teachers in the audience to hand their phone to the person to their right, who then put it away. After 15 minutes he asked how the teachers, who ranged from those just out of college to veteran educators, felt about their missing phone, and most of the audience agreed that it was making them crazy to the extent that many could not focus on the ongoing talk. Our dependence on technology and our inability to be away from it for even a few minutes is just one clear indicator that we are not functioning at our best level. If our minds are always worrying about what we are missing then how can we focus attention on what we are getting?

THE BOTTOM LINE

Avoiding an iDisorder does not mean getting rid of your technology. Most assuredly the solution is about balance and moderation. But how do you teach people to moderate the use of something that they have plugged into their ears, eyes, and minds every waking (and non-waking) hour of the day?

That is the goal of this book. I am going to provide you with strategies and tactics to reset your mind and make sure that you stay sane in a potentially insanity-producing world. In each chapter I will show you how each potential iDisorder comes with its own triggers and how to avoid them and stay healthy.

Because each chapter tackles a different psychological disorder, the book can be read in any order. Pick your favorite diagnosis and start there. You will most likely see yourself manifesting many of the signs of each disorder. It's not entirely your fault. No, the technology didn't make you do it. But an iDisorder is an easy road to take when everything can be done behind a screen with the touch of a button. My job is to help you recognize the signs and symptoms of your own iDisorder and take simple, straightforward steps toward controlling your world before it controls you.

TWO

Media Starts with "Me"

My friend Damon is such a glory hog. He is always on Facebook posting where he is at every moment. It's like he is sounding a trumpet to announce that he has arrived! He has like 2,500 FB friends including most of the popular kids at school. He puts their photos on his page and comments on their wall all the time. He must do five status updates a day and if nobody says anything he starts commenting on his own updates. His photo doesn't even look like him; I think he had it done professionally. Man, it just looks too good. He says no, but we all think yes. The weirdest thing is that if you tag him in a photo and he doesn't like the way he looks he will ask you to untag him.

—Jarrod, age 16, New Rochelle, CT

I met this guy on eHarmony and he seemed to be just what I was looking for—competent, cute, smart, funny—so we set up a coffee date. He got there first and already had a cappuccino waiting for me. I was secretly pleased that he remembered that's my favorite coffee drink. And then he started to talk, and talk, and talk . . . about himself. In the 90 minutes that we spent together he didn't ask me one thing about me, not one question. He just kept boasting about his job and his boat and his everything. How do these people seem so interesting and engaging online and then so self-centered in person?

—Diana, age 32, Los Angeles, CA

According to the *Diagnostic and Statistical Manual (DSM)*, narcissistic personality disorder (NPD) is a pervasive pattern of grandiosity (in fantasy or behavior), need for admiration, and lack of empathy, beginning by early adulthood and present in a variety of contexts. Someone with NPD exhibits five (or more) of the following traits:[1]

1. Has a grandiose sense of self-importance (e.g., exaggerates achievements and talents, expects to be recognized as superior without commensurate achievements).
2. Is preoccupied with fantasies of unlimited success, power, brilliance, beauty, or ideal love.
3. Believes that he or she is "special" and unique and can only be understood by, or should associate with, other special or high-status people (or institutions).
4. Requires excessive admiration.
5. Has a sense of entitlement (e.g., unreasonable expectations of especially favorable treatment or automatic compliance with his or her expectations).
6. Is interpersonally exploitative (e.g., takes advantage of others to achieve his or her own ends).
7. Lacks empathy: is unwilling to recognize or identify with the feelings and needs of others.
8. Is often envious of others or believes others are envious of him or her.
9. Shows arrogant, haughty behaviors or attitudes.

It's not much of a stretch to see Damon possessing at least five of the nine signs of NPD just by looking at Jarrod's account of his Facebooking behaviors. Damon most certainly acts entitled and wants his "friends" to know what he is doing at every moment. He collects friends (or perhaps he hopes that they are admirers) and wants to be popular by associating with (or friending) the cool kids at school. He needs to look his best and will only allow perfect photos of himself to be shown to the world. He is living the narcissistic lifestyle at the young age of 16.

But isn't that what Facebook, Twitter, blogs, Flickr, YouTube, and other social networks and posting sites are all about? The objective of a social network—if there is a goal or an objective—is to be social. How you do that is up to a set of moment-by-moment choices. And many of those choices encourage a sort of narcissism. What should I use for my profile picture? Does this one make me look more interesting? Smarter? Cuter? Should I use Foursquare to alert everyone that I am shopping at the mall, out to lunch, or at a club? Should I try to friend the smart kids? The cool kids? The football players? Sure, there is a section on every Facebook page called "About Me," where you can talk about anything you feel defines you. But just because it is called "About Me" does not mean that it has to be grandiose or self-promoting or provide an inflated view of YOU. It can say anything. You choose how to present yourself.

Facebook presents numerous opportunities or choice points for someone to sketch out how they want the world to see them. What profile picture do you choose? Does it just show you, or you interacting with others? Who are your "Friends" and how do others see them? What is your "Philosophy" and what "Activities and Interests" do you feature? In short, there are many opportunities to present yourself online, and they often prove to be a window to the psyche. Do you tweet often about what you are doing, thinking, and feeling? Do you post YouTube videos of yourself? Do you have your own website? To a narcissist social networks provide a virtual playground for self-expression.

Social networking is not the only technological area that we see narcissistic behaviors played out for an audience. Consider the ubiquitous cell phone. Although the cell phone has been around for quite some time now it has become more visible recently. It is out on the table during meals instead of in a pocket or purse. When someone emerges from a movie it is immediately checked, often even before discussing whether they liked the movie or not. One of my closest friends recently told me that whenever he is having a conversation with someone and it has gone on for more than 15 minutes or so he excuses himself to go to the restroom so that he can check his iPhone. Smartphones are wonderful and the fact that you can check your e-mail, monitor your social networks, and keep in touch with your world ensures that they will have a draw that is extremely strong for the narcissist.

There are many more ways for people who share some of these narcissistic tendencies to express them through their technological interactions. The man who sends a mass e-mail boasting about his accomplishments to everyone on his contacts list is sharing his feelings of grandiosity. The woman who obstructs the grocery store aisle, speaking on her cell phone about her troubles in a loud voice and ignoring the fact that she is possibly bothering other people, is showing signs of narcissism. The teen who responds to a text from his friend who is sad about breaking up with his girlfriend by telling the friend about the fun evening he had with *his* girlfriend is certainly demonstrating his lack of empathy. The bottom line is that any technology that allows us to function behind a screen—where people cannot see us and we cannot see them or their reactions to our behaviors— presents numerous opportunities to emulate the characteristics in each of the nine narcissistic signs. I will explore this in more detail in the rest of this chapter.

DO WE ALL HAVE A TOUCH OF NARCISSISM?

NPD is a controversial topic among psychologists. Sigmund Freud adapted the term *narcissism* from the Greek mythological character, of Narcissus, who was so self-absorbed that he fell in love with his own reflection in a pond of water. While it is presented in the *DSM* as a set of traits leading to a personality disorder, which psychologists believe to have no specific "cure," some prefer to view it as something that all normal, healthy people have to a greater or lesser degree. Psychologists refer to it as "trait narcissism," "normal narcissism," or "subclinical narcissism." This makes sense to me. After all, when you look at the nine *DSM* signs for NPD, they could apply to many people around us and not particularly "abnormal" people.

"Normal" narcissists are grandiose, have an inflated self-concept, are self-promoting, use their social world to display a sense of status and esteem, desire to be popular and admired, know that they are smarter than others, know that they are good looking, feel entitled, and need constant affirmation of their intellect, beauty, and success. They may be exhibitionists, and at the very least they are very concerned about their appearance and being fashionable. In addition to these qualities, narcissists do worry— somewhat obsessively at times—about what others think of them and attempt to present themselves only in a positive framework. They are great at starting relationships that they feel will make them look better and also great at ending relationships when they have gotten what they want out of them. They are not interested in forming deep, long-lasting relationships, but rather seek any relationship that may serve to enhance their status and how others see them. In general, they feel entitled to all that is coming to them and lack empathy toward others. I can think of at least a half-dozen people who fit many of these characteristics but I would not say they have a personality disorder. They are simply more narcissistic than other people in my world.

TO KNOW ME IS TO LOVE ME (AT LEAST FOR A SHORT TIME)

One of the interesting things about a narcissist is that at first glance they seem so nice and so likeable. In a fascinating study,[2] Professor Delroy Paulhus of the University of British Columbia had four to six students work together in groups seven times for 20 minutes each to discuss a range of topics. After the first and last sessions the students anonymously rated the behavior of each other and themselves during the meeting. Students also completed a series of psychological tests including the Narcissistic Personality Inventory (NPI), which you will hear more about later in this chapter. After spending the first 20 minutes together, those students who had more of a sense of entitlement and a tendency to exploit others (as seen on the NPI) were rated as more agreeable, conscientious, open, competent, entertaining, and well adjusted. After the final session— after two hours and 20 minutes of total interaction—the same narcissists were rated as less agreeable, less well adjusted, less warm, more hostile, and arrogant. So, what happened over the two hours following the first 20-minute meeting? One possibility that has been raised is that the positive reactions that narcissists get at this "zero acquaintance" or first meeting may actually confirm their belief that they are superior and deserve to be the center of the show, and this reinforces their behaviors, which become more problematic as the meetings progress.

In an interesting article in *Psychology Today,* Scott Barry Kaufman, a New York University cognitive scientist and personality psychologist and author of the blog *Beautiful Minds,* speculates that

the positive social reactions that narcissists evoke in others at first sight might play an important role in maintaining their problematic interpersonal behavior and intrapersonal coping mechanisms that are dysfunctional in the long run. Being admired by others is like a drug for narcissists. The problem for narcissists is that their addiction to admiration hinders them from establishing relationships or from sticking with social contexts in which they are embedded for a longer period of time . . . the positive interpersonal reactions narcissists evoke at zero acquaintance [upon first meeting] are an important part of the vicious interpersonal cycle that narcissists experience.[3]

The fact that narcissists are loveable at first can be a major problem as it may only serve to enhance the feeling that they are great and admired, and they then do everything in their power to maintain that feeling of superiority. I can only imagine that during the first session in Dr. Paulhus's student meetings the narcissists received both verbal and nonverbal feedback about their likeability, including smiles, nods, and compliments, and as the meetings progressed, and as people in the group discovered their narcissistic tendencies, the feedback turned negative and the narcissist felt the need to do anything to feel admired again. It is, indeed, a vicious cycle, and one that is easy to play out on social networks, online dating sites, blogs, tweets, and any environment where the narcissist can put his best foot forward and gain positive first impressions. Diana, who I introduced at the top of this chapter, experienced how a person can seem so wonderful and positive on an online dating site and then be self-absorbed and narcissistic in person.

NARCISSISTIC INJURY AND NARCISSISTIC RAGE

Recently I was chatting with a colleague at a conference about how technology is making it easier for people to act out in ways that they would not do in person, and he recounted a story about a patient of his, a 38-year-old single woman named Susan. Susan told my colleague that her phone rang at 11 P.M. and because of the late hour she didn't answer it. She did listen to the voice mail that her friend Amy left in case she was in trouble and needed help. Amy's message said that she needed to talk about something important but it didn't seem like an emergency so Susan decided that she could wait to get back to her in the morning on her way to work. Much to Susan's surprise she awoke to a nasty e-mail in the morning. Evidently

Amy had called three different friends and sent all of them the following e mail message when nobody had responded to her phone messages:

> Dear friends, I am appalled that none of you answered your phone last
> night. I was having a major crisis and I needed to talk to you, any of you.
> I called all of you because a friend of mine came to visit and talked about
> killing himself. I needed some feedback and advice. Nobody called me
> back. I suggest that you all look at your priorities and figure out why you
> did not return my call. Amy

Although Amy felt that she was justified in being angry, her e-mail suggested that Susan was a bad person for not responding immediately, and further, that not responding meant that Susan did not care about her. This hurt Susan since these are issues that she is dealing with in therapy. I am not suggesting that Amy is narcissistic, but in terms of the characteristics I listed above, she certainly qualifies as having some level of "normal narcissism."

Narcissists also react strongly to negative feedback. Sigmund Freud discussed the concepts of a "narcissistic injury" or, in an extreme case, a "narcissistic scar" that arises from a feeling of inferiority. Others have extended Freud's ideas from early development and sexuality to everyday life where a narcissistic injury refers to any threat to a person's grandiose sense of importance or even to lack of acclamation for a narcissist's accomplishments. Clearly Susan not answering Amy's phone call was viewed as a narcissistic injury. This can also be seen in Damon's behavior (as Jarrod's account continues):

> One day a friend of mine decided to have some fun with Damon and
> posted a phony comment about how he had been seen shopping at Target
> for clothes. Damon went into a rage that surprised all of us. We were just
> having some fun but he acted like we had said that he was a criminal or
> a thief or something. He posted stuff on his wall and everyone else's wall
> telling them that this was someone's idea of a joke and it wasn't funny.
> He railed against my friend on FB and also sent an e-mail out to all of the
> students at school spreading rumors. Finally my friend removed the post
> and Damon acted like nothing had happened.

Narcissists often react to their injury with what has been called "narcissistic rage," which is usually an angry, nasty outburst directed at the person or persons who inflicted the injury. This is exactly what Damon did when he felt injured by his friends' comments on Facebook, and it is what Amy did in her caustic, accusatory e-mail. Heinz Kohut, an Austrian-born psychologist known for the development of Self Psychology, which looks at mental disorders as having arisen from disrupted or unmet developmental needs, wrote a fascinating article titled "Thoughts on Narcissism and Narcissistic Rage," in which he explained how when narcissists feel that they are being attacked they go into a frenzy and attempt to denigrate the person or persons who are striking a blow to their feelings of self-worth. According to Kohut, this is a protective mechanism for the self so that narcissists can continue to exist in the belief system that all is well, they are superior, and everyone knows that to be true.[4]

In my previous books I have talked about how, when we are communicating with people while sitting behind a computer screen or even a cell phone screen, there is a feeling of safety and anonymity, even with those people we know, which compels us to act uninhibited and say things that we might not say in a face-to-face setting or even on the phone, when the person at the other end has the ability to interrupt the conversation and display cues of upset and anger. Consider how easy it is for the entire narcissistic cycle to exist and be repeated over and over when the parties are behind the safety of the screen. This whole process—starting from feelings of grandiosity and deservedness and leading to injury and then rage—is expressed all the time on social networks and through other communication tools such as tweets, blogs, e-mails, or text messages. Online communication not only makes it easy to play out the narcissist's grandiosity but is a natural forum for narcissistic rage in an environment where off-the-cuff, thoughtless remarks abound.

TROPHY FRIENDS

Narcissists are known for having shallow, superficial relationships with many people, particularly focusing on "trophy friends" who can make them look more popular and enhance their public glory. What better place to parade their greatness than a social network?

In her book *Life on the Screen: Identity in the Age of the Internet*, MIT professor Sherry Turkle discussed how technological interaction could act as a Rorschach test.[5] In a Rorschach test, a psychologist or psychiatrist shows you cards with ink blot designs and asks you to tell her what you see. The answers are analyzed and dissected and can be used to learn about a person's underlying psychological mechanisms and potential personality disorders. Although Turkle's book was written in the early 1990s, before social networking, it is not too far of a stretch to see Facebook or Twitter activities as a sort of Rorschach test. What you post, what you say, and what pictures you present are all a representation of your underlying psyche. And when we look at many people's social networking behaviors we start to see what looks like a world of narcissists.

I was introduced to Janine through a friend because she thought we might share interests in movies. After Janine accepted me as a Facebook friend, I looked at her wall and the friends who had posted there and I was immediately impressed—and a bit awed—by the number of "artistic" people who Janine had as Facebook friends. From reading her wall postings, I discovered that she was always meeting this person at a party or that person at a wine tasting, and her Friends list included ultra-hip artists and people whose names I knew from television and movies. When I mentioned to my friend how amazing Janine's life was, she said that it was all a façade and that Janine was a very sad and lonely person whose posts glorified her life and her world through association with other people who had interesting lives. Janine's world was a treasure trove of trophy friends that made her feel better about herself and her life.

SELF-SERVING, ILLUSORY SUPERIORITY, AND ME, MYSELF, AND I

Trait narcissism has been connected to several phenomena, including "self-serving bias," "illusory superiority," and overuse of first-person pronouns. Michael, a 22-year-old college senior, provides us with an excellent example of the self-serving bias.

> My best friend, Becka, is a great person and I love her dearly but she is always full of excuses when things don't go right for her. The other day she got back a paper and was outraged that she got a C. She ranted and

raved about how the professor was an idiot and he probably let the dumb TA grade the papers and how she had no respect for him anymore. This was the same class that she got an A on the midterm and was raving about how smart she was and how the teacher knew it, too. She told me that whenever the prof asked a question of the class she felt he was looking at her and smiling and nodding even when he didn't call on her.

Michael nailed it with Becka. When things were going right she was the first to jump up and take credit for being smart and believed that everyone knew it. When something went wrong, she was also the first to blame others, rather than herself.

Illusory superiority is an interesting phenomenon. Certainly we all like to look good and to feel that we are good. This effect can be seen among many groups, including studies of professors at the University of Nebraska, where, when asked where they fell in terms of teaching ability, 68 percent of them rated themselves in the top quarter of all teachers.[6] Illusory superiority studies have been duplicated often, with people rating their own driving ability, intelligence, and nearly every characteristic way above average.

Narcissists take that to the extreme. No matter what the issue, they believe they are on top of their game and much better than the average Joe (or Josie). They are smarter, look better, act better, work harder, and, in fact, do nearly everything better than most anyone else. Imagine asking a narcissist if they felt they were better than others at a phony, made-up trait called *spranging*—they would say, "Of course I am!"

Recently I gave a talk on narcissism in the world of social networking at a national psychology convention, and one audience member, a middle-aged psychologist, suggested that I visit the blog of one of his friends, William. William, a 38-year-old stockbroker, was, he said, "full of himself" and would be a perfect example of what I presented in my talk. I copied down just a few of William's most recent posts—he appears to post as many as 10 or 20 times a day. Here is a sampling:

I watched the first episode of Body of Proof last night. Great show and I loved it! I think that Dana Delany is gorgeous!

My office mate is such a jerk. He brings in the smelliest lunches and I can't stand it. I think I may have to talk to my boss about this.

[via Foursquare] William just checked in at @ Starbucks (Orange, CA)

I went to the gym this morning and feel so great! I plan to go 4 days a week and will be buff in no time.

OK, so count the number of personal pronoun references that William made in his four posts. I count at least 11 and perhaps more if you infer the existence of an "I" in front of statements such as "feel so great!" Now, count any references to other people. I see just one when he talks about his office mate and says "he." William certainly seems to overuse the personal pronoun, which may signal that he has more trait narcissism than others. According to an often-quoted study by Professors Robert Raskin of the University of California at Berkeley and Robert Shaw of Yale University, when people were asked to talk about any subject for five minutes, those who were more narcissistic used "I" and "me" more often and used words such as "we" or "you" far less often.[7] Another study found that narcissists who used more personal pronouns on their Facebook "About Me" page had a more self-promoting and sexy main photo and used more aggressive words and more profanity.[8] This certainly confirms the psychologist's comment that William is "full of himself." Along the same lines, glance back at Amy's e-mail and count the number of personal pronouns that she used. If you dare you might also try it yourself by looking at an e-mail you may have sent or a Facebook posting you made. You may or may not be surprised. If you have a Twitter account you will be able to see substantially more personal pronouns because Twitter is geared to declarations of someone's personal feelings and thoughts. But Facebook is supposed to be a social gathering place and social gatherings are about many people, not just one.

A GENERATION OF NARCISSISTS?

There are those who would argue that the new generations of children, teens, and young adults born after 1980 and known as Millennials, the Net Generation, or the iGeneration are, by their nature, more narcissistic than those of earlier generations. Jean Twenge, a professor of psychology at San Diego State University and co-author of *The Narcissism Epidemic: Living in the Age of Entitlement* with Keith Campbell of the University of Georgia, places the blame on parenting that has emphasized self-expression and freedom in children since the mid-1980s.[9]

Twenge and her colleagues examined scores obtained from more than 16,000 college students who all took the same measurement tool— the NPI—between 1979 and 2006 and found that post-millennial college students scored substantially higher than their cohorts from just 20 years prior. Strikingly, they discovered that two-thirds of recent college students scored above the average on the NPI compared with only 50 percent with those who took the same test in the late 1970s and early 1980s.

Twenge and Campbell argue, "Understanding the narcissism epidemic is important because its long-term consequences are destructive to society. American culture's focus on self-admiration has caused a flight from reality to the land of grandiose fantasy." Further, they said, "permissive parenting, celebrity culture and the Internet are among the causes of the emerging narcissism epidemic."

Twenge and Campbell's research confirms that 60 percent of college students agreed with the statement: "People in my generation use social networking sites for self-promotion, narcissism, and attention-seeking." In commenting on these results, Twenge said, "A blatant example of Facebook narcissism is the person who's posted 200 pictures just of themselves."

But are they truly narcissists? Does this mean that they have an incurable personality disorder?[10] I would argue that they have an iDisorder, and, if you bear with me, you will see that there are ways to rethink your online persona so you avoid looking narcissistic in your online world.

Nathan DeWall, a professor at the University of Kentucky and colleague of Twenge and Campbell, also found support for these long-term changes. He examined a major cultural product stretching across decades: popular song lyrics. In a detailed investigation of lyrics from the ten biggest Billboard Hot 100 hits between 1980 and 2007, the words "*I*" and "*me*" increased over time and the use of words such as "*we*" and "*our*" decreased, mirroring Twenge and Campbell's reported increase in narcissism over the same period.[11] It appears that culture reflects our increasing narcissism ... or is our narcissistic nature driving changes in the music that pervades our lives and inhabits our iPods, social networks, and Internet domain?

TOO MUCH MEDIA = ME, ME, ME

In Chapter 1 we discussed a 2011 study that examined the relationship among psychological disorders, media use, multitasking, and attitudes toward the value of technology. One scale we used measures narcissism with statements such as the following (the subject answers *true* or *false*):

I know I'm a superior person, so I don't care what people think.

Other people envy my abilities.

I do what I want without worrying about the effect on others.

As you can see, these phrases clearly represent narcissistic attitudes. After combining 24 such statements and comparing the answers to a national representative sample, the survey produced some interesting and, I think, quite telling results. First, those people of all generations who spent more hours a day using certain media, including being online, sending and receiving e-mail, instant messaging, texting, listening to music, and watching television, were more narcissistic. Second, those young people of the iGeneration who used social networks more were far more narcissistic than those who used them less or not at all. Third, those (of all generations) who were more anxious when not checking in with their text messages, cell phone calls, and Facebook were more narcissistic than those who were less anxious about continually looking at their phones or jumping on Facebook to read posts and status updates.

These results paint an interesting picture of people—and this refers to all people, not just young adults and teenagers—who are gobbling up media and social networking and displaying attitudes and behaviors that define narcissism. The bottom line is that a lot of people pounding away on their laptops, constantly checking their smartphones, and living the high-tech, media-rich life are showing strong signs of being narcissistic. Let's take one aspect of this media diet—social networking—and see what researchers have discovered about how it relates specifically to aspects of narcissism.

IT'S ALL ABOUT ME

Although Facebook (FB) and Twitter are fairly new, the former appearing in 2004 and the latter in 2006, psychologists have already begun to study how they might impact narcissism. Laura Buffardi and Keith Campbell of the University of Georgia found that more narcissistic Facebook users—as assessed by the NPI, which you, too, can take later on in this chapter—had more self-promoting content on their pages (more wall posts), used their main profile photo for self-promotion, and had more online social interaction (more FB friends) than those who were less narcissistic. In their study, independent raters could tell which Facebook users were more narcissistic simply by noting whether they had a large number of friends and had a "glamorous" and staged-quality profile photo.[12]

Since the profile photo appears on every Facebook post, it is clear that narcissists take it very seriously and want it to be very attractive. As evidence of this, Soraya Mehdizadeh of Canada's York University found that more narcissistic Facebook users had a more attractive main photo as well as more attractive top 20 photos, had more status updates, and spent more than an hour a day on Facebook.[13] Other researchers have found similar relationships between narcissism and status updates. In a recent study Tracii Ryan and Sophia Xenos of RMIT University in Melbourne, Australia, compared Facebook users and nonusers and found that Facebook users are more narcissistic and the most narcissistic of the Facebookers had more photos and more status updates.[14]

Freud and others have posited that narcissism develops in early childhood and can even be measured in children as young as 8 years old. Sander Thomaes and his colleagues at Utrecht University examined Facebook pages of preteens, aged 8 to 12 years old, who got fake feedback from peer judges about their profiles. As expected, those who heard that their peers liked their profile had an increase in self-esteem while those who heard that peers did not approve of their profile showed decreased self-esteem. However, those children who were high in narcissism showed a much larger hit to their self-esteem than those children who were lower in narcissism, showing the profound impact of a narcissistic injury. Interestingly, across all of Thomaes's preteens, peer disapproval had a 50 percent larger (negative) impact on self-esteem than the impact of peer approval, and even more so to narcissists. To narcissists, an "injury" is more profound and harmful than approval.[15]

The impact of parenting on narcissistic behaviors was shown to be even more pronounced in a recent doctoral dissertation by Christopher Lootens of the University of North Carolina at Greensboro. In this study college students were asked to recall how they were parented and then answer questions pertaining to their narcissistic tendencies. Students who were raised by either an authoritarian mother or father—where rules were rules and parental warmth was largely absent—were decidedly more narcissistic than those raised by parents who showed warmth and compassion and/or had no rules for the child's behavior.[16]

In a very interesting study of college student FB users, Shawn Bergman of Appalachian State University and colleagues found that the more-narcissistic users had more friends (online friends), wanted to have as many friends (virtual and real) as possible, and posted more self-focused pictures than group pictures. However, in contrast to others who scream about the Internet and Facebook being a hotbed of narcissism, Dr. Bergman concluded that,

> Surprisingly, we found that narcissism was not a strong predictor of the reported amount of time spent on SNSs [social networking systems] or frequency of status updates. This suggests that Millennials' SNS usage is not solely about attention-seeking or maintaining self-esteem, but is also a means of staying connected and communication. While previous generations accomplished this via letter, telephone, or email, the Millennials may simply prefer to connect and communicate via SNSs. Thus, this may not be a sign of pathology, but a product of the times.[17]

I will get back to this later but I think that Dr. Bergman has a valid point. Is it narcissistic to use communication tools that, by their nature, promote narcissistic tendencies? Is this really narcissism or is it simply adapting to technology?

TWEETING THE NIGHT (AND DAY) AWAY

If narcissism is rampant in online social media, what about Twitter, which is a more obvious and blatant vehicle for "all about me" rants? In a recent study of more than 3,000 tweets from 350 Twitter users, Mor Naaman, Jeffrey Boase, and Chih-Hui Lai of Rutgers University discovered two types of tweeters:

- *Meformers,* who posted updates on everyday activities, including their daily feelings, thoughts, and emotions, and had little interaction with followers.
- *Informers,* who shared information, had more friends and followers, and interacted more with followers than did meformers.

Guess which was the most prevalent tweeter? If you guessed *meformers* you were right! Eighty percent of all the tweets studied were classified as coming from meformers. According to a press release about the study,

> "Informers" are more likely to post messages that share information (such as news links), where "meformers" tend to focus on what the researchers call "Me Now" messages—posts that update a user's followers about that user's thoughts, location or immediate situation. Informers tend to be embedded and active in social awareness streams. They have more friends and followers and they interact with those people much more than "meformers," the study results found.[18]

I have heard Twitter referred to as "140 characters of mediocrity," but that may only refer to the writing itself. For narcissists, the draw is not the content, but the audience. Just ask Lady Gaga (nearly 14 million followers as of this writing), Kim Kardashian (10.3 million), or Ashton Kutcher, who in 2009 had a contest with CNN to see who could be the first Twitter user to reach one million followers the quickest. I am not saying that any of these

celebrities have been diagnosed as narcissistic, but their texting behavior
certainly sounds like narcissistic behavior to me.

The grandiosity often seen in social networking can be even more salient on television. Popular reality TV shows are merely vehicles for narcissists to play to a larger audience. But while very few people get to be reality
TV stars, video-sharing sites such as YouTube, where a posted video can
"go viral," can turn someone into an instant celebrity. After all, if Justin
Bieber can go from a YouTube video to a superstar, anyone can be a superstar, right? Susan Boyle was just another singer on the show *Britain's Got
Talent* until her version of the song "I Dreamed a Dream" went viral and
made her a household name. Daniel Tosh plays web videos on his syndi-
cated Comedy Central show *Tosh.0* and makes unknowns into instant celebrities. And on the hugely popular show *iCarly,* Miranda Cosgrove plays
a teen who gets famous hosting a web show with her friends.

The Internet has made it easy for narcissistic expression in many modalities. The written word can be seen on blogs, wikis, and social networking
and personal websites. Visual representations are easily accessible for free
on video-sharing sites as well as on photo-sharing sites. In fact, the Internet
is one big canvas for strutting one's stuff. Why then are we not all showing
massive amounts of trait narcissism online? Why do some of us boast and
brag and write the word "I" hundreds of times while others are content to
share information, comment on our friends' postings, and act in a way that
indicates our motives are altruistic at best or at least not narcissistic?

WE ARE ALL ACTORS ON A STAGE

Professor Erving Goffman, an eminent Canadian sociologist who died in
1982, prior to the Internet revolution, published a seminal book entitled
The Presentation of Self in Everyday Life. Goffman must have antici-
pated social networking because he described it perfectly when talking
about how we are all actors in a play and are presenting the image of
ourselves that we want others to see. One of Goffman's major tenets was
that as we present ourselves we continually monitor how others perceive
us and adapt our presentation of self to look best to all people. He uses
the term *performance* to refer to "all the activity of a given participant

on a given occasion which serves to influence in any way any of the other participants." In addition, Goffman talked about how a person shares two selves, one on the front stage and one on the back stage. Our front-stage self mirrors how we want others to see us while our back-stage self is the one doing all the work keeping up appearances.[19] Doesn't this sound a lot like what we see people doing online?

In *Me, MySpace, and I,* I interviewed danah boyd (yes, Dr. boyd spells her name with lowercase letters), a social media researcher at Microsoft Research New England and a Fellow at Harvard University's Berkman Center for Internet and Society, about Goffman's ideas and how she felt they applied to MySpace, which was the rage of the day *way* back in 2007. Here is what she had to say:

> The way you develop your identity is to put things out there, get feedback, and adjust accordingly. You develop an internal model of yourself and balance this with reactions from other people; this is what Erving Goffman calls, "impression management." Doing this online allows you to be more reflective earlier about whom you are. On MySpace, for example, you have to write yourself into being; in other words, you have to craft an impression of yourself that stands on its own. Is it the end-all and be-all in developing your sense of self? Of course not. But online expressions are a meaningful byproduct of identity formation.[20]

So, if I take Goffman's approach, as adapted to social networking by Dr. boyd, who calls this our *networked identity* evidenced through *public displays of connection,* then I would say that our online self is an invention that, for most people, is a continual approximation of presenting our sense of self to the world. However, when a person has characteristics of NPD, the self we are presenting may actually be the idealized self that we want others to see rather than the "true self"—as we really are—as proposed by Dr. Carl Rogers, founder of humanistic psychology, and by other psychologists. Perhaps the phrase "On the Internet, nobody knows you're a dog" should be translated as, "On the Internet, you can be whomever you want to be whenever you want."

THE PSYCHOLOGY OF CYBERSPACE

Judging from research done over the past decade or two, the study of Internet use is complicated. Data on how much time we spend online is inherently flawed because many people carry the Internet with them at all times on their smartphones, iPads, or laptop computers. If you open your phone and check your e-mail for a moment does that count as being online? Even deciding what someone is doing online is difficult since all browsers allow you to maintain multiple open websites and there is no way to know which website you are viewing at any given time.

What we can tell, or at least what psychologists have been able to discover from years of research, is why people choose certain Internet behaviors. Two overlapping theories make sense to me: Uses and Gratifications Theory, and Social Capital Theory.

Uses and Gratifications Theory was originally intended to describe why people used more traditional media, such as television and even newspapers and magazines. Its basic tenet is that there are many forms of media that can gratify our social and psychological needs and they all clamor for our attention. People need to choose the particular form of media that meets their personal needs and provides internal gratification. Since the Internet explosion Uses and Gratifications Theory has been applied to a variety of platforms, including blogs, Facebook, and Twitter. For example, one study found seven separate uses and gratifications for maintaining personal journal blogs (online diaries or social networking sites): They keep a record of one's thoughts, improve writing, allow self-expression, afford access from anywhere at any time, allow the sharing of information with others, help pass the time, and provide a social community.[21] Other researchers have found that different forms of media fulfill needs for communication and connection, information, and, of course, the need to look good, to feel special, to look smart, and to cultivate all of those components of normal narcissism.[22]

One study examined the different uses and gratifications from Facebook and instant messaging and discovered that for social networking, people are gratified through six mechanisms: entertainment, affection, fashion, problem sharing, sociability, and social information, while instant messaging promotes gratification through relationship development and maintenance.[23] Another study of 1,715 college students at the University of Texas found that social networking fulfilled four needs: socializing, entertainment, self-status seeking, and information. Still another often-quoted study by John Raacke and Jennifer Bonds-Raacke found many gratifications for Facebooking, including keeping in touch with old friends and current friends, posting and looking at pictures, making new friends and locating old ones, and keeping up with social events.[24] Finally, a recent study in the journal *Computers in Human Behavior* portrayed tweeters as gaining their gratification from an informal sense of camaraderie that comes from social connection.[25]

Clearly, again, these interactions can be benign or they can be played to excess and start to resemble narcissistic tendencies. One further idea from psychology—Social Capital Theory—will help to clarify my sense of the role technology plays in promoting narcissism. Social capital includes all of the benefits that we gain from our social relationships. Psychologists have found three different types of social capital:[26]

- *Bonding social capital* comes from our close family and friends and is how we feel a special closeness to and caring from our loved ones.
- *Maintaining social capital* involves keeping our old friendships intact so that they may provide support when needed.
- *Bridging social capital* includes all of our "acquaintances," or people who we would not necessarily go to for social support but find useful for different purposes, such as providing information. Often bridging social capital refers to what people who study relationship networks call "weak ties" as opposed to "core ties" such as those provided by bonding social capital.

Charles Steinfield, Nicole Ellison, Cliff Lampe, and Jessica Vitak of the University of Michigan have studied the impact of media on social capital. In one study they found that time spent on Facebook was a predictor of all three types of social capital. In another study they discovered that the *intensity* of Facebook interaction is strongly related to bridging social capital or the building of weak ties.[27] In essence, social networking is all about collecting your own social capital.

Putting the two theories together, we find that there are a variety of reasons to spend time doing online activities, and many of them can be beneficial to the psyche. However, the narcissist sees the world differently. He sees it as a continual need for gratification and commendation from others, and that is usually obtained through weak ties or bridging social capital. If we could put all of the uses and gratifications and all of the social capital on a scale, I would predict that the more narcissistic that someone is, the more they exploit their bridging social capital and the more gratification they get from those weak ties. Less narcissistic people would make use of bonding and maintain social capital and gain their gratification in other areas and for other reasons that have less to do with the self and more to do with others.

THE NARCISSISTIC BRAIN

It is pretty clear that narcissistic behavior gets played out through various media. In an article for *The New Atlantis,* Christine Rosen called it "the age of egocasting," which she defined as "the thoroughly personalized and extremely narrow pursuit of one's personal taste."[28] Social networking provides a palette for the egocasting narcissist to present herself any way she wants, through words, pictures, and videos, and will continue to do so with any new modality invented. My question is: *Does technology make people narcissistic or are narcissists attracted to technology because it is a good platform from which to express themselves?* Professor Judith Donath, director of the Sociable Media Group at the Massachusetts Institute of Technology's Media Lab, says, "Social networking provides a series of mini mental rewards that don't require much effort to receive. These rewards serve as jolts of energy that recharge the compulsion engine, much like the frisson a gambler receives as a new card hits the table. Cumulatively, the effect is potent and hard to resist."[29] It sounds like narcissists don't stand a chance, do they?

Brain research can teach us about how the mind works and which areas of our white matter appear to control which processes. Studying narcissism is complex because, as you might guess, no one brain structure houses the propensity for the expression of grandiosity, self-enhancement, and all other characteristics of trait narcissism. Several recent studies, however, do give us a glimpse into the mind of the narcissist. In one clever research study, Tong Sheng and his colleagues at the University of Southern California examined brain activity during rest and found that narcissists had higher activity in the posteromedial cortex, a region that is connected to having thoughts about yourself. They also discovered that narcissists have higher activity in the medial prefrontal cortex (MPFC), which is associated with impulsive action without regard to consequences.[30]

Using a slightly different twist, Franco Amati and his colleagues at Arizona State University looked at what happens when you stimulate the MPFC. Participants were given what was billed as a cultural IQ test in which words were presented and the participants had to say whether they knew what the words meant (50 percent of the words were not real words!). Narcissists are known for "false claiming," which is saying that they know something when in fact they don't. In Amati's study, stimulation of the MPFC reduced the narcissist's behavior of "false claiming," which suggests that increased activity in the MPFC is responsible for reflection and social monitoring.[31] Other research indicated that the MPFC was also related to "self-enhancement bias," in which narcissists perform actions to make themselves look better in the eyes of others.[32]

One further piece of information about the narcissist's brain might shed light on the complexity of this attack on the psyche. University of Chicago neuroscientist John Cacioppo, co-author of *Human Nature and the Need for Social Connection,* studied brain activity when people were exposed to pictures that were designed to arouse positive feelings and those that would promote negative feelings.[33] When shown pleasant pictures, lonely people showed less response in the ventral striatum, which is the brain area that recognizes rewards. In contrast, lonely people showed more activation of the visual cortex when shown unpleasant pictures of people than to unpleasant pictures of objects; this finding suggests that they are attracted more to the upset and discomfort of others. According to Cacioppo, "When you're lonely, your brain is in a heightened state of

alertness for social threats, even if you're not explicitly looking for them."
This is particularly apt for narcissists, who are always anxious that some
one might not see their most "perfect" self. Consider the narcissistic person who posts something online and then waits for responses, counting
the seconds and imagining the worst. From the research, the narcissist's
brain must be continually activated in areas that encompass loneliness,
rewards, self-enhancement, impulsive thoughts, and social monitoring. No
wonder the narcissist is constantly in a state of despair and need.

WHAT CAN YOU DO TO STAY HEALTHY
IN A HIGH-TECH WORLD THAT
PROMOTES A NARCISSISTIC ¡DISORDER?

Sigmund Freud said that NPD, as with most if not all personality disorders, is incurable. However, if we make the leap and talk instead about
normal narcissism or trait narcissism as something that we all have to a
lesser or larger extent, it is possible to take steps to appear (and be) less
narcissistic. First, however, you have to have a sense of how much or little
trait narcissism there is either in yourself or someone else. If you are a
narcissist you may not even recognize the signs. If you suspect someone
else has narcissistic tendencies you may want to have an idea of the level
of that person's trait narcissism. The well-established NPI can be used to
assess the level of trait narcissism. A version of the NPI is in Figure 2.1
on the next page. There are 40 questions and each includes a choice between two options. I recommend that you complete this for yourself first,
following the scoring instructions at the bottom, and then complete it for
another person who you feel may be showing strong trait narcissism.

 If someone you know has a high level of trait narcissism, there are
some ways that you might help. You may be able to do some things to reduce that person's narcissistic tendencies, but helping most likely means
helping yourself deal with the grandiosity, feelings of superiority, narcissistic rage, and any other signs that that person directs at you.

FIGURE 2.1. NARCISSISTIC PERSONALITY QUIZ[a]

Below you will find a list of 40 statements, one in Column A, and the opposite in Column B. For each line, choose a statement from Column A or B that **best matches your typical attitudes and behaviors**. If neither one fits you perfectly just select the one that comes the closest to matching your typical attitudes and behaviors.

	Column A		*Column B*
1	☐ I would prefer to be a leader.	☐	It makes little difference to me whether I am a leader or not.
2	☐ I see myself as a good leader	☐	I am not sure if I would make a good leader.
3	☐ I will be a success.	☐	I am not too concerned about success.
4	☐ People always seem to recognize my authority.	☐	Being an authority doesn't mean that much to me.
5	☐ I have a natural talent for influencing people.	☐	I am not good at influencing people.
6	☐ I am assertive.	☐	I wish I were more assertive.
7	☐ I like to have authority over other people.	☐	I don't mind following orders.
8	☐ I am a born leader.	☐	Leadership is a quality that takes a long time to develop.
9	☐ I rarely depend on anyone else to get things done.	☐	I sometimes depend on people to get things done.
10	☐ I like to take responsibility for making decisions.	☐	If I feel competent I am willing to take responsibility for making decisions.
11	☐ I am more capable than other people.	☐	There is a lot that I can learn from other people.
12	☐ I can live my life in any way I want to.	☐	People can't always live their lives in terms of what they want.
13	☐ I always know what I am doing.	☐	Sometimes I am not sure of what I am doing.

14	☐	I am going to be a great person.	☐	I hope I am going to be successful.
15	☐	I am an extraordinary person.	☐	I am much like everybody else.
16	☐	I know that I am good because everybody keeps telling me so.	☐	When people compliment me I sometimes get embarrassed.
17	☐	I like to be complimented.	☐	Compliments embarrass me.
18	☐	I think I am a special person.	☐	I am no better or worse than most people.
19	☐	I wish somebody would someday write my biography.	☐	I don't like people to pry into my life for any reason.
20	☐	I am apt to show off if I get the chance.	☐	I try not to be a show off.
21	☐	Modesty doesn't become me.	☐	I am essentially a modest person.
22	☐	I get upset when people don't notice how I look when I go out in public.	☐	I don't mind blending into the crowd when I go out in public.
23	☐	I like to be the center of attention.	☐	I prefer to blend in with the crowd.
24	☐	I would do almost anything on a dare.	☐	I tend to be a fairly cautious person.
25	☐	I really like to be the center of attention.	☐	It makes me uncomfortable to be the center of attention.
26	☐	I like to start new fads and fashions.	☐	I don't care about new fads and fashions.
27	☐	I can read people like a book.	☐	People are sometimes hard to understand.
28	☐	I can make anybody believe anything I want them to.	☐	People sometimes believe what I tell them.
29	☐	I find it easy to manipulate people.	☐	I don't like it when I find myself manipulating people.
30	☐	I can usually talk my way out of anything.	☐	I try to accept the consequences of my behavior.

31	☐	Everybody likes to hear my stories.	☐	Sometimes I tell good stories.
32	☐	I like to look at my body.	☐	My body is nothing special.
33	☐	I like to look at myself in the mirror.	☐	I am not particularly interested in looking at myself in the mirror.
34	☐	I like to display my body.	☐	I don't particularly like to display my body.
35	☐	I will never be satisfied until I get all that I deserve.	☐	I take my satisfactions as they come.
36	☐	I expect a great deal from other people.	☐	I like to do things for other people.
37	☐	I want to amount to something in the eyes of the world.	☐	I just want to be reasonably happy.
38	☐	I have a strong will to power.	☐	Power for its own sake doesn't interest me.
39	☐	I insist upon getting the respect that is due me.	☐	I usually get the respect that I deserve.
40	☐	If I ruled the world it would be a better place.	☐	The thought of ruling the world frightens the hell out of me.

Scoring Instructions[b]

For each of the pairs give yourself 1 point for each "A" answer and 0 points for each "B" answer.

The average score for the general population is 15.3

The average score for celebrities is 17.8

Narcissists score over 20[b]

[b]If you are interested, there are also specific items on the NPI that match narcissistic traits according to the popular psychology website "PsychCentral" (http://psychcentral. com/quizzes/narcissistic.htm). Higher scores on any of the traits can indicate how the narcissism is exhibited.

Authority: Items 1 through 8

Authority refers to a person's leadership skills and power. People who score higher on authority like to be in charge and gain power, often for power's sake alone.

Self-sufficiency: Items 9 through 14

This trait refers to how self-sufficient a person is, that is, how much you rely on others versus your own abilities to meet your needs in life.

Superiority: Items 15 through 19

This trait refers to whether a person feels they are superior to those around them.

Exhibitionism: Items 20 through 26

This trait refers to a person's need to be the center of attention, and willingness to ensure they are the center of attention (even at the expense of others' needs).

Exploitativeness: Items 27 through 31

This trait refers to how willing you are to exploit others in order to meet your own needs or goals.

Vanity: Items 32, 33 and 34

This trait refers to a person's vanity, or their belief in thir own superior abilities and attractiveness compared to others.

Entitlement. Items 35 through 40

This trait refers to the expectation and amount of entitlement a person has in their lives, that is, unreasonable expectations of especially favorable treatment or automatic compliance with one's expectations. People who score higher on this trait generally have a greater expectation of entitlement, while those who score lower expect little from others or life.

HELPING REDUCE NARCISSISTIC TENDENCIES IN SOMEONE YOU KNOW

As long as someone does not have an extremely high NPI score you may be able to take some action from your side to help out. Here are some suggestions:

1. Help the person reduce time spent using media and increase time spent with nature. Marc Berman, John Jonides, and Stephen Kaplan of the University of Michigan have developed Attention Restoration Theory, which talks about how getting someone out of an urban or media-rich environment gives the brain time to restore parts that are directly connected to voluntary or direct attention, which may help the person reduce their knee-jerk re-actions online.[34]

2. There are many who assert that narcissism arises from a combination of positive, overly effusive, but indiscriminate parental

praise and cold, rejecting parental messages. Knowing this can help you better understand a narcissist and, perhaps, find ways of responding to their narcissistic tendencies that are neither too positive nor rejecting.

3. If you experience narcissistic rage from someone the best strategy is to not engage him. If, for example, you see an online post from a friend who is immediately attacked by a narcissist, the best strategy is to back off and avoid making a comment even if you feel you need to support your friend. You will only fuel the rage. The best bet is to hide the person on your Facebook page, which means you won't see any of his posts and will have no reason to respond.

Narcissists usually have a very acutely attuned psyche that searches out adoration and ways to promote a sense of self and simply cannot and will not deal with criticism. It may be the case that nothing you do will make any difference. There are those who believe that even trait narcissism is next to impossible to fix.

COPING WITH YOUR OWN NARCISSISTIC TENDENCIES

If you took the NPI in Figure 2.1 and scored 20 or above, the following suggestions should help reduce the signs and symptoms of a narcissistic iDisorder.

1. Moderate your personal technology input. Spend more time in nature. It will have a restorative effect and make it less likely that you will react to someone without thinking through the ramifications of your comments.

2. Social networks are designed to be social. That is, they are there for an interchange of ideas and for fun. If you find yourself fretting over every comment and constantly pounding out comments, status updates, and wall postings, you might be in danger of hurting others' feelings and losing the fun part of social networking.

3. Always remember that there is a real person on the other end of any e-communication you put out. It is just too easy to say nasty,

cruel things to people who you can't see, and real people get their feelings hurt by unkind words. I know it is difficult, but I believe that everyone should adopt an "e-waiting period" between writing a message and sending it on its way through cyberspace with no chance to retrieve it once the send key is pressed. Waiting for a minute or so can give you time to reread your message and reassess whether the language might be too harsh and in need of softening.

4. Modulate your use of personal pronouns in your electronic communication. When you write something, stop just before you click "send" or "post" and read it carefully. Count the number of times you use the words "I" and "me" compared with the use of references to other people. Try replacing some of the personal pronouns with "we," encompassing more people and making the comment less about you and more about sharing experiences with others. Become more of an "informer" rather than a "meformer."

5. When dealing with e-communication of any type—social networking, text messaging, Twitter, blogging—remember that behind that screen there is a human being with feelings who can be easily hurt by words that are unaccompanied by cues that we use during face-to-face communication, including gestures, facial expressions, and voice tone. Also remember that your communication is "asynchronous," meaning you may be sending your message when you are in a narcissistic rage but you have no idea what state the person will be in when she receives it. She may be in a bad mood and your words may spur more nasty arguments or she may be sad about something else and your hastily sent missive may exacerbate her dark mood. If you take just a few minutes to let a draft message sit you may find ways to soften the message.

6. Where do you gain your social capital? Psychologists are clear that healthy people should concentrate on bonding social capital (good friends and family) and maintaining social capital (old friends) and downplay those weak ties gained through bridging social capital. Check your social networking pages and examine

your Friends list. Classify each friend as providing one of the three types of social capital. Do you have a lot of bridging social capital coming in from your friends? If so, you may want to consider locating old friends and engaging them or making sure that your Facebook page includes family and close friends so that you are more apt to gain social capital from strong ties who know you and appreciate you rather than weak ties who may spur more narcissistic behaviors.

We spend as much time communicating online as we do offline, and our new online world may be promoting a narcissistic iDisorder. If you follow my suggestions you will be able to nip this debilitating state in the bud or at least reduce your tendency to slip into an iDisorder.

THREE

Obsessively Checking in with Your Technology . . . 24/7

I'd go crazy if I had to go one day without my phone.

—KMX (online ID)[1]

35 per cent of Americans with smartphones also open up apps before washing the sleepy dust out of their eyes.

—Kat Hannaford, editor, *Gizmodo UK*[2]

No matter where I am, whether it is in a restaurant, at the movies, or even in a public restroom, I see people holding onto a slim device that allows them to do just about anything that they can do from any Internet-enabled computer at home. But this device—what we call a "wireless mobile device" (WMD)[3]—has become, for many, an object of obsession. People check their phone constantly regardless of where they are or who they are with. People no longer think twice about pulling out their WMD in a social situation and sending a text while supposedly conversing with other people. We seem to have lost some of the common rules of etiquette in the service of constant worldwide connection. Have WMDs become true weapons of mass destruction, not of our physical world, but of our emotional world?

Jared, a 42-year-old businessman, lost his work cell phone while on a family vacation in the snowy mountains and got really grumpy, then difficult to be around, then panicky. This went on for the whole day, with arguing and fighting between him and his wife about what he *had* to do to replace the phone, which involved leaving early and driving immediately to the phone store. They fought during the entire car drive down the mountain and all the way home from their interrupted vacation. Jared was so worked up that he was convinced that he'd lost all of his contact information, many work-related e-mails, and some important files. However, after they had driven all the way home, their little four-year old girl, said "Here Daddy . . ." and pulled out the cell phone from her car seat. She had been hiding the phone since it first went missing and was afraid to say anything when her parents started fighting.

Are you a compulsive technology user? Are you constantly checking your e-mail, your text messages, or your voice mail? If so, you're not alone. In a recent study in my laboratory, we used a standard measure that assessed compulsive behaviors among Americans and found that those who showed more compulsive personality traits: (1) spent more time online each day, (2) communicated more by all modalities (instant messaging, texting, social networking), (3) played more video games, (4) listened to more music, (5) spent more time checking for texts, cell messages, and Facebook updates, and (6) was more prone to multitasking than other people.[4] People seem to use their technologies compulsively in two different ways: (1) because they either love their device, crave surfing the Internet, and love their software and phone apps so much that they cannot get enough of them; or (2) because they become so worried about missing out on some important news that they can't keep themselves away from the Internet or their phones. The first kind of compulsive behavior is driven by the pleasure that people receive from keeping in touch with others, knowing the latest stock market values, or watching humorous YouTube videos. This kind of compulsive behavior, associated with an "addiction" to technology, will be discussed in Chapter 4. The second kind of compulsive behavior, driven by worry and "obsessive" thoughts, is the subject of this chapter.

WORRY IN A TECHNOLOGY CONTEXT

Most people enjoy the benefits and pleasures of their WMDs. The people I know value their devices for accessing information 24/7, for serving as portable video players, for listening to music, and for enhancing social connectivity. But what many people don't seem to realize is that their WMD use also leads to great anxiety. I see people who need to check their smartphones all of the time. I observe people who worry about messages that they may be missing if they are "off the grid" for even a short period of time. And, especially, I notice people who are greatly concerned when they are away from their devices. If we leave our WMD somewhere—even for just a few minutes—we get that nagging feeling that we are missing out on something . . . or is it everything? When we awaken, we ask ourselves, what did we miss while we were sleeping? And then at least a third of us check our WMD even before getting out of bed.[5] The same happens when our devices are lost or misplaced and even when we go on vacation and purposely silence them or leave them behind. Consider the kids at Lincoln High School in Portland, Oregon. They were part of an experiment within the school to go without all technology for a week. One of the students complained,

> I feel really anxious because I don't know if I'm missing something important. I keep thinking I can't wait for this to end because I need to check my e-mail. How many Facebook notifications am I going to have after this?[6]

Have you noticed that some people won't go out camping or on a trip into a remote area because they know that they won't get cell reception? My colleague John, a 61-year-old university professor, was planning to go on a cruise and was worried that there would not be Internet access. I tried to convince him that he would be much more relaxed and enjoy himself much more if he turned off his phone and ignored e-mails while he was away. Even though he promised that he would relax and enjoy himself, he also spent a considerable amount of mental work prior to the trip investigating when and where he could get Internet access from the ship and how much it would cost.

According to a July 2011 Harris Poll, eight in ten vacationers brought or planned to bring at least one technological device on their summer 2011 vacation, with half bringing their laptop computer and stating that their plan was to work on their vacation, including checking e-mail (35 percent), checking work voice mail (22 percent), and taking work-related phone calls (22 percent).[7]

Recent studies have looked at the long-term risks when people do not take quality vacations, risks that include employee burnout and health problems. For example, Brooks Gump at the State University of New York, Oswego, and Karen Matthews at the University of Pittsburgh performed a large-scale study of American men at risk for heart disease and found that those men who vacationed more had fewer risk factors for death.[8] This does not bode well for those "Crackberry" addicts and smartphone junkies who fail to leave their devices behind to relax on vacation. They might experience physical symptoms of anxiety—including chest pain, heart palpitations, shortness of breath, or dizziness—in addition to worrisome thoughts.

Like most people, I am attached to my devices. When I am away from them I get that uncomfortable feeling that I am missing something. When I am in a meeting where phones are not allowed I find myself thinking about who and what I might need to deal with when the meeting is over. Text messages, voice mails, and e-mail pile up rapidly and I feel as though I am falling behind if I am not connected. MTV coined the term *FOMO,* or "fear of missing out," to give this feeling a label. The television station polled a large number of young people and found that 66 percent agreed that they find it "exhausting to always be 'on,'" but, at the same time, 58 percent agreed that "when I'm unplugged, I worry that I'm missing out on something."[9]

We love those WMDs and it appears that we can't live without them, but most people are being slowly pulled toward an obsessive iDisorder. MTV's FOMO appears to be a worldwide phenomenon to which anyone can fall prey. For example, an interview study of cell phone "addicts" in Australia found that worrying about being out of the loop in one's social circle compels individuals toward excessive cell phone use. One interviewee in that study said, "If I go to work or somewhere and accidentally leave my phone at home, I literally get anxious. Because I'm like 'who's calling me, what have I missed.'"[10] Business people carrying around their BlackBerry devices all of the time is a great example of this problem, but the situation also exists in my own profession, higher education. Thirty years ago, we professors could leave our offices or labs at the end of the day, go home, and get away from committee work, administrators, and student queries. In contemporary times, with our smartphones and tablet computers, all of these work tasks come home with us . . . and to the restaurant . . . and the coffee shop . . . and the dinner table. I confess that I am hopelessly attached to my iPhone, and when I am at dinner with my family I often spend time glancing at messages and focusing on what I am missing at work, or what I could (or should) be doing that is work related. And whether I need to respond immediately to that email from a colleague from India, rather than putting the phone away and completely enjoying my family time.

These are all symptoms of panic disorder, an anxiety disorder defined in the *DSM*.[11] A second anxiety disorder that seems very relevant is obsessive-compulsive disorder (OCD). OCD is an anxiety disorder in which people have unwanted and repeated thoughts, feelings, ideas, and sensations (obsessions) that make them feel driven to engage in behaviors (compulsions). A key feature of OCD is that these obsessions or compulsions cause major distress and interfere with daily life. There are many types of obsessions and compulsions, such as an excessive fear of germs and the compulsion to repeatedly wash one's hands to ward off infection. Obsessive-compulsive disorder affects about 1 percent of the American population and has an average age of onset of 19 years old.[12] However, nearly 90 percent of the general population experiences similar obsessions that are not sufficiently severe to be classified as OCD, and it is in this group that we find behaviors that might be indicative of an iDisorder.[13]

Often the iDisordered person carries out behaviors—for example, pulling their phone out of their pocket to check for new messages or jumping onto their laptop as soon as they get home to check for Facebook activity—to get rid of obsessive thoughts, but this only provides temporary relief. Not performing the obsessive rituals can cause great anxiety. Additionally, in traditional OCD, obsessions involve a perceived lack of control by the afflicted person, and persons with OCD are aware that their obsessions are not real and that there is not a rational reason for performing the compulsions.[14] Constantly checking one's pocket to make sure your cell phone is still there is not rational but I have seen people do it. Actually, to be honest, I probably do this at least a few times a day myself.

For some people, the anxiety from being disconnected is severe and leads to extreme behaviors. New Jersey resident Carl Ippolito had his phone stolen and was able to track it down to a location using cell phone tracking software. When Mr. Ippolito arrived at the location, he confronted a man named Brent Johnson, who he saw on a similar phone. Mr. Johnson denied stealing the phone, so Mr. Ippolito lost control and attacked him. When the dust settled it turned out that Mr. Johnson was using his own phone, and the "stolen" phone was really just a lost phone, found shortly afterward at the snack shack at a local baseball field where Mr. Ippolito had been umpiring a youth baseball game. Apparently, someone failed to use the phone tracking software properly.[15] Was Ippolito a hot-head prone to solving problems in a physical manner . . . or did he show signs of obsessive behavior? A more extreme story comes from the state of Washington. There, a young lady had her cell phone taken away by her father. Upset, she complained and complained about her dad's decision, but complaining was not enough to satisfy her negative feelings. The daughter retrieved a hunting bow and fired an arrow at her father, striking him in the head. As her father lay bleeding, the daughter refused to let him use the cell phone to call for help. She made him crawl to the neighbor's house, instead.[16]

Clearly, an iDisorder related to technology anxiety and OCD is becoming increasingly prevalent as we become attached to devices for all aspects of our life. Consider what happened to my colleague's wife, Mary, on the first day that she got her new smartphone. Mary and her family picked up her new phone on the way to a restaurant for dinner. The server came, took everyone's orders, and left. As the food arrived everyone realized that Mary had nothing to eat. She had been too busy playing with her new phone and hadn't looked at the menu, hadn't ordered, and hadn't even noticed that their server had come and gone. When my colleague asked his wife why she hadn't ordered, without looking up Mary said that she was captivated by the phone and all the new features it had!

MEASURING ANXIETY OVER DEVICES

Jim Taylor from the University of San Francisco and the Wright Institute in Berkeley wrote online about seeing increasing numbers of people around him experience symptoms of what he calls *disconnectivity anxiety* (DA). Here's how Dr. Taylor describes the anxiety:

DA typically presents itself during a breakdown in the technology that makes communication today instantaneous and continuous, whether

telephone (landline or mobile), Internet, text messaging, or simply when
someone else doesn't respond immediately. DA is associated with symptoms of worry, negative emotions, such as fear, anger, frustration, and despair, and physical distress.[17]

In our laboratory, we measured how much anxiety people felt about
an inability to utilize their devices using the scales shown in Figure 3.1.
Take a moment and answer honestly how anxious you would feel if disconnected from each means of communication and then take a look at how
the anxiety rates differ when we asked a group of Americans of all ages,
shown in Figure 3.2. As you can see from the latter figure, young people

FIGURE 3.1. IF YOU CAN'T CHECK IN WITH THE FOLLOWING TECHNOLOGIES AS OFTEN AS YOU'D LIKE, HOW ANXIOUS DO YOU FEEL?[18]

Technology	Level of Anxiety			
	Highly Anxious	Moderately Anxious	A Little Anxious	Not Anxious at All
Text messages	O	O	O	O
Cell phone calls	O	O	O	O
Facebook/other social networks	O	O	O	O
Personal e-mail	O	O	O	O
Work e-mail	O	O	O	O
Voice mail	O	O	O	O

FIGURE 3.2. PERCENTAGE OF PERSONS WHO BECOME HIGHLY ANXIOUS OR MODERATELY ANXIOUS WHEN THEY CANNOT CHECK THEIR DEVICES

Device	iGeneration	Net Generation	Generation X	Baby Boomers
Text messages	51%	51%	29%	15%
Cell phone calls	34%	50%	31%	18%
Social networks	28%	29%	10%	6%
Personal e-mail	10%	21%	20%	15%
Work e-mail	14%	20%	17%	19%
Voice mail	11%	18%	14%	15%

are very anxious about checking their text messages: Half of all iGeneration teenagers and Net Generation young adults are highly or moderately anxious when they can't check their text messages. From the data in the table you may also notice that they don't get anxious much at all when they can't check their personal e-mail, work e-mail, or voice mail. For older generations (Generation X and Baby Boomers), the majority told us that they are "not anxious at all" about checking their text messages, and three out of four are only "a little anxious" or "not anxious at all" about checking their cell phone calls or social networks. In fact, very few members of the older generations appear to get anxious about missing their technologies, certainly not at the level of teens and young adults. How did you fare?

In my earlier books, I described how most children and teens are increasingly obsessed with technology.[19] A recent study found that 35 percent of Americans open up smartphone apps, 18 percent check Facebook, 23 percent use a web browser, and 24 percent check e-mail before even getting out of bed in the morning.[20] Constantly checking our devices becomes an out-of-control feedback loop, with the checking serving to lower our anxiety (our FOMO) until the checking must be repeated over and over again, perhaps even causing sleep interruptions.

PHANTOM IN YOUR POCKET

Have you ever felt your pocket vibrating, but when you grabbed your phone there was neither a call nor any activity that would have made it shake? This is known as *phantom vibration syndrome* and it is real. Phantom vibrations were nicely described by one user in an online forum:

> Whenever I travel a certain distance away from my phone I start to hear it vibrate even though no one is texting or calling me. Same thing happens when my phone is in my pocket. I start to hear/feel it vibrate even though no one is calling/texting me. My phone keeps playing mind games with me.[21]

This user is not alone, as shown in a dissertation by David Laramie at Alliant International University in which he found that about two-thirds of users experienced phantom phone buzzes.[22] Michael Rothberg and colleagues at Baystate Medical Center in Massachusetts questioned hospital medical staff and found that almost 70 percent of the participants experienced phantom vibrations from an electronic device (pager or cell phone). Only 2 in 100 medical staff found the vibrations to be very bothersome but six in ten of them had tried to stop the vibrations by adjusting their phone or pager. Analyses done by the researchers showed that the phantom rings were linked to how much a person used their phone, with frequent phone users being more prone to the syndrome.[23]

In order to find out how compulsions and anxiety levels are related to checking our devices, my laboratory asked the question shown in Figure 3.3 to thousands of Americans. Take the questionnaire on page 56, and then, in Figure 3.4, see the percentages of people who checked their devices most frequently. iGeneration teens and Net Generation young adults were significantly more likely to be checking their text messages, cell phones, and social networks than Gen Xers, who were significantly more likely than Baby Boomers to be doing so. More than half of teens and young adults combined indicated that they check their text messages "all the time" even though they could have chosen to answer "every 15 minutes"! Three out of four check their text messages hourly or more frequently and 55 percent check their cell phone calls hourly or more frequently. Teens and young adults did better with checking their social network accounts, but still, almost one in three check them "all the time." How did you fare?

How much anxiety is too much? Consider the possibility that the anxiety over technology can ruin a vacation and interfere with one's relationships. One of my neighbors, Mark, is a young professional, an insurance agent, who is married and has two young children. He gets more than 100 e-mails a day from work, and he says that he must be constantly checking his e-mail in order to stay caught up with the messages. He says that the e-mails continue in the evenings and on the weekends so he has to keep checking during those times, too. Recently, the family tried to go on a weekend vacation to the beach in San Diego. I say "tried" because Mark couldn't keep himself away from his laptop and e-mail. He was checking e-mail whenever the family was in the hotel room, including in the evening after having spent the day out having fun. After the kids would go to bed,

FIGURE 3.3. FREQUENCY OF CHECKING YOUR DEVICE[24]

Technology	How Often Do You Check Each of the Following?							
	Never	A Couple of Times a Month	A Couple of Times a Week	Once a Day	Every Few Hours	Every Hour	Every 15 Minutes	All the Time
Text messages	○	○	○	○	○	○	○	○
Cell phone calls	○	○	○	○	○	○	○	○
Facebook/other social networks	○	○	○	○	○	○	○	○
Personal e-mail	○	○	○	○	○	○	○	○
Work e-mail	○	○	○	○	○	○	○	○
Voice mail	○	○	○	○	○	○	○	○

FIGURE 3.4. PERCENTAGES OF PERSONS WHO CHECK THEIR DEVICES ALL THE TIME

Technology	iGeneration	Net Generation	Generation X	Baby Boomers
Text messages	49%	56%	34%	17%
Cell phone calls	27%	36%	31%	18%
Facebook/other social networks	27%	32%	16%	8%
Personal e-mail	14%	25%	20%	11%
Work e-mail	10%	20%	20%	12%
Voice mail	9%	17%	14%	15%

Mark's wife wanted to relax and have some quality time together, but Mark would be busy answering e-mail on the laptop he set up on the nightstand right next to the bed. The ensuing fight between Mark and his wife was so upsetting to him that he told me (via e-mail, of course) that he was never going on vacation with the family again!

HOW DO YOU DEAL WITH AN OBSESSIVE-COMPULSIVE iDISORDER?

The evidence is all around us that people are attached to their devices and oftentimes driven to use them obsessively by fear and worry. Missing out on social information, work information, and our personal pursuits can put us in a state of anxiety and even cause panic attacks, sometimes with serious consequences.

Anxiety related to technology can be extreme. Are you the kind of person to chase down and beat someone who might have taken your device? Are you the kind of person who becomes so irritable about being away from your e-mail that you would risk offending your family just to be back on your computer? Are you the kind of person who is so obsessed with checking your text messages that you are driving with one hand (or two knees) on the steering wheel and one hand on your cell phone? If so, then you might need to make some changes in how you relate to your technological devices. These changes might be difficult enough that you cannot do them alone; you might need the help of a professional therapist to do so.

Those of us who are strongly attached to our devices put our lives on hold when we misplace our devices. We cannot focus on what is going on around us. We stop all conversation with others, neglect our tasks, and become single-minded in our search for what is missing. We develop great anxiety about not being able to check our e-mail or our text messages. As the search stretches on, our initial feelings of concern might transform into worry and then fear of what will happen if the device is never found. For some of us, that fear is associated with intense negative feelings, including irritability, nervousness, and panic. Anger and hostility might also occur.

I have collected a variety of techniques for resetting yourself so that you will reduce your dependence upon your devices. You must recognize when you are experiencing anxiety so that you can take a break. You can "adjust the volume" on your online connections. Naomi Baron at American University described how we have the flexibility to choose how much we want to "hear" from our devices.[25] For example, in a social networking website, you can often choose whether you want to receive notifications for all events or just selected events. Choosing the latter can reduce the amount of information that you are exposed to and perhaps break you from the FOMO cycle.

Also, you can consider taking the advice of Daniel Sieberg, a science and technology journalist. He provides a four-step program for bringing physical human contact back into your life if you feel that you are overrun with technology. The four steps are Rethink, Reboot, Reconnect, and Revitalize. In the first step, Rethink, you should assess how much time you spend connected to your technological devices. When you add up how much time you spend texting or e-mailing, in one year, the total can be very eye-opening. In 2010, the average American spent about 2.5 hours per day online.[26] Multiply that by 365 days in a year and the total comes to 912.5 hours! In the second step, Reboot, you should disconnect from your devices and software programs for a period of time. In the third step, Reconnect, you should gradually reintroduce technological gadgets into your life, but do so sparingly. Finally, in the Revitalize step, you should put a priority on human contact over electronic contact whenever possible.[27] If you are concerned that you might have severe anxiety related to your devices, and if you feel you might need to talk to a professional about it, then you should consider contacting a therapist or psychologist.

Figure 3.5 is a checklist that you can use to help you decide if you might need to make changes to your technology lifestyle or if you might need to seek professional help to make those changes. You might also consider making changes if you have already worried that you might have a problem. And you should consider making changes if you notice negative effects of your technology-related behaviors on the people around you in your daily life. The checklist includes the behaviors described in this chapter.

FIGURE 3.5. CHECKLIST FOR ANXIETY PROBLEMS CONNECTED TO TECHNOLOGY AND MEDIA

Problem or Concern	Yes	No
I have thoughts that my use of technology is out of control.	☐	☐
I make attempts to control my use of technology but am not successful.	☐	☐
I am concerned about how often I use my technological devices.	☐	☐
My use of devices gets in the way of everyday tasks.	☐	☐
My use of devices gets in the way of my social interactions.	☐	☐
My family, friends, or co-workers tell me that I have a problem with my attachment to my devices.	☐	☐
I experience an intense "fear of missing out" when I am not around my devices.	☐	☐
I have experienced phantom vibrations from my phone.	☐	☐
I get irritable when I am not near my technological devices.	☐	☐
I cannot go on vacation without checking my cell phone or e-mail.	☐	☐
I have gotten into arguments with my family or friends when I cannot use my devices.	☐	☐
I become highly anxious when I can't check my text messages, cell phone calls, or social networking account.	☐ ☐	☐ ☐
I feel tense and nervous when I am online or when I am using my cell phone.	☐	☐

You will notice that some of the items on the checklist are more severe than others, so that interpreting your results is not just a matter of how many items you checked "yes" to, but also which items. You should be especially concerned if you checked off any of the items that show that your anxiety is interfering with friends, family, or work obligations. However, if you have checked off three or more items, then you ought to consider making some changes.

Anxiety-related problems, such as OCD, seem quite likely to develop given the attachment we have to our technology and technological devices. They can interfere with our social relationships, cloud our thinking, and cause intense negative emotions. These forms of iDisorders might be affecting you; use this checklist as a guide, and don't be afraid to seek help if you are concerned that your anxiety has gone beyond your control.

FOUR

Getting High on Technology

Hooked on Smartphones, Social Networking, and Texting

I am an addict. I don't need alcohol, cocaine or any other derailing form of social depravity. . . . Media is my drug; without it I was lost.
—Student asked to go a day without technology-based devices[1]

If you can make use of something that makes your life easier while maintaining enough inner strength and freedom to avoid dependence, you are the master. If you do not cultivate this inner strength and freedom, you become the slave.
—Ulrich Weger, senior lecturer in Psychology, University of Kent[2]

Jim, a 32-year-old manager at a computer company, cannot leave a room without his Blackberry. At least three or more times a day he pats his pocket to make sure it is there and he checks it all day long. At dinner with his wife and daughter, he has his BlackBerry on the table in front of him, and he spends most of the dinnertime staring at the phone screen.

Jane is hooked on social media. Before she gets out of bed in the morning, she grabs her iPhone from the nightstand and checks for status updates from her friends. Checking Facebook throughout the day is the primary way that she keeps up with her social circle, and she hates having to make phone calls to find out what her friends are up to.

Rick, a 70-year-old grandfather, loves to take photos with his smart-phone and then post them online. He especially likes to shoot pictures of his family and then put them online so that distant relatives can see them. He never asks anyone for permission to post the photos publicly despite getting several complaints from family members.

You have heard people talk about friends who they claim are addicted to the Internet and you may have even wondered whether you are addicted. Scientists began developing measurement instruments to identify Internet and technology addicts when stories of such fanatics came to the surface in the mid-1990s. Mostly, these measurement tools are based on several core concepts that come from psychiatrists' and psychologists' understanding of other confirmed addictions, including substance abuse and pathological gambling, both outlined in the *DSM*.[3]

Of course, compulsive use is a key part of Internet addiction. An "addict" must overuse the Internet, the cell phone, or other technologi-cal devices to be considered abnormal. However, overuse is not the only important part of being addicted to technology, nor is it even a defining feature of addiction. An addict also experiences withdrawal, tolerance, in-terpersonal and/or health problems, and time management problems. But how do we gauge these experiences when we are dealing with an environ-ment that we all use every day?[4]

Symptoms of withdrawal might include agitation, depression, anger, and anxiety when the person is away from technology or computers. These psychological symptoms might even turn into physical symptoms such as a rapid heartbeat, tense shoulders, and shortness of breath.

And just like with other addictions, technology addiction presents the problem of habituation or tolerance. Tolerance means that an addict grows accustomed to the "high" received from technology use and therefore must do something more extreme to achieve the same high the next time that technology is used. For example, a video game addict could thoroughly en-joy a particular game, but soon he will need to get an even more challeng-ing, more violent, or more interactive game to achieve the same feeling of enjoyment.

As with most iDisorders, an important aspect of technology addiction is that it interferes with "normal" life activities. In other words, just playing lots of video games is not necessarily bad unless playing interferes with one's personal relationships, hygienic behaviors, or work and chores.

Finally, an addict can easily spend more time in technology-based activities than planned. That can result in the addict losing sleep, being late to work or school, and/or skipping face-to-face social activities.

ADDICTED TO WHAT?

Internet addiction is the most researched form of a technology addiction, but other related addictions have been proposed by scientists. Some have proposed television addiction,[5] while others have proposed video game addiction.[6]

Mark Griffiths at Nottingham Trent University in the United Kingdom has defined the concept of a generic technology addiction that could apply to any computer-based technology.[7] Technology addictions are defined by Dr. Griffiths as nonchemical (behavioral) addictions that involve human-machine interaction. According to him, these addictions can be passive (e.g., television) or active (e.g., computer games).[8] Some psychologists have proposed that the concept of technology or Internet addiction is too broad and general and needs to be refined. For example, Dr. Kimberly Young, a professor at St. Bonaventure University and author of *Tangled in the Web,* suggested that addicts become hooked on specific applications on computers.[9]

This possibility of an application addiction does not seem at all far-fetched to me when I consider what is happening to the people who I encounter in my life. For example, consider the case of Richard, a student who works with me in my research laboratory on various psychology projects. Richard is extremely intelligent and bright, and he participates regularly in our laboratory discussions. However, he also can get intensely moody on some days and can be a downright smart-ass on those days. In my first work encounters alongside Richard, I thought that this moodiness was part of his personality, but through getting to know him better, I have since come to realize that the moodiness is a side-effect of staying up all night before coming to work. What is Richard doing when he stays up all night? It turns out that he is playing the online video game *Halo,* which involves a space soldier battling in a virtual world.

Other characteristics associated with technology addiction might include salience, mood changes, and relapse.[10] Salience means that a person is obsessed with the technology-based activity. They think about it all of the time, even when they are away from their devices. The mood changes occur as a result of using the technology, the software, or the device. Both negative and positive mood changes are possible. For example, going online and posting one's status as a social network update might begin to lift one's spirits when they are feeling down. Seeing a friend respond with a "like" to the status update could elevate their mood even more. Relapse is the idea that an addict might start up the problem activity even after having quit for a while. Each measure of Internet addiction created by scientists includes all of these concepts or some subset of them. For example, the Chen Internet Addiction Scale (CIAS) was developed mainly to measure Internet addiction in Chinese adolescents. (It turns out that technology addiction is a huge problem in Asian countries, potentially much worse than in Western countries.[11]) The CIAS measures compulsive use, withdrawal, tolerance, interpersonal and health problems, and time-management problems.[12]

Figure 4.1[13] shows a measure of Internet addiction developed by Kimberly Young, one of the first researchers to describe and measure the concept of Internet addiction. Answer each question with "yes" or "no." Dr. Young considered people to be "addicted" if they answered "yes" to five or more of the questions and if their behavior could not be accounted for by a period of mania (temporary, highly energetic activity).

Not surprisingly, addiction to cell phone use is now being identified and studied by researchers. Cristina Jenaro and her colleagues at the University of Salamanca in Spain found that, while many students were frequent phone junkies, 10 percent of the students in her sample exhibited problematic cell phone overuse and, additionally, 3.9 percent of the students had both problematic cell phone and problematic Internet overuse. Further, the researchers found that students exhibiting cell phone overuse also were more likely to exhibit bodily complaints, insomnia, social dysfunction, anxiety, and depression. Do you think that you might suffer from cell phone

FIGURE 4.1. SCREENING INSTRUMENT FOR ADDICTIVE INTERNET USE

Question	Response	
Do you feel preoccupied with the Internet (think about previous online activity or anticipate next online session)?	Yes	No
Do you feel the need to use the Internet with increasing amounts of time in order to achieve satisfaction?	Yes	No
Have you repeatedly made unsuccessful efforts to control, cut back, or stop Internet use?	Yes	No
Do you feel restless, moody, depressed, or irritable when attempting to cut down or stop Internet use?	Yes	No
Do you stay online longer than originally intended?	Yes	No
Have you jeopardized or risked the loss of a significant other, significant relationship, job, educational, or career opportunity because of the Internet?	Yes	No
Have you lied to family members, "a therapist," or others to conceal the extent of your involvement with the Internet?	Yes	No
Do you use the Internet as a way of escaping from problems or of relieving a dysphoric mood (e.g., feelings of helplessness, guilt, anxiety, depression)?	Yes	No

overuse? You can try a sample of the questions from the Cell-Phone Over-Use Scale developed by Dr. Jenaro and colleagues (Figure 4.2).[14] When you answer the questions, use the following response scale: 1 = "Never," 2 = "Almost never," 3 = "Sometimes," 4 = "Often," 5 = "Almost always," and 6 = "Always." The higher your total score on the measure, the greater your chances of being identified as a compulsive overuser of a cell phone.

Some researchers have proposed a subset of cell phone addiction called "text-message dependency," and it has primarily been studied in Asian countries. Text-message dependency applies not only to text messages sent via mobile phones but also to e-mail sent on cell phones. It has been observed, for example, that kids in Japan who exhibit text-message dependency will leave their cell phones on while they sleep so as not to miss messages. This could lead to interference with sleep. It also has been shown that kids with text-message dependency will experience nervousness when they do not have their cell phones with them.[15]

FIGURE 4.2. EXAMPLES OF STATEMENTS FROM THE CELL PHONE OVERUSE SCALE (COS)

Question	Response					
	Never	Almost Never	Some-times	Often	Almost Always	Always
Do you feel preoccupied about possible calls or messages on the mobile phone and do you think about it when your mobile is off?	(1)	(2)	(3)	(4)	(5)	(6)
How often do you anticipate your next use of the mobile phone?	(1)	(2)	(3)	(4)	(5)	(6)
Do you feel the need to invest more and more time using the mobile phone to feel satisfied?	(1)	(2)	(3)	(4)	(5)	(6)
How often do you try to reduce the importance of the time spent using the phone, even though it has been many hours?	(1)	(2)	(3)	(4)	(5)	(6)
Have you ever restricted your time spent using the phone due to previous overuse?	(1)	(2)	(3)	(4)	(5)	(6)
Have you ever tried to not use the mobile phone and failed?	(1)	(2)	(3)	(4)	(5)	(6)
How often do you get angry or do you shout if someone tries to interrupt you when you are using the mobile phone?	(1)	(2)	(3)	(4)	(5)	(6)
Do you use the mobile phone to escape from your problems?	(1)	(2)	(3)	(4)	(5)	(6)
Do you lie to your relatives and friends regarding the frequency and duration of your mobile phone use?	(1)	(2)	(3)	(4)	(5)	(6)
Have you risked an important relation, a job, an academic opportunity, or a career development opportunity due to the overuse of the mobile phone?	(1)	(2)	(3)	(4)	(5)	(6)
Do you refrain from going out with your friends in order to spend more time using the mobile phone?	(1)	(2)	(3)	(4)	(5)	(6)

WHAT'S WRONG WITH OVERUSING THE
INTERNET (OR OTHER TECHNOLOGY)?

There are serious negative outcomes that can occur as the result of a technology addiction. Researchers have noted that the consequences of technology addiction are similar to the consequences of chemical addictions such as drugs or alcohol and can include financial problems, job loss, and relationship breakdowns.[16] Kimberly Young provides a case study that demonstrates the financial and relationship problems that can occur as the result of addiction.

Dr. Young's patient, who we will call Jo, described herself as initially computer illiterate, but she became quite enamored with computer use (especially social chat rooms) over time. She began to feel depressed when she wasn't online and, to avoid this, spent more and more time on the computer. She canceled appointments and stopped calling her real-life friends. Significant family problems developed: Her daughters felt ignored and her husband complained about the financial cost of her constant online behavior. She eventually became estranged from her daughters and separated from her husband.[17]

Sleep patterns are often totally disrupted by technology addiction. Technology addicts use their devices or the Internet 40 to 80 hours per week, or they might go on "net binges" in which a single session can last up to 20 hours or more. Given that there are only 168 hours in a week, using technology this much will nearly always result in sleep disruption. Being sleep deprived can impact academic or work performance and even weaken one's immune system. Additionally, sitting around at the computer or on the couch for long periods of time can lead to a loss of exercise, an increased risk of carpal tunnel syndrome, and eye or back strain.[18] For example, a study by the Benesse Institute of Education in Japan found that Japanese youth who used cell phones excessively were likely to come home after midnight and likely to go to bed after one in the morning. They also were more likely than less-frequent cell phone users to be late for school and late for class.[19] In a later study of Japanese youths and cell phone use, it was found that more than one-third of eighth-graders—kids barely out of their preteen years—agreed that cell phone use interferes with their daily schedules.[20]

HOW USERS BECOME ADDICTED TO TECHNOLOGY

Researchers have begun to identify certain personality traits that lead to an increased chance of becoming an addict. Some of the characteristics of a technology addictive personality that have been suggested are impulsivity, sensation seeking, psychoticism, and social deviance.[21] In other words, persons with a tendency to become addicted might already be likely to take actions without much thinking (impulsivity), to seek out intense or intensely pleasurable stimulants (sensation seeking), to be aggressive (psychoticism), and to avoid following rules (social deviance). Impulsivity and sensation seeking are related to each other, with sensation seeking seen as a form of impulsivity.[22]

The results of some studies examining sensation seeking and impulsivity with respect to Internet addiction have found that persons who have Internet dependence or persons with high Internet use also are sensation seekers.[23] One study of adolescents by Chih-Hung Ko and colleagues at the Kaohsiung Medical University in Taiwan suggested that individuals who have an inherent need to seek novelty might be particularly attracted to Internet activities. Novelty seekers quickly grow bored and need new stimuli to be aroused. Online games might especially satisfy the needs of these individuals as such games provide a highly varied environment with constantly changing scenarios and feedback.[24]

Dr. Ko identified another personality factor that was linked to Internet addiction called "harm avoidance," which reflects the idea that some people go out of their way to avoid uncomfortable situations. Dr. Ko and colleagues speculated that the online world is often perceived by adolescents as requiring less responsibility and causing less harm than the real world. Additionally, there is a "disinhibition" effect in which being online and "behind the screen" causes individuals to be less cautious about their actions.[25] Therefore, the online world might make persons high in harm avoidance especially vulnerable to Internet addiction. An additional personality-related factor investigated by Dr. Ko and colleagues was "reward dependence," which refers to how well people respond to pleasing stimuli—for example, rewards—from the environment. Surprisingly, individuals low in reward dependence were more likely to fit the criteria of Internet addiction. The researchers explained the relationship and reward dependence (RD) this way:

> Adolescents with low RD are impaired in their responsiveness to verbal approval and social reinforcement, and they have poor persistence. They demonstrate little tolerance for unpredictable frustrations in real life. Immediate and predictable achievement from Internet activity such as online gaming could therefore provide satisfactory resources for novelty and esteem without unpredictable frustration.[26]

There is good evidence that one's natural way of behaving (i.e., one's personality) can influence susceptibility to technology addiction, with sensation-seeking, harm avoidance, and reward dependence being three factors that influence your chances of addiction. How much of this is biochemical?

WHAT'S KNOWN ABOUT THE BIOLOGICAL BASIS OF TECHNOLOGY ADDICTION?

Scientists recently began considering whether the brain structures and functions responsible for technology addiction are the same as the ones responsible for classic drug addictions. For drug addictions, much evidence points to an altered reward system in the brain, perhaps involving changes in brain chemical levels (e.g., dopamine and/or serotonin).[27] Recent reviews of the non-substance or behavioral addictions reveal an overlap in the brain circuitry and chemistry with those brain systems involved in substance abuse.[28] Behavioral addictions that have been studied run the gamut from well-investigated ones like gambling addiction to less studied ones like sugar addiction and pornography addiction. The evidence that a behavioral addiction is the same as a drug addiction as far as the brain is concerned appears to be strongest for gambling addictions; however, there is some evidence that Internet addiction might function like a drug addiction.[29] A recent study of brain tissue in adolescents afflicted with Internet addiction leaves no doubt that there are differences between addicts and non-addicts in terms of brain systems. The researchers found that there were significant differences in the gray matter and white matter—measures related to the structure and functions of neurons—between the addicted adolescents and their "healthy" counterparts.[30]

THE PULL OF TECHNOLOGY

Technology addiction is probably not just attributable to individuals with certain personality characteristics or brain chemical levels. The technology itself lures us into using it, sometimes for extreme lengths of time. Even when people are not online, they might often be thinking about being online. A relative of mine, Rob, is a 52-year-old father of three boys and consumed by online fantasy football. Rob, who has a very busy job as a contract manager for an international computer consulting firm, provides a good example of the "pull" of technology. When the professional football season starts, Rob becomes obsessed with managing his own fantasy football team. Although football games (real and fantasy) are almost exclusively played on the weekends, the fantasy football website provides plenty of exciting opportunities for checking in and participating during the work week. There are daily posts by sports experts giving advice as to which players should be picked, almost daily "simulations" of head-to-head matchups between players, constantly streaming live "discussions" between fantasy football team owners over who are the best football players, hourly (or faster) news updates about what is happening in the real world of professional football, and a variety of online tools for managing one's own fantasy football team. In other words, there is always something exciting happening online. How can a football fanatic like Rob resist checking in on a frequent basis during the work day, especially when he has a company-issued BlackBerry device that gives him free web access?

As corroboration of Rob's addiction to online fantasy football, Kimberly Young found that interactive programs and software were likely to be linked to Internet dependency. The interactive programs that she observed as critical were Internet chat programs and multi-user domains (MUDs). MUDs are addictive because they provide multi-sensory information (sound and video), realistically portrayed virtual environments, and real-time interaction with other users. Have you ever tried *World of Warcraft?* There is a good chance that you have gone on a quest in this virtual fantasy world given that more than 12 million users were playing it as of 2010.[31] In fact, it is often referred to as *World of Warcrack* because it is so addictive!

In contrast, Dr. Young's study found that programs used for information-gathering or for maintaining relationships that were not real-time or synchronous (e.g., e-mail) were associated with non-dependent Internet users who were not technology addicts. In other words, it appears that the interactive types of programs and applications might have certain features that make them very appealing and prone to addictive behavior.[32] This is a critical issue and is particularly important since social networking is interactive, as are many websites and online activities. In fact, the computer and the technology environment allow for a number of factors that might encourage addiction. In addition to specific programs or applications, a person might become addicted to the act of typing, the type of communication that occurs on the computer or device, the avoidance of face-to-face communication, the kind of information that can be accessed online, or game playing. The fact that so much information and so many activities are available online might intensify the addictive qualities of being on the Internet.[33]

A more complex picture of how the technology itself may spark addictive behaviors involves the rather limited costs and potentially major psychological benefits of our Internet or technology experiences. For example, for minimal time and cost, the Internet in general and social networks in particular allow us to correspond with others who share our interests, meet people we would never otherwise meet, download entertaining software such as games, and keep in touch with friends. Psychologically, we benefit: We gain a feeling of status and trendiness, we are taken seriously and listened to, we can manipulate our online profile to suit our needs, and we are allowed to go on and on about interests that our physical family and friends might find very boring.[34]

And we should not forget the fact that programs and applications are designed by humans and companies to be interesting and fun. One of the most important factors that influences our desire and willingness to use technology is the interactivity of the program behind the technology. Psychological rewards, such as those earned while playing video games, also are important and built into the programs by the software designers.[35] Some researchers have likened the sense of excitement associated with using the Internet to a "high" that video game addicts receive when they play games or that gambling addicts receive when they place a bet.[36] With respect to cell phone use, it has been suggested that overuse of the phone (specifically, sending and receiving text messages) results from a need to receive approval from one's friends.[37]

Another possibility is that Internet and technology addiction are part of a larger pattern of technology obsession that goes all the way back to the introduction of radio in the 1930s. With radio, people began getting information and engaging in quasi-social activities through technology-mediated sources. Families gathered around the radio receiver after dinner to listen to the latest shows and to hear up-to-date news. Television continued the trend and the Internet is the latest installment, with smartphones as the ultimate personal resource that allows 24/7 access wherever and whenever.[38]

THOUGHTS THAT LEAD TO ADDICTION

Generally speaking, addictive behavior has been linked to low self-esteem. When a person has low self-esteem, several thought processes occur. There is a focus on negative self-evaluations. There also is a suspicion of praise. In other words, a person with low self-esteem might think, "How could people say nice things about me when I am not worth much? Those people must have ulterior motives." In one study, Dr. Lynette Armstrong and her colleagues found that self-esteem was a predictor of the number of hours spent per week on the Internet. It also was a strong predictor of Internet addiction.[39] It's quite possible that having low prior self-esteem increases the "high" that one gets from technology use by making relatively small rewards (for example, a high score in a game) even more compelling than normal. However, the authors of the study caution that low self-esteem might be the result of Internet addiction as much as it is likely that it is the cause of Internet addiction.

Negative feelings and thoughts are not just associated with low self-esteem but also with other mental disorders. Depression and social anxiety might also be involved, especially as they are associated with disordered thoughts.[40] Other conditions that can lead to negative thoughts include poor social skills and being lonely.[41] Addictive substances, in this case technology, the Internet, and smartphones, provide, for many, an escape from these distressing thoughts.[42] For example, I'm sure that most people know someone who lifts their spirits and distracts themselves by watching silly YouTube videos. Additionally, the anonymity of the Internet might allow for individuals to (virtually) overcome their perceived inadequacies.[43]

There are other possible factors influencing the development of addiction, too. For example, Dr. Young noted that negative life events—such as job dissatisfaction, medical illness, unemployment, and academic instability—could trigger addiction. The rewarding qualities of the Internet and the anonymity of being online could help these individuals avoid their suffering and dull their pain.[44]

TREATMENT

Internet addiction is a serious problem and has been considered for inclusion in the new version of the *DSM*. There have been several attempts at applying the standard psychotherapeutic approaches to individuals with Internet addiction, but no one approach appears to be sufficient.[45] The personality factors that might contribute to technology addiction suggest some approaches for dealing with individuals who experience the problem. First, healthy activities that provide novel and interesting stimulation ought to be considered in place of Internet-based or technology-based activities. Going outside and gardening or playing a sport would be excellent substitutes. Second, interventions that provide psychologically satisfying rewards ought to be substituted for Internet-based activities, as well. Reading a good book, perusing the (physical) newspaper, or playing (real) cards come to mind.[46]

Dr. Young provided several practical approaches to dealing with problematic technology use:

- Being offline at the times when you are normally online.

- Setting alarms to remind you when it is time to log off and get to work (or school).
- Setting a schedule for being online and offline.
- Avoiding problematic applications such as online chatting.
- Reminding yourself of the bad and good of the Internet.
- Examining what activities are lost due to excessive Internet use.
- Trying support groups and family therapy if necessary.[47]

Technology addiction is a real phenomenon and can have serious problems associated with it as an iDisorder. Although Internet addiction is the most widely studied form of technology addiction, you can be addicted to many different forms and aspects of technology, including text messaging, social networking, and cell phone calls. Addiction is not just about compulsive use, but also withdrawal, relapse, and other symptoms. Some personality types might be prone to technology addiction. Interestingly, the neural basis of technology addiction might be the same as the neural basis of drug addiction. If you find that you are an addict or that you have a potentially addictive personality, then you should consider trying to reduce your compulsive technology use with the tips mentioned here.

FIVE

The Ups (and Downs) of Leading a Cyberlife

Social Networking Among Teens Can Lead to "Facebook Depression."
—G. S. O'Keefe, K. Clark-Pearson, and
Council on Communications and Media [1]

I have a 35-year-old patient, Nathan, who has rapid cycling bipolar disorder. For the last six months or so I have been working with his psychiatrist and Nathan is finally on a medication that seems to be working. In therapy we have been working on the underlying issues that confront him on a daily basis and I think that we have been reasonably successful. A couple of months ago, I went to get him in the waiting room and found Nathan looking disheveled and furiously typing on his new iPad and flipping back and forth from screen to screen. He looked like he hadn't slept in the week since we last met. We spent the entire session, and much of the next month or two, dealing with his manic online behavior. With cognitive behavioral techniques I thought that we had successfully worked toward understanding how the Internet can exacerbate mania and then when I went to get him for his next session I found him sitting in the waiting room staring at the iPad and sobbing. Seeing this behavior I realized that the same online world that had spurred a manic episode was now potentiating a bout of depression.

—Personal communication from an anonymous psychologist

I n 1995, Dr. Robert Kraut and his colleagues at Carnegie Mellon University tracked 93 households and the time they spent online. Dubbed the HomeNet Project,[2] Kraut provided these households with a computer and Internet access and then carefully monitored the families' use and their psychological health. In their first HomeNet report, which examined the initial year or year and a half of Internet use, Kraut concluded, "Greater use of the Internet is associated with increases in loneliness and

symptoms of depression."[3] However, when the HomeNet Project continued to check in with these families, they found that by the third year of
Internet access those signs of loneliness and depression were gone.[4] This
portion of the HomeNet Project was completed before the new millennium, before ubiquitous Internet use, and most certainly before the rapid
rise of social networking. Does having access to the entire world of both
information and communication make us more prone to depression or
does it provide us a vehicle with which to express our feelings of being
sad and lonely?

According to the National Institute of Mental Health (NIMH),[5] nearly
one in five adults will suffer from some form of depression—either major
depression or a milder dysthymia—during their lifetime, with an additional
4 percent of adults suffering from bipolar disorder, which encompasses both
depression and mania. In addition, 11 percent of children and adolescents
will suffer from depression. Each of these mood disorders—major depression, dysthymia, and bipolar disorder—has unique and distinct symptomology, which can get played out through our relationship with technology and
media. In this chapter I will explore these three disorders and show you
why I think that technology plays an often-prominent role in exacerbating
an existing mood disorder or perhaps even encouraging its development.

According to an article in *Pediatrics,* the official journal of the American Academy of Pediatrics, "Researchers have proposed a new phenomenon called 'Facebook depression,' defined as depression that develops
when preteens and teens spend a great deal of time on social media sites,
such as Facebook, and then begin to exhibit classic symptoms of depression."[6] Whether there is truly an affliction called Facebook depression is indeed controversial.[7] However, there is no doubt that our interactions with
technology are making us *appear* as though we may be depressed or manic
or both.

Let's begin with the combination of both depression and mania. Bipolar disorder, often referred to as manic depression, has an average age of
onset of 25 years old and affects nearly 4 percent of the population. Bipolar disorder is a combination of waves of depression and waves of mania.
These waves may come rapidly, with one wave of depression followed by

a wave of mania, or may slowly cycle from the lows of depression through normalcy through manic highs. Here is the NIMH website description of bipolar disorder:

> Bipolar disorder, also known as manic-depressive illness, is a brain disorder that causes unusual shifts in mood, energy, activity levels, and the ability to carry out day-to-day tasks. Symptoms of bipolar disorder are severe. They are different from the normal ups and downs that everyone goes through from time to time. Bipolar disorder symptoms can result in damaged relationships, poor job or school performance, and even suicide. People with bipolar disorder experience unusually intense emotional states that occur in distinct periods called "mood episodes." An overly joyful or overexcited state is called a manic episode, and an extremely sad or hopeless state is called a depressive episode. Sometimes, a mood episode includes symptoms of both mania and depression. This is called a mixed state. People with bipolar disorder also may be explosive and irritable during a mood episode.[6]

NIMH describes the symptoms of mania as:

- Experiencing a long period of feeling "high," or an overly happy or outgoing mood.
- Experiencing an extremely irritable mood, feeling agitation, feeling "jumpy" or "wired."
- Talking very fast, jumping from one idea to another, having racing thoughts.
- Being easily distracted.
- Increasing goal-directed activities, such as taking on new projects.
- Being restless.
- Sleeping little.
- Having an unrealistic belief in one's abilities.
- Behaving impulsively and taking part in a lot of pleasurable high-risk behaviors, such as spending sprees, impulsive sex, and impulsive business investments.

The other side of bipolar disorder, the down times or depression, is described as:

- Experiencing a long period of feeling worried or empty.
- Experiencing a loss of interest in activities once enjoyed, including sex.
- Feeling tired or "slowed down."
- Having problems concentrating, remembering, and making decisions.
- Being restless or irritable.
- Changing eating, sleeping, or other habits.
- Thinking of death or suicide, or attempting suicide.

Depending on the type of bipolar disorder, people may have episodes lasting anywhere from weeks to changing states from depressed to manic within the same week or even the same day.

As you read the psychologist's description of his patient Nathan, you get a picture of someone who is cycling between bouts of depression and mania, but since the trigger seemed to be tied to the Internet, the psychologist wanted to talk to me about the role that technology might be playing in these waves of high and low feelings. Although I have never met Nathan, I know many adults and teenagers who manifest manic behaviors, appear depressed, or, like Nathan, cycle through the two, going from high highs down to low lows. Whether this is a genetic or biologically related psychological disorder may be an open question. However, the research is now showing that technology may act as a trigger to induce these mood swings. This is the precise definition of an iDisorder.

FEELING DOWN AND GOING ONLINE

The bulk of the work that psychologists have done over the last decade on mood disorders and their link to technology has focused on the depressive side. According to the NIMH, nearly 17 percent of American adults will be diagnosed as having major depression during their lifetime, with another nearly 3 percent having dysthymic disorder (persistent depression for at least two years but no major depressive episodes during the first two years and no manic episodes either). Add in another 4 percent of adults who will be diagnosed with bipolar disorder and subtract the overlap and you have one in five adults who will manifest symptoms sufficiently severe to carry a diagnosis of a mood disorder. NIMH statistics also show that one in seven children and adolescents will be diagnosed as having a mood disorder, with most of them showing major depression or dysthymic disorder.[9]

Research has shown that the average ages of onset are 32 for major depression[10] and 31 for dysthymic disorder.[11] The Net Generation and Generation X, who came of age just as the Internet became part of our American lifestyle, would be around these ages right now. As you may recall from Chapter 1, these generations spend a large amount of time online and use a variety of technologies that may become prime fodder for depressive symptoms. In the large-scale study of psychiatric disorders that I described in Chapter 1, we found the following interesting results when examining the relationship between a variety of technology uses, attitudes, and behaviors when compared to symptoms of major depression, dysthymia, and mania. Figure 5.1 displays the relationships that were statistically valid after controlling for any and all relevant demographic variables.[12]

Examining the two Axis II depressive disorders in Figure 5.1,[13] it is clear that there are both similarities and differences in people who manifest symptoms of major depression or dysthymia. For example, when it comes to the specific technologies, instant messaging, texting, playing video games, and watching television are related to both forms of depression, while listening to music for hours on end is only related to being dysthymic. Consider the following example from one of our research studies of Mitchell, a 35-year-old construction worker who is on disability leave for depression.

> I work for a construction company and we have been working on a huge office building for more than a year now. When I was working I would have my iPod on all day long and would listen to music that I grew up with. Most of this was heavy metal with dark lyrics about death and destruction. When I would come home I would barely say hi to the kids and the wife and go

FIGURE 5.1. TECHNOLOGY AND MEDIA USE, TECHNOLOGY BELIEFS AND ATTITUDES, AND TECHNOLOGY BEHAVIORS RELATED TO SPECIFIC MOOD DISORDERS

	Disorder		
	Major Depression	*Dysthymia*	*Mania*
Technology and Media Uses Most Associated with the Disorder	Engaging in excessive instant messaging	Engaging in excessive instant messaging	Using a lot of media and technology each day
	Texting constantly	Texting constantly	Being on Facebook often
	Playing video games often	Playing video games often	Spending lots of time online
	Watching a lot of television	Listening to music constantly	Engaging in excessive instant messaging
		Watching a lot of television	Texting constantly
			Playing video games often
			Listening to music constantly
			Watching a lot of television
Technology-Related Behaviors Most Associated with the Disorder	Getting anxious when can't check texts, cell calls, Facebook	Constantly checking voice mail and e-mail	Constantly checking texts/cell calls/Facebook
	Getting anxious when can't check voice mail or e-mail	Getting anxious when can't check voice mail or e-mail	Constantly checking voice mail and e-mail
	Preferring to multitask		Getting anxious when can't check texts, cell calls, Facebook
			Preferring to multitask
Technology-Related Beliefs and Attitudes Most Associated with the Disorder	Believing that technology is a negative societal influence	Believing that technology is a negative societal influence	Believing that technology is a negative societal influence
	Believing in getting emotional support online	Believing in getting emotional support online	Believing that technology is a positive societal influence

downstairs in the basement to play one of the GTA [*Grand Theft Auto*] games. My wife kept telling me to go to the doctor because I always seemed so down and grouchy. When she dragged me away from my games to watch TV with her I always wanted to watch war movies while she wanted to watch the *Tonight Show*. Over time the kids started acting strangely toward me and acting up at the dinner table and even at school. My wife was getting angry often and I heard her crying in bed quietly when she thought I was sleeping. Finally I went to a psychiatrist on my medical plan and he immediately diagnosed me as having been really depressed for almost an entire year. He put me on disability and some medication to help improve my mood swings and now that I am home all day long all I do is play games, listen to music, and watch Netflix movies. I can't figure out why I am not getting any better. My wife says it's because I am playing depressing games and watching people killing each other on TV all day long. She is worried and very sad about what is happening to me.

In order to understand Mitchell's problems, we turn to a clever study entitled "I'm Sad You're Sad," designed by Jeffrey Hancock, a professor at Cornell University. Dr. Hancock and his colleagues found that depressing movie clips and sad music induced negative affect in their viewers and listeners compared with those who watched a neutral movie or listened to a neutral song.[14] Hancock also found that these depressive symptoms could be transmitted to another person through what he called "emotional contagion," where the mood of one person (in this case a singer or an actor) can affect someone's mood drastically.

To demonstrate emotional contagion the researchers followed a five-minute sad movie presentation with a 15-minute instant messaging task in which each participant was asked to learn something they had in common with their IM partner—who they had not met before the study—and discuss something that was worrying that partner. While they were conversing, the person who had viewed the sad movie listened to sad music and tried to solve difficult (and often impossible) anagrams. Those participants who experienced the negative movie and music were frustrated trying to solve anagrams, expressed fewer words and more sad words in the IM, and took longer to do so than those who had IM partners in the neutral conditions. Strikingly, their partners—who did not hear the music, see the movie, or solve the anagrams—also used less positive words compared with partners of those in the neutral condition. This is emotional contagion at work. It is not surprising that Mitchell, who spent his entire day watching sad images and listening to sad music, was deeply affected.

Now consider Brandon, a 19-year-old college student who is away from home for the first time in his life. Brandon lives in a dorm with two roommates and attends college 500 miles away from his home. He is constantly texting (he showed me his current month's phone bill and he had sent and received a whopping 6,359 text messages), and he has long instant message conversations deep into the night with his high school girlfriend—she is a senior and still lives in his home town—and his best friend who goes to a community college near home. After just five weeks at school Brandon is behind in all four of his classes and hasn't even started the readings for two of them. He can't seem to get out of bed in the morning and he is feeling like every day is a burden. According to Brandon, "Maybe I am not cut out for college right now. I just don't seem to be doing well. I lie in bed staring at the walls and then can't get up in the morning for class. Even on those nights that I do get enough sleep I just can't get motivated to do anything. I try to read for my Poly Sci class, which I like but it is all so confusing and I can't seem to follow the book or the professor. I just want to go home."

Brandon is most likely suffering from some sort of depression and his symptoms sound like a potential case of major depression. Although there is no way to directly "blame" the technology for his lack of interest and lethargy, it seems that he retreats into electronic communications as a way of keeping in close contact with his friends back at home. When I asked him about those texts and IMs, he told me, "For the most part my conversations with my friends are like 'Hey, are you feeling crappy, too?' or me complaining about life. My girlfriend and I fight constantly on IM and by texts. She wants me to see a shrink and I just want to come home. I think that she wants to break up with me and that makes me feel even worse although I understand that I am a major downer in her life."

Several studies have found similar links between media use and depression. One study, which used data collected from a 1994–2002 project entitled "The National Longitudinal Study of Adolescent Health," found that among its 4,142 middle-school and high-school students who had no signs of depression when the study began, more current television viewing and more time currently spent online were related to more depression eight years later.[15] The authors explored several contributing factors, including the fact that media activities displace sleep, and lack of sleep is known to cause depression. In addition, they suspected that other causes might include the fact that the content of their activities may be negative (as in Hancock's emotional contagion study), they might be spending less time interpersonally interacting with friends and family, and they may be making negative comparisons to themselves, including comparisons about their body type[16] and their intelligence. Regardless of the cause, the study extended the impact of these media to depression among adolescents who, as we know, are now consuming massive quantities of media in all forms.

If you look at the middle portion of Figure 5.1 you also get a hint of some additional technology-related behavioral signs that might indicate a specific mood disorder. For example, people who suffer from either major depression or dysthymia get anxious when they can't check their e-mail or voice mail while those with more severe depression issues also get anxious when they can't check ANY of their other e-communication modalities, including text messages, cell phone calls, and, of course, Facebook. Finally, and not surprisingly, those afflicted with the manic component of bipolar disorder prefer to multitask—or task switch—and are constantly checking in with all of their communication tools. If those with mania cannot access their cell or social networks they tend to exhibit more symptoms associated with this disorder.

The research results in the lower section of Figure 5.1 also highlight some other issues that might shed light on someone who demonstrates different mood disorder symptoms. Again, there are similarities and, I think, quite meaningful differences that capture each disorder. For example, while people with all three mood disorders believe that technology has a negative influence on society, those with depressive symptomology believe that they can garner emotional support in their online world. Those with mania do not hold that belief, but instead they see technology as having *both* positive and negative societal effects, which perhaps creates an environment that promotes manic symptoms similar to an approach-avoidance conflict, where a person has to choose something that is attractive and engaging but has negative repercussions. We will further explore these issues at the end of the chapter when I talk about strategies for helping yourself or someone you know deal with mood disorder symptoms that are being manifested through their technology use.

CAN SOCIAL NETWORKING MAKE YOU DEPRESSED?

According to the latest statistics more than 800 million people in the world are Facebook users, including 48 percent of Americans; 36 percent of Australians, New Zealanders, and South Pacific Islanders; 26 percent of Europeans; and 21 percent of Latin Americans. Overall, 10 percent of the world's population use Facebook and only 30 percent of them are from the United States.[17] Whether or not Facebook survives as the dominant social network, it is clear that the Internet has become a place to socialize and communicate with other people, both friends and strangers. With mobile devices making access available whenever you want and wherever you might be located in the world, we are always connected to our social worlds. The question then becomes, when we are behind the safety of our computer screen (whether it be the large one on our desk or the small one in the palm of our hand), are we able to understand the true dynamics or what language experts call the *pragmatics*[18] of communication?

If you are communicating directly, face to face, with someone and you say something that hurts their feelings, they will most likely react and express their upset and sadness through both words and nonverbal cues such as body language, facial expressions, and tears. In most cases you, as the person who elicited those hurt feelings, will notice these cues and respond to them, often with an apology or words of comfort and empathy. What happens when someone's feelings are hurt but you cannot see them react because they are not in the same physical space as you? In the online social networking universe, the only vehicle available in which to express those feelings is words. Certainly the person could add some emoticons such as a frowning face to indicate upset. Or they could go even further and pour out their emotions in a video that they post on Facebook. But the dominant mode of person-to-person e-communication uses two-dimensional words, flat on a page, which are mostly devoid of all those cues that we use to understand another person's emotional state.

In 2006, a Missouri teenager, Megan Meier, began communicating on MySpace with a boy named Josh. He expressed caring feelings for her until he started saying unkind things and telling her that she was a bad person and that she should go kill herself. Megan did not know that Josh was really the mother of a former friend of Megan's intent on hurting her, and sadly, Megan hung herself. She has become emblematic of the dangerous impact two-dimensional words can have on people who socialize online.

Megan is not the only teenager or young adult to become depressed by something someone wrote on her wall. There are many cases of depression and suicide that involve a social network. Tiong-Thye Goh and Yen-Pei Huang of Victoria University of Wellington, New Zealand, conducted a comprehensive study of 15,107 teen and young adult MySpace bloggers in Australia, New Zealand, and the United Kingdom. The researchers used a computer program to search for key words that would indicate the existence of depression and suicidal ideation. Strikingly, they found one in six had expressed these negative thoughts and were found to be at risk for depression and potential suicide.[19] There is no way to tell from this research whether MySpace activities were making teens and young adults more depressed or more depressed kids used MySpace. Regardless, however, social networking sites can reflect depressive ideation.

Although the New Zealand study focused on keywords that might indicate potential suicidal ideation, is there anything specifically that might provide an early warning flag that one of our social network friends is depressed? This question has been the topic of three extensive research studies with interesting results. Joanne Davila and her colleagues at Stony Brook University studied nearly 4,000 social network users and found that depressive symptoms appeared to be moderated not by the amount of time spent on social networks but rather on the quality of those online interactions.[20] Those students who had more negative interactions on their Facebook or MySpace pages were more likely to be depressed, regardless of whether they were heavy or light users of the sites. Interestingly, Davila found similar results for text messaging and instant messaging, both important communication modalities for teens and young adults. More importantly, however, Davila and her colleagues found that those young people who "ruminated" (fixated or dwelt on) and "co-ruminated" (talked to others) about these depressing encounters online were more likely to stay depressed. In essence they showed that online social interactions have the same qualities as real-world interactions. More negative interactions thought about more often are more likely to evoke depressive symptoms regardless of whether it is face to face or on Facebook. According to Dr. Davila, "Social networking is just another salient venue where problematic relationships can play out and have an impact on depression."[21]

Using a different approach, Megan Moreno, a professor at the University of Wisconsin, examined 200 university student Facebook profiles in an attempt to identify potential depressive symptoms by inspecting status updates.[22] Moreno and her colleagues were able to discern that one-fourth of the profile status updates displayed depressive symptoms and 2.5 percent of them could be categorized as indicating a major depressive episode. More important, I believe, is that Moreno discovered that those students who received at least one comment to their status update were more likely to discuss their depression publicly on Facebook. A study by a Dutch research team found results that suggest one way people can be positively impacted through this same modality: Adolescents who received positive feedback on their social networking profiles showed increased self-esteem and increased sense of well-being.[23] According to Moreno, her results plus those of the Dutch research team indicate that, "Given the frequency of depression symptom displays on public profiles, social networking sites could be an innovative avenue for combating stigma surrounding mental health conditions or for identifying students at risk for depression."

Following up on Moreno's notion that Facebook may provide an avenue for detecting depression, I discovered an interesting recent doctoral dissertation study by Shannon Holleran of the University of Arizona, who attempted to determine if social networking websites could be used for early detection of depression among college students.[24] Holleran' s theory was that given the public nature of social networking postings, as well as the perceived anonymity and invisibility behind the screen, people might engage in less *impression management* and thus be more likely to provide signs and symptoms of depression. In a series of three studies, Dr. Holleran asked judges— who were just other college students— to read a full MySpace page, a full Facebook page, or portions of a Facebook page and determine whether the person penning those words was depressed. Using an independent, well-researched depression measurement tool, Dr. Holleran was then able to relate characteristics of social networking use with actual levels of depression in the Facebook or MySpace users who posted those pages.

Interestingly, while the judges were able to accurately determine depressive symptomology from a full MySpace page or Facebook page (which include both the person's thoughts as well as interactions with others), they did a slightly better job if they only read the person's Facebook status updates. However, when judges were asked to predict levels of depression three months down the road from the current Facebook pages, the person-to-person interactions on Facebook were helpful because they allowed the judges to detect changes in the quality and quantity of interpersonal exchanges. Further, Holleran examined the exact words used in the status updates and found that more depressed people used fewer positive emotion words, more death-related words, more religious words, more metaphysical words (e.g., *faith, moral*), more swear words, and more negative emotion words (e.g., *worthless, sad*).

So, is there such a thing as Facebook depression, or depression caused by being on a social network? The answer to the question is best summed up by Larry Magid, a well-respected *Huffington Post* journalist and long-time commentator on the impact of technology. He wrote: "Clearly, there are people who use Facebook who are depressed but what isn't clear is whether Facebook users are any more likely to be depressed than non-Facebook users and, even if that's the case, whether that's because Facebook causes depression or because depressed people are more likely to turn to Facebook to help them deal with their depression. I haven't done the research, but I'm pretty sure that children who visit pediatricians (except for regular checkups) are more likely to be sick than children who don't visit them. Does that imply that pediatricians cause illness? Of course not."[25]

MORE MEDIA-INDUCED DEPRESSION

From Jeffrey Hancock's study "I'm Sad You're Sad," discussed previously, we know that the mood of one person can, and does, affect the mood of others, acting as an emotional contagion. Moods are expressed through all electronic modalities including television, music, and the Internet. Do they, too, provide venues for eliciting depressive symptoms? The answer is a resounding YES! Our own study (see Figure 5.1) showed that depression and mania both were related to various forms of electronic communication, including instant messaging and texting as well as playing video games, watching too much television, and listening to music. Of course those are only correlational results that don't answer the question: Does the technology cause the mood disorder symptoms, or are depressed people more likely to use the technology?

For a partial answer to the impact of technology and media on depressive symptomology, we once again turn to solid research across a variety of fields around the world. For example, The National Longitudinal Study of Adolescent Health mentioned earlier[26] pinned the blame for depression on total daily media use and television and did not find any increased depression from playing video games, listening to the radio, or watching movies on television. Dr. Scott Frank of Case Western University studied 4,000 high school students and found that hyper-networking—which he defined as spending more than three hours per school day on social networking websites—and hyper-texting—more than 120 messages per school day—were related to depressive symptoms.[27] Similarly, a national study of college life in Taiwan found that both male and female students who played more online video games and spent more time chatting and information seeking were more depressed.[28] Finally, several Dutch researchers[29] as well as many other international scholars[30] have found a link between Internet use, instant messaging, e-mailing, chatting, and depression among adolescents while numerous studies have shown strong relationships between video gaming and depression, with one even demonstrating that over the course of two years more video game use among children and adolescents predicted more depression.[31] Overall, it appears that no single technology or media can be identified as a trigger for depressive symptoms.

Finally, the results of my own research show how the various types of media or technology might elicit signs of depression. In a study discussed in more detail in Chapter 9, my colleagues and I examined whether the use of a variety of media or technology devices was related to poor health regardless of personal information, family demographics, the person's eating habits, or their (lack) of exercise. Those young children who used more media in any and all forms for more hours on a daily basis (with no particular device culprit) had worse psychological health. For preteens, using too much daily media in general also predicted poor psychological health; however, one specific potential cause of depression was also identified: video gaming. Finally, for teenagers, the same set of predictors (too much media in general and video gaming specifically) was identified as a cause of depression, but now another causal factor—excessive time spent online—was also identified as predicting depression and other psychological maladies. Putting all of these studies together gives us a picture that too much of any form of media might lead to—or, more accurately, might be related to—depressive symptomology.

WHY DEPRESSED PEOPLE USE MORE MEDIA . . . OR WHY MEDIA MAKES PEOPLE MORE DEPRESSED

Psychologists have offered a multitude of theoretical explanations for the link between media and depression. Cognitive behavioral scientists—those who focus on the interface between our thoughts and behaviors—have likened the current state of our cyber world to the "wild, wild west": There are few rules and anything goes.[32] A cognitive behavioral psychologist would argue that we are continually deriving responses from faceless and disembodied people who exist behind a screen and feel free to say anything at any time without much regard for our personal feelings. A photo that we post on Facebook might garner some "likes" from friends, and then that one nasty, negative comment from a friend of a friend hits us like a fist-sized rock. Literally our world can be turned upside down by one thoughtless, off-the-cuff remark made by someone identified only by a profile picture and words. Recent work out of Harvard University[33] confirms that these negative responses hit us at a cellular level in our brain in an area responsible for feedback-related negativity, so it is no wonder that a single bit of negative feedback can send us spiraling emotionally downward.

The early behaviorists argued that any responses could be traced directly to the stimuli that elicited them. Albert Bandura of Stanford University proposed a more social version of this theory, dubbed Social Learning Theory or Social Cognition. Bandura's theory describes how we gain our sense of *self-efficacy,* beliefs about our own abilities and competence, from our social interactions. Positive interactions leave us feeling better while negative ones pose a threat to our coping abilities. If we are already experiencing depressive symptoms, negative evaluations—such as someone mocking a posted Facebook photo—can have a devastating impact on our self-evaluations and, in turn, on our depression. This is particularly true given the wealth of research and robust findings showing that depressed people demonstrate selective attention to negative comments far more than positive ones and allow those negative comments to linger and occupy attention far longer than positive ones.[34] No wonder that negative post can hit us so hard and for so long even when it is one among dozens. People who are depressed tend to miss the positive and overaccentuate the negative, which means that if we are showing even the mildest depressed feelings, negative communications can have a much more pronounced effect on us. And in our wild west Internet world we often encounter those nasty slaps, which can cut us deeply, even when the person delivering the blow isn't someone we know or consider part of our friendship network.

HOW DO YOU KNOW IF SOMEONE IS DEPRESSED OR MANIC?

The signs of depression are clear: feeling tired or down, having problems with concentration and memory, feeling tearful or on the verge of tears, feeling irritable, sleeping more than normal, thinking about death, losing appetite, losing interest in pleasurable activities, and changing normal daily functioning. Similarly, the signs of mania are fairly clear: being easily distracted, talking rapidly, having racing thoughts, feeling restless, behaving impulsively, engaging in more high-risk activities, and showing changes in sleep habits, with shorter sleep cycles and longer waking cycles. There are many tested questionnaires that can gauge your level of depression as well as others that deal with the combination of mania and depression. Take a few moments and answer the questions in Figure 5.2 and use the information below the questions to score your mood disorder level. NOTE: You can also use the same questionnaire to assess another person's mood disorder.

After you have answered each of the nine questions in this instrument, add up the total points circled for your depression score. Although the PHQ–9 is used with a variety of diagnostic criteria, the most common is shown in Figure 5.3.[35]

If you are at all concerned that the problem might also include manic symptoms, you might want to take the Goldberg Bipolar Screening Quiz developed by Dr. Ivan Goldberg.[36]

COMBATTING A DEPRESSION OR MANIA IDISORDER

Once you've taken the PHQ–9 you should have a sense of your depressive signs as well as the potential mood swing symptomology. It is important to note that all mood disorders are serious and if you, or someone close to you, is feeling depressed and/or manic you need to discuss this with a professional. The treatment of choice is most often a combination of drugs and some form of therapy, which has been shown in numerous research studies to be optimally effective, particularly for treating depression,[37] However, if someone is exhibiting this type of iDisorder it may be helpful to consider the following suggestions.

It's all about balance. The research that we have done in our lab as well as numerous studies by other scientists has shown that using excessive media is related to mood disorders. When you are continually dealing with the world through the written word you tend to lose sight of emotional connotations behind those two-dimensional printed characters on the screen. Everything in your world becomes two-dimensional and all words share the same meaning, regardless of whether they are from your best friend, your parent, or some person you friended on Facebook. Consider the following as a way of keeping it "real."

FIGURE 5.2. PATIENT HEALTH QUESTIONNAIRE TO MEASURE DEPRESSION

PATIENT HEALTH QUESTIONNAIRE (PHQ–9)[a]

Over the *last 2 weeks,* how often have you been bothered by any of the following problems? (Circle one answer per row.)

Problem	Not at All	Several Days	More than Half the Days	Nearly Every Day
Little interest or pleasure in doing things	0	1	2	3
Feeling down, depressed, or hopeless	0	1	2	3
Trouble falling or staying asleep, or sleeping too much	0	1	2	3
Feeling tired or having little energy	0	1	2	3
Poor appetite or overeating	0	1	2	3
Feeling bad about yourself—or that you are a failure or have let yourself or your family down	0	1	2	3
Trouble concentrating on things, such as reading the newspaper or watching television	0	1	2	3
Moving or speaking so slowly that other people could have noticed or the opposite—being so fidgety or restless that you have been moving around a lot more than usual	0	1	2	3
Thoughts that you would be better off dead or of hurting yourself in some way	0	1	2	3
Scoring (add the total circled for each column)				
Total score (add the total of the 1s, 2s, and 3s)				

[a]Kroenke, K., Spitzer, R. L., & Williams, J. B. W. (2001). The PHQ-9: Validity of a brief depression severity measure. *Journal of General Internal Medicine, 16(9),* 606-613.

FIGURE 5.3. PHQ–9 ASSESSMENT OF DEPRESSION

Score Range	Depression Severity
1 to 4	Minimal depression
5 to 9	Mild depression
10 to 14	Moderate depression
15 to 19	Moderately severe depression
20 to 27	Severe depression

- For one week keep a chart with your various technology and media uses. Consider using the one in Figure 5.4 as a model. I have entered some sample data for myself from one day. When I woke up at 8 A.M. I immediately grabbed my cell phone and checked my e-mail, voice mail, texts, etc. I basically have my cell phone with me all day long so the "end time" was actually when I turned it off at night. During the day I used my cell phone, laptop, and tablet. I watched the news, so I added television to the list. There are several aspects of this list that are important for you to monitor.

  - First, how much time are you spending using technologies? More time with technology is related to more depression and mania symptoms. Use this as a guide to monitor and perhaps pace your media and technology time.

  - Second, how are you communicating with people during the day? Are you mostly conversing electronically? Are you getting enough face-to-face communication time? This is important since the research shows that when our communications are electronic we are missing essential cues that we need to have a complete communication.

  - Third, note overlap between time spent using one device (or multiple windows on a device) and another device, when you are ripe for multitasking or switching from one task to another. Remember that those who preferred to task switch more showed more signs of mania!

FIGURE 5.4. SAMPLE MEDIA AND TECHNOLOGY USE CHART

Technology/Media Use	Start Time	End Time	Total Time	Who Did You Communicate with During this Time?
Cell phone	8:00 A.M.	11:00 P.M.	15 hours	Text: son, daughter, colleague E-Mail: 18 received, 3 sent
Laptop computer	9:00 A.M.	6:00 P.M.	9 hours	E-Mail: 53 received, 17 sent IM: son Facebook: 2 "likes," 1 status update, posted comments on three walls, five posts on my wall
Tablet computer	10:00 P.M.	11:30 P.M.	1.5 hours	None—reading only
Television	10:00 P.M.	12:30 A.M.	2.5 hours	None—watching only

- During the same week keep a specific list of all the communications you received and how each made you "feel" on a –10 (horrible, upset) to +10 (fantastic, great) scale. I recommend using a simple chart for this, such as the one that you see in Figure 5.5. I just plotted my early morning communications and already I can see that the only communication that was uncomfortable was one on Facebook from JS, someone I barely know. And notice further that the impact of that one communication was quite substantially negative, a –7 on my –10 to +10 scale. If I had been feeling depressed, the fact that this one Facebook post affected me so strongly would be very important information. Based on this I might want to ask: "Why did a FB post on my wall from someone I don't even know have such a major impact on my mood? Who is this person and why am I letting JS impact me so strongly?"

- I also recommend paying attention to the other end of your communication scale. Why did a positive communication from my colleague only register a +4 and an e-mail from MM only reach a +3 when my "feelings" indicated that they were both positive in how they made me feel? When negative information weighs far more heavily in impacting your mood compared to positive information, this is a sign of depression. This is why I like to use a +10 to –10 scale so that I can directly compare the impact of negative communications with that of positive ones.

Guard against emotional contagion. Remember that Dr. Hancock's research demonstrated that we are emotionally impacted by the emotions of others through technology. This implies that you should pay attention to the types of messages that you are getting from your various entertainment media.

- What television shows are you watching? Are they depressing? Are they showing human misery or unhappiness? If so, then you should change what you watch. The same thoughts go for

FIGURE 5.5. CHART TO ASSESS HOW E-COMMUNICATIONS AFFECT YOUR MOOD

Communication Partner	Modality	Relationship to You	How Did It Make You Feel?	How Did It Affect Your Mood? (+10 to -10)
CW	IM	Son	Great! Nice to connect	+10
KW	Text—multiple	Daughter	Wonderful	+10
MC	Phone	Colleague	Good productive work time discussing a book chapter	+4
JS	Facebook	Friend of friend	Uncomfortable—somewhat snippy and nasty	−7
MM	E-mail	Colleague on East Coast	Felt positive—discussed my recent article and the feedback was fair and positive	+3

the music you listen to and any other form of media that enters your mind during the day. Try to listen only to neutral or positive messages.

- In the same vein, negative communications can be emotionally contagious. Who are you connecting with and are they spreading their depressive symptoms to you? Obviously you cannot remove certain people from your life and it is important to maintain those family ties and friendships. However, just because someone is an online friend doesn't mean you have to read every post about their unhappiness and their rants and raves. Hide anyone who might be emotionally contagious. If they need to reach you, there is always the telephone and e-mail.

- A quick side note: In Dr. Holleran's study she found that more depressed people used fewer positive emotion words, more death-related words, more religious words, more metaphysical words (e.g., faith, moral), more swear words, and more negative emotion words (e.g., worthless, sad). Pay attention to the use of these words in your own writing and that of others, as they may signal a depressed person.

Social compensation. Research has shown that those people who use the Internet for communication often do so to compensate for their less-than-satisfying friendships in the real world.[38] Although there are those who would argue that you cannot really be friends with people you only know online, there are many who feel the opposite. And the evidence seems to support the latter with a recent Pew Internet & American Life Project study showing that people who are on social networks have more close friends and get more social support than those who are not on social networks.[39]

- Make a list of those people who you consider good enough friends (including family members) that you would talk to them about feeling down or upset. For each indicate how much time you spend with them per week both online and in the real world.

Now list those people who you consider acquaintances. In this list also indicate how much time you spend with them online and/or offline. If you are depressed look at the first list and make sure that you are spending more time with those people than the ones on the second list. Also notice how you contact your good friends and which way will work best for you to get support for your feelings. Don't worry if there are good friends on your list that you connect with more online. As you will see, you can derive empathy in a virtual world.

Virtual empathy is real (and potentially valuable). A recent study done by senior psychology students Alexander Spradlin and John Bunce and colleagues in my research lab highlighted a very important message about where you might go to obtain support and empathy. Spradlin and Bunce administered an anonymous online survey to nearly 1,400 young adults that measured empathy shown in the real world, virtual empathy shown online, feelings of social support, and a variety of detailed questions about the types of technology that people use in their daily lives. Several interesting results were found, including the fact that virtual empathy is not only a real concept but it is linked to a feeling of social support,[40] although real-world empathy is more strongly related to positive feelings, that is, you feel more supported if you receive empathy in person than if you receive it online. The more interesting results for this discussion are:

- Those who spend more time on social networks and who instant message more often are the best at dispensing virtual empathy and social support. So, look for those "friends" who share these characteristics to message about your sad and lonely feelings. In Figure 5.6 you can see a brief example of how virtual empathy can be dispensed on a social network. Lauryn is stressed and upset about her mom's surgery and several of her friends have sent good thoughts her way. Lauryn feels so good that she sends back hugs and kisses in one post and a big "Thank uuuu!!!!!!" in another. And it is not just the comments from Marlene, Jennah, Adam, Nguyen, and Mavel that make her feel better. It is also the

FIGURE 5.6. EXAMPLE OF VIRTUAL EMPATHY

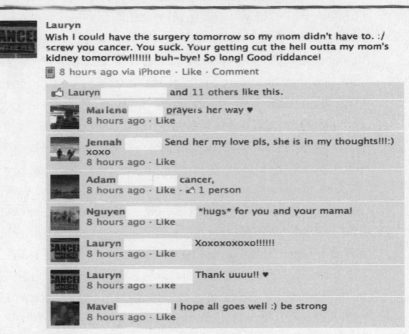

Lauryn
Wish I could have the surgery tomorrow so my mom didn't have to. :/ screw you cancer. You suck. Your getting cut the hell outta my mom's kidney tomorrow!!!!!!! buh–bye! So long! Good riddance!
8 hours ago via iPhone · Like · Comment

Lauryn   and 11 others like this.

Marlene   prayers her way ♥
8 hours ago · Like

Jennah   Send her my love pls, she is in my thoughts!!!:)
xoxo
8 hours ago · Like

Adam   cancer,
8 hours ago · Like · 1 person

Nguyen   *hugs* for you and your mama!
8 hours ago · Like

Lauryn   Xoxoxoxoxo!!!!!!
8 hours ago · Like

Lauryn   Thank uuuu!! ♥
8 hours ago · Like

Mavel   I hope all goes well :) be strong
8 hours ago · Like

11 Facebook friends who "liked" her post. This is the new millennial way of saying "I am thinking of you," and all together the posts and "likes" made Lauryn feel supported.

Pay attention to signs of childhood depression. One in nine children and adolescents will experience a serious bout of depression. This means that, as parents, grandparents, aunts, uncles, older siblings, or even family friends, we need to be extra vigilant about children and their online behaviors. Although these suggestions are not unique to combating childhood depression, they will be helpful to parents who want to make sure their children, pre-teens, and teens stay mentally healthy. Remember the study from my lab where we found different activities predicted poor psychological health at different ages? These lead to three suggestions:

- Monitor the use of all technology and media for children. This does not mean that children cannot watch television, play on a computer, or even use a smartphone. What it means is that parents must be extraordinarily alert to the specific activities their children are doing with their media. Practice "co-viewing"[41] where you either participate in your child's media-driven activities or you make sure that they are doing these activities where you can observe them at all times. Resist the temptation to have your young children play with their technology quietly in their bedrooms.

- Pre-teens who use more technology in general and play more video games were more depressed in our research. Just as with children, monitor the use of all technology and practice co-viewing as much as possible. Be a proactive parent when it comes to video gaming. Most video game systems allow people to play with others on the Internet, and this may be problematic if your pre-teen is at risk for being depressed. The dialogue online in these games can be intense and upsetting, so if you do allow your pre-teen to play with others make sure that you discuss proper conduct.

- Those teens who appear to be the most negatively affected psychologically are the ones who use more technology of all types, including being online, using social networks, and playing video games. Although it may be difficult to practice co-viewing with your teen it is still important to discuss their experiences. This can best be accomplished with family dinners and family discussions. Research shows that families who eat dinner together three or more times a week have healthier children and a higher functioning family system.[42] Here's how to exploit this. Family meals need to be sacrosanct. That means that they are mandatory and each family member must know that all technology must stop and time is set aside for dinner and talk. Here's my version of how to run an effective family meal:

  - It should last no longer than 45 minutes. This is a long time for the attention span of a child or teenager and you want these meals to be positive, not aversive.
  - All technology should be turned off at the beginning, including laptops, televisions, and, the most difficult and controversial item, cell phones and smartphones. This includes mom's and dad's cell phones, too!

- Parents should ask their children questions about their technology use and then listen to the answers. This is a time for information gathering, not discipline or critique. Ask about how people interact with them online, particularly while on social networking sites or other collaborative Internet activities. Parents should also share some examples of how they interact with technology as a tool at work and when keeping up with social obligations.

- If you find that your children cannot stand being without their phones, and it is likely that they will have problems with this, institute a "tech break" part way through dinner. A tech break is where everyone at the table gets to check in with their technology for a minute or two and then turn it off and participate in the family conversations without being interrupted.[43]

- Children and teens need to be taught the pragmatics of conversations whether they are online or face to face. Teach them that there is a real person at the other end and just because they can't see the other person's reactions to a communication doesn't mean that there wasn't a strong, negative, hurt reaction. The more they understand this dynamic behind the screen the better able they will be to deal with those who don't understand the pragmatics and are intentionally hurtful.

Watch for "cognitive" signs of depression. Dr. Aaron Beck, the father of Cognitive Therapy, believes that the cause of depression can be traced directly to distortions in a person's thinking through false ideas such as all-or-none thinking ("I didn't get the job and I will never get a job"), overgeneralization ("John said I am a loser. Everyone thinks I am a loser"), and magnification ("Jean unfriended me. Nobody likes me at all and I have no friends"), among other cognitive distortions. Pay attention to this kind of thinking in yourself and your friends. The brain is a marvelous organ but it can get stuck in a rut, which can reflect depressive symptomology. If you find yourself (or a friend) making any of these distorted statements, Dr. Beck would tell you to dispassionately approach the statements and not the feelings behind the statements and dispel the falsehoods with logical reasoning.

Multitasking and mania go together. We all switch our focus from one task to the next. This is a skill that we have cultivated as a human race. However, research is showing that this task-switching behavior (also known as multitasking) may not be healthy or beneficial. Worse yet, the precise technologies that we embrace daily, including our computers, the Internet, and smartphones, encourage task switching by providing multi-sensory environments that are present in our visual and auditory fields. The beeping phone draws our attention away from what we are doing—regardless of its importance—in order to check who just texted us. The popup YouTube video entices us to watch even if it is not a good time. Our newest research shows that those who prefer to task switch more are those who show signs of mania. One suggestion is to institute your own personal "tech breaks," where you focus on work without switching for, say, 15 minutes, and then allow yourself a minute or two to check in with your technologies and then return for another 15 minutes of focused work time. This only works if you remove those tempting blinking websites and mute your phone.

Bright light therapy. A recent study in the Netherlands confirmed the important role of light in regulating mood. Dr. Ritsaert Lieverse and his colleagues found that just three weeks of additional bright lighting dramatically improved depression scores in elderly people facing major depression.[44] Other studies have shown that not only is bright light good for reducing depression but it can be as effective as medication.[45] I should note here that bright light does not mean sitting closer to your computer screen. Bright light can be gained from special light boxes or sunshine.

If you find yourself or others exhibiting signs of depression linked to specific use of technology or media then try implementing some of the suggestions above. The bottom line, however, is that serious mood disorders require the attention of a qualified physician or mental health practitioner.

Next, we tackle a very important psychological disorder that has garnered a lot of press and speculation over the last decade or two: attention-deficit hyperactivity disorder (ADHD).

SIX

Sorry I Missed the Meeting . . . I Went to Check My E-Mail and the Next Thing I Knew It Was Two Hours Later

ADHD is a medical condition, but it's [also] a brain condition. We know that the brain adapts and changes based on the environmental stimuli to which it is exposed repeatedly. Therefore, it is not unreasonable to believe that environmental stimuli can increase the risk for a medical condition like ADHD in the same way that environmental stimuli, like cigarettes, can increase the risk for cancer.[1]

—Douglas Gentile, associate professor of Psychology, Iowa State University

Colby is a 29-year-old, unmarried insurance salesman who is struggling to keep his job. At his last review his supervisors wrote that Colby's excessive tardiness, absence at company meetings, and lack of completed paperwork are substandard and prevent him from doing his job correctly. If he doesn't remedy these issues soon, Colby may be out of work— again. In 2009, he lost his job as an account manager for the same reasons. Colby has a bachelor's degree in marketing from a southern university, but he struggled there as well, receiving mostly Cs from his professors. His primary issue is that he has trouble completing tasks, and distractions prevent him from being on time or even showing up to important meetings and consultations.

Colby has always had a bit of trouble focusing. While he was never formally diagnosed with attention-deficit hyperactivity disorder (ADHD), his behavior mirrors the symptoms. As an adult Colby cannot resist the temptation that the online world offers, from texting all day long to checking ESPN every ten minutes for updates on his favorite sports teams. He toggles back and forth between his Facebook page and CNN regularly. Colby is typical of today's young adult. He grew up playing video games until the wee hours of the morning and struggled in school starting in first grade. In Colby's case his ADHD symptoms may have been caused or exacerbated by his excessive game playing.

ADHD is a common and potentially destructive disorder that causes people to have severe inattentiveness and lack impulse control, and it creates problems at work and school for those afflicted. According to the Centers for Disease Control, 5.2 million U.S. children ages 3 to 17 have ADHD,[2] and 8.4 percent of all children 3–17 years of age have been diagnosed with ADHD at some time. The percentage of boys 3–17 years of age ever diagnosed with ADHD is 11.2 percent, while the percent of girls the same age ever diagnosed with ADHD is 5.5 percent. About 1 percent, or eight million, of adults ages 22–45 are currently taking medication for ADHD,[3] but according to the Anxiety Disorders Association of America, less than 20 percent of people who actually have ADHD are treated for it. About 60 percent of the children who have ADHD continue to have it through adulthood.[4]

The percentage of children diagnosed with ADHD rose 33 percent from the late nineties to 2008, with ten million children ages 3 to 17 diagnosed with a developmental disorder.[5] In the past decade alone the percentage of children with ADHD rose an additional 30 percent.[6] With such rapid increases in ADHD-diagnosed children, this is clearly a major problem, although some believe that the rise is due to more sophisticated diagnostic tests. But, there may be other associated causes—namely, technology and media use—that make this an iDisorder.

While a percentage of the population has been diagnosed with this disorder, our dependence on technology, the 24/7 availability of the Internet, and our constant use of devices makes us *all behave us if we have ADHD.*

Let's face it, we live in a plugged-in world. We communicate through electronic and wireless devices, listen to music through tiny gadgets plugged into our ears, carry around small computers that allow us access to zillions of pieces of information—and we do this all at the same time, often while in the company of other "real people." Most young people have multiple screens open on their laptops as they watch TV, listen to music, and update their Facebook status. Our devices make us unable to focus or concentrate on one thing for a long time. It even appears that babies may be getting their starter dose of an ADHD iDisorder from television programming, with its quick scene changes and bright, colorful, moving pictures.[7]

According to psychologists the classic symptoms of ADHD include the following:

1. Making careless mistakes in homework, work, or other activities.
2. Not paying close attention to details.
3. Having trouble keeping attention on tasks.
4. Not listening when spoken to.
5. Not following instructions and failing to finish work.
6. Having trouble organizing activities.
7. Avoiding, disliking, or not wanting to do activities that take significant mental effort for long periods of time.
8. Losing tools for completing tasks.
9. Being easily distracted.
10. Being forgetful in daily activities.
11. Having associated hyperactivity and impulsiveness (blurting out answers, interrupting).

It is not a stretch to see how many of those signs and symptoms could be a result of constant media and technology use, including, as I will discuss in this chapter, social networking, video gaming, smartphone use, and much more. Many claim that it is not just the use of any single device or website but rather our propensity for trying to use so many of them at the same time, so let's first explore the often confusing issue of multitasking.

MULTITASKING MADNESS

One of the pervasive buzzwords out there is multitasking, often blamed for much of the ADHD-like symptoms we exhibit.[8] This is the notion that people can do several tasks at the same time. However, the more tasks we take on—with the assistance of very attractive and distracting sounds and visuals from advanced technology—the more our brain gets stressed and overloaded, and the worse we do at all of the tasks. Research tells us there is no such thing as multitasking—that all we can really do is task switch. In other words, people lack the ability to pay full attention to two tasks at a time. Take the case of Cathy Cruz Marrero, dubbed "Fountain Girl" on the Internet. She was so focused on her phone that she fell into a fountain pool at a mall in January 2011.[9]

This is a comical example, but using our technological devices may have more serious consequences—they may be permanently ruining our focused attention. A study on instant messaging and focused attention in college students shows that those students who do more IMing score lower on a focused attention scale.[10] Also, several studies show that even experienced computer users are distracted when trying to read online or in hypertext documents.[11] The consensus among medical and mental health practitioners is that there are more costs than benefits to multitasking, including:

1. Attention difficulties
2. Poor decision making
3. Lack of depth of material
4. Information overload
5. Internet addiction
6. Poor sleep habits
7. Overuse of caffeine

In our lab we studied multitasking among 1,319 adults across three generations—Baby Boomers, Generation X, and the Net Generation—by asking them about how they performed 12 typical daily activities, including nine technology/media-based activities (being online, using a computer without being online, playing video games, listening to music, watching television, texting, talking on the telephone, instant messaging and chatting, and sending and receiving e-mail) and three additional daily activities not involving technology (eating, reading a book, and talking face to face). We examined all 66 dual-task combinations to measure the perceived ease of simultaneous tasks. We found that some task combinations are easier to do than others, and the number and type of activities change depending on how old you are. For instance, almost all of our research participants reported being able to listen to music and do other activities at the same time. Baby Boomers had the most trouble doing more than one task at a time. Watching television, listening to music, and eating were the easiest tasks for them to do coupled with other tasks, while the younger generations found it easier to do more tasks at the same time. Just 67 percent of Baby Boomers reported being able to do more than one task at a time compared with 77 percent of Generation Xers and 87 percent of the Net Generation. More poignantly, when you looked at each generation and how they felt about the ease of doing each of the 66 total task combinations, Net Geners led the way with 65 percent of the task combinations deemed very easy to use, while only 23 percent of the task combinations were assessed this way by Baby Boomers; Generation X was somewhere in the middle, with 42 percent of the tasks combinations labeled as easy to do by those adults in their thirties and forties.[12] For all generations, however, there was agreement that text messaging, reading a book, and video game play were the hardest tasks to do with others.

We know people multitask using media simply by the statistics on media use. In the latest research on people's media use, the Nielsen Research Company found that during the final quarter of 2010 teens sent and received 3,705 texts each per month, which equals approximately six per hour. Young adults ages 18–24 sent and received 1,630 texts a month and even pre-teens weighed in at a whopping 1,178 per month. Among young adults 62 percent sent photos, 49 percent used mobile Internet, and 38 percent downloaded software and other applications.[13] It is clear that young people are using just this one form of media—text messaging—at a dizzying rate, and, though this is one of the most difficult technologies to multitask with, they are clearly doing so. Children, teens, and young adults have grown up in an era of massive influx of technology. This is obvious, but consider this—

before the year 2000, none of these existed: iPod, iPhone, Wii, MySpace, Facebook, Google Plus, LinkedIn, iTunes, YouTube, Pandora, Twitter, iPad, Xbox, Satellite Radio, Flickr, Skype, camera phones, Kindle, Firefox, Black-Berry, 3-D TV, Android, Club Penguin, TiVo, Broadband, Farmville, Groupon. An amazing array of new technology, media, and software, all designed to consume our time, entertain us, make it easier for us to connect, and ultimately turn us into master multitaskers. Maybe. Let's see what psychological laboratory research has to say about this.

In a classic study back in the 1950s, Colin Cherry at the Massachusetts Institute for Technology tested how people pay attention through what are called "dichotic listening tasks." In Cherry's studies, his participants listened to voices in one ear at a time and then through both ears in an effort to determine whether we can listen to two people talk at the same time. One ear always contained a message that the listener had to repeat back (called "shadowing") while the other ear included people speaking. The trick was to see if you could totally focus on the main message and also hear someone talking in your other ear. Cleverly, Cherry found it was impossible for his participants to know whether the message in the other ear was spoken by a man or woman, in English or another language, or was even comprised of real words at all! In other words, people could not process two pieces of information at the same time.[14]

Cherry's work was validated and extended to our modern day media-rich world in a fascinating study out of a Stanford University laboratory. Researchers Eyal Ophir, Clifford Nass, and Anthony D. Wagner conducted a series of experiments to determine systematic differences in the way people process information by comparing chronically light and heavy media "multitaskers." The two groups were each shown a combination of letters and numbers at alternating times and asked whether the numbers were odd or even and whether the letter was a consonant or a vowel. This is a very easy task, but the researchers discovered that heavy media multitaskers were less capable of answering correctly, or not as good at task switching, because they were more distracted by the wrong answers. Wondering if this was because the tasks involved language elements (numbers, letters), one study found the same result when participants were presented with different shapes and colors and asked to identify them.[15] The authors concluded that, "Heavy multitaskers are distracted by the multiple streams of media they are consuming or, alternatively, that those who infrequently multitask are more effective at volitionally allocating their attention in the face of distractions."[16]

Researchers have also studied the effect of multitasking in the workplace and found that technology is distracting to even the best of us. For example, Gloria Mark and her colleagues at the University of California, Irvine, observed computer programmers—whose jobs are very detail oriented—for three days, eight hours a day, and found that these programmers were interrupted every three minutes.[17] Other researchers have shown that using laptops during meetings leads to interruptions every two minutes[18] and that even medical students switched tasks every five minutes while studying in the school's computer lab.[19]

In many workplace studies the culprit is e-mail. In one study, 85 percent of employees at a British company responded to an e-mail within two minutes of its arrival and 70 percent responded within *six seconds*![20] This was all driven by the individuals as the company had no policy about responding to e-mail messages within any time frame. With constant interruptions it is not hard to see how we are distracting ourselves right into the signs and symptoms of an ADHD iDisorder.

Researchers have also found it is difficult to return to a task once interrupted. One study of computer programmers showed that the resumption lag—the time it takes to return to an interrupted task—was five minutes or longer for more than half of 10,000 programming sessions, and only one in six times did the programmer return to the main task within a minute.[21] Further work by Gloria Mark showed an even more profound impact: Computer programmers in her study took an average of more than 25 minutes to return to their original task after they interrupted themselves.[22] And although they were able to complete all of their tasks, those programmers who self-interrupted more often were more stressed at work than those who spent more time focusing on a single task.

As we have talked about throughout this book, we know that people are consuming massive amounts of media and technology, way more than time would permit if they used each device or each website alone without multitasking or task switching. And it is causing them to behave as if they have ADHD—the constant distractions are leaving them less focused and more prone to rapidly switching between screens and devices, with serious consequences.

DISTRACTED DRIVING

One of the major problems associated with multitasking—for both individuals and society as a whole—is distracted driving, which, according to the U.S. Department of Transportation, is responsible for up to 25 percent of all automobile accidents and 18 percent of all car-related fatalities.[23] Distracted driving includes any activity that takes your attention away from driving, but technology use gets the most attention since it is still a relatively new phenomenon and distracts us more than any other activity. We used to hear stories about people eating or putting on makeup in the car and then swerving out of control into oncoming traffic. Now we mostly hear stories about driving-while-texting. People from Southern California will surely remember the horrible Metrolink crash in September 2008, when a train carrying passengers through the San Fernando Valley hit a freight train, killing 25 people and injuring 135. The engineer, Robert Sanchez, was texting with a teenage train enthusiast seconds before the deadly collision. He was also killed.[24] Another case from Southern California is 42-year-old Martin Burt Kuehl, an Orange County man who killed a pedestrian during a car accident in August 2008. Martha Ovalle, a 32-year-old nanny, was crossing the street when Kuehl fatally struck her. He had been sending and receiving texts non-stop for 30 minutes prior to the accident.[25] Finally another case involved a woman updating her Facebook page while driving through Chicago city streets in 2010. A 70-year-old motorist, Raymond Veloz, was out of his car looking at the damage from a fender-bender when he was hit and killed by Araceli Beas, who was logged into Facebook through her mobile device at the time of the accident, uploading a photo of herself to her profile page.[26]

Here are some statistics from the official U.S. government "distracted driving" website:[27]

- 20 percent of injury crashes in 2009 involved reports of distracted driving.
- Of those killed in distracted-driving-related crashes, 995 involved reports of a cell phone as a distraction (18 percent of fatalities in distraction-related crashes).
- In 2009, 5,474 people were killed in U.S. roadways and an estimated additional 448,000 were injured in motor vehicle crashes that were reported to have involved distracted driving.
- The age group with the greatest proportion of distracted drivers was the under-20 age group—16 percent of all drivers younger than 20 involved in fatal crashes were reported to have been distracted while driving.
- Drivers who use hand-held devices are four times as likely to get into crashes serious enough to injure themselves.
- Using a cell phone while driving, whether it's hand-held or hands-free, delays a driver's reactions as much as having a blood alcohol concentration at the legal limit of .08 percent.

While these examples are extreme and show just how destructive it can be to operate machinery while distracted, there are other technology-related conditions that contribute to attention problems, particularly in kids. Iowa State University doctoral student Edward Swing and associate professor of psychology Douglas Gentile discovered that playing video games and watching television both contribute to a diminished attention capacity in children. They found that elementary school-aged children who watched or played more than two hours of TV or video games per day were 1.5 to 2 times more likely to have "above average" attention problems.[28] Ironically, ADHD kids are good video game players. This is why technology can be so engaging for them—it sucks the focus into these kids so that they are actually more focused and stay focused longer on them than on other tasks such as homework.

The bottom line is that technology appears to be extremely distracting and those distractions lead to behaviors that mimic the same behaviors shown by people with ADHD.

THE ADHD BRAIN

We now know that ADHD can persist over one's lifespan,[29] and most researchers agree that genetics and biological factors are the underlying cause of the disorder. We have examined how using technology and media can make us *behave* as if we have ADHD, but some researchers have examined how the brain can actually cause people to be distracted. Ryota Kanai and his colleagues at University College London tested whether a particular region of the brain—the superior parietal cortex on the left side of the brain—influenced distraction. The team temporarily disrupted the brain function in this specific area in 15 volunteers using transcranial magnetic stimulation. "In what Kanai calls a 'psychologist's version of Where's Waldo?'" writes Laura Sanders of *Science News,* "people hunt for a circle and filter out irrelevant details, such as a distracting red diamond. With dampened brain activity in the left superior parietal cortex, people took longer to find the target than when brain activity was not reduced, suggesting that this brain region influences attention. Dampening activity in an unrelated part of the brain didn't have an effect."[30]

When the researchers compared the brains of easily distracted individuals to those who are more focused, they discovered that the easily distracted had denser brain tissue with more nerve cells. Kanai calls this counterintuitive effect "too much brain," or a large volume of gray matter with more neural connections. "Kanai speculates that it may be linked to the fact that as we mature, the brain's grey matter is pruned of neurons in order to work more efficiently."[31] This may explain why signs of ADHD are predominantly found in children and teenagers, since the brain continues to develop and mature by consolidating good neural connections and pruning unneeded ones in the prefrontal cortex—the major area controlling decision making—which is not completely mature until young adults reach their mid- to late twenties or even into their early thirties.

Further evidence that children's brains are not fully developed can be found in a recent study by Stuart Washington, a neuroscientist at Georgetown University Medical Center. In a study of what is called the "default-mode network"—a set of five brain areas that scientists believe control the way people see the world, form beliefs, and coordinate attention—Dr. Washington had 6- and 27-year-olds perform a task in an MRI machine and examined the brain activity that took place after the children and young adults completed the task. The older the participant, the more the activity in the default-mode network showed coordinated neural activity essential for seeing the world as an adult.[32]

What is truly baffling to people is that many of those with ADHD seem to have little trouble focusing as long as the material is compelling. For example, Missy, a mother of three children, was told by the school counselor that her 8-year-old son Dexter needed to be tested for ADHD because he was not able to sit still in class and pay attention to the teacher and to his work. Missy was puzzled. "How could Dex have ADHD when he can sit and play his video games for hours and hours? He has a wonderful attention span!"

Well, it turns out that video games require a different type of attention than schoolwork. In a video game the player is constantly gaining rewards, which stimulate the brain to release a neurotransmitter called dopamine. Schoolwork most definitely does not provide constant rewards. In fact, it is based more on the process of intermittent reinforcement or rewards and not nearly as much dopamine is released, nor is the reward center of the brain being constantly activated.

There is another major difference between attention in school and the kind of focus seen playing video games. School moves slowly with paced education while video games (and other technologies such as television and the Internet) move fast with rapid scene changes and dazzling colors, shapes, and forms. According to Dr. Dimitri Christakis, a pediatrician at the University of Washington School of Medicine, "If a child's brain gets habituated to that pace and to the extreme alertness needed to keep responding and winning, the child ultimately may find the realities of the world underwhelming, understimulating."[33]

Brain research paints us a picture of how someone can get so engaged by technology that their focus seems almost too good to be true, while at the same time engaging, distracting technological devices and websites can encourage rapid task switching with little regard for completing any one task.

PROBLEMS AT WORK AND SCHOOL

Exhibiting the symptoms of ADHD can have a profound negative effect on people's work and home lives. Children like Dexter often get in trouble in school when they can't sit still or pay attention to their teachers. This may lead to the child believing he is not competent or lacks the aptitude for schoolwork. The repercussions for adults can be even more severe, with an ADHD-affected person missing an estimated three weeks of work a year due to lessened productivity.[34] They miss meetings, have memory problems, and cannot stay focused on one task for very long.[35]

Further, people are using technology not only for work purposes, but also to check in with their Facebook friends, play games, and go online.[36] In fact, one study found that 76 percent of computer-based task switching in the workplace centers on "distracting activities," while only 13 percent focuses on work-related activities.[37] As mentioned earlier, studies have shown that computer programmers could only stay on task for three minutes at a time, and most distractions were technologically induced. Further, it took those distracted workers extra time to resume their task, most likely because once distracted, they encountered more distractions along the way.

University of California's Gloria Mark and her colleagues at Humboldt University in Berlin, Germany, examined whether the type of interruption (e.g., picking up a telephone, answering an instant message) made a difference in work performance. The researchers discovered that the context of the interruption did not have an impact on performance, but to their surprise, while their participants completed the interrupted tasks in less time than the group that had no interruptions with no difference in quality, they were not immune to the ramifications of constant task switching. They concluded that "people compensate for interruptions by working faster, but this comes at a price: experiencing more stress, higher frustration, time pressure and effort."[38]

In our own research laboratory at California State University, Dominguez Hills, we conducted a study in which we observed college, high school, and middle school students studying for 15 minutes in their natural study environment. Trained observers sat unobtrusively behind a studying student and observed all activities at each minute of the study time. As with the work of Gloria Mark's programmers, these students appeared to lose focus about every three minutes, and one of the main causes of that disrupted focus included the number of windows that were open on a nearby computer screen. From about the 8- to 11-minute mark students had their lowest focus and this was precisely when the number of open computer windows peaked. The predictors of good performance included how much the students were able to stay focused on task and whether they had pre-developed study strategies; the predictors of poor performance included their preference for task switching versus completing a single task before moving on to a new one, their daily media consumption, and if they checked their Facebook page just once during the 15-minute study period. Media, multitasking, and social networking appear to be immensely distracting to students.

In another observational study we sent student researchers into college and high school classrooms to eavesdrop and see what the students were doing while they were supposed to be paying attention to a lecture. As you can see from Figure 6.1 below, a lot of activity is going on that has nothing to do with the ongoing lecture. For example, we discovered that a fifth of college students have their cell phones out on their desks during lectures, and about a quarter of them were texting during class. Although the data show fewer distractions in the high school classroom, still one in seven students was texting during class. A few even had their iPod ear buds in and were apparently listening to music while the teacher lectured.

In an effort to determine the potential negative impact of these distracting technologies in the classroom, we conducted a study to see whether

FIGURE 6.1. OBSERVATIONAL STUDY OF TECHNOLOGY USED IN THE CLASSROOM DURING A COLLEGE OR HIGH SCHOOL LECTURE

Technology Used	College Classroom	High School Classroom
Laptops	11%	2%
Cell phone on desk	22%	7%
Cell phone in lap	10%	12%
Texting during class	24%	15%
iPod ear buds	2%	4%

texting during classroom lectures had an impact on test scores. In advance of this study we collected cell phone contact information from students in four psychology classes. In each class we randomly assigned students to one of three groups: One group received no text messages from the experimenters during the lecture, one group received four text messages, and the final group received eight text messages. Each class watched a 30-minute videotaped lecture while the experimenters sent them their text messages.

Two features of this study are important in understanding the results. First, students were asked to respond to our text messages (e.g., "What is your college major and why did you select that major?"), and, in fact, they did, with a typical response being about nine words. Second, the text messages were timed to coincide with information on the videotape lecture that would appear on an exam immediately after the lecture.

As predicted, we discovered that those students who received and responded to eight texts scored significantly worse on the test—about one letter grade—than those who got either zero or four text messages. Surprisingly, however, the group that got "only" four texts in the 30 minutes did not suffer on the exam. What we did find, however, when we looked more closely at the data, was that our instructions were a bit vague. We only asked that the students "respond" to our texts and did not tell them when to respond. It turned out that those who did not respond immediately, but instead waited for a minute or two, did as well as those who received no texts. In fact, if they waited three or four minutes they got two letter grades higher than those who responded immediately.[39] This was both serendipitous and surprising and will be discussed later in the chapter in terms of strategies for helping reduce distractions.

In the same study we also administered a follow-up questionnaire that included the students' opinions about texting and other technology-related behavior. Figure 6.2 shows the percentage of students who agreed that certain disruptive practices were acceptable in the classroom. Notice that although the vast majority agreed that sending and receiving text messages hurts their ability to learn, and a third agreed that they personally get distracted by someone else receiving or sending a text during class, half the students still felt that it was acceptable to text during class.

FIGURE 6.2. CLASSROOM TEXTING BEHAVIOR

Question	Percent Who Strongly Agreed or Agreed
It is OK to text during class lecture.	49%
Receiving text messages hurts my ability to learn lecture material.	77%
Sending text messages hurts my ability to learn lecture material.	72%
I get distracted when someone receives a text during class.	37%
I get distracted when someone sends a text during class.	31%

One more piece of the puzzle to explain why technology and media might be producing symptoms of an ADHD iDisorder comes from another study from our lab. A graduate student, Julie Felt, and I queried more than 1,000 parents using an anonymous online survey to gain information about the potential relationship between media and health. The kinds of technology that we found most kids have at hand were quite surprising and unexpected. Figure 6.3 shows the percentage of children, pre-teens, younger teens, and older teens who had various technologies in their bedrooms. As you can see, a majority of even the youngest children had a television in their bedroom plus a video game console to boot. In addition, all youngsters had multiple technologies at their fingertips without ever leaving their bedrooms.

Most researchers agree that having a television in the bedroom is not beneficial for children[40] and adolescents,[41] and recent research from my own lab found that teens who had a computer in the bedroom were more likely to have parents who were indulgent or neglectful, two types of parenting styles that are related to behavioral and psychological problems in adolescents.[42] Obviously if "normal" children and teens have problems having technology available in the bedroom, then those with ADHD would even be more in jeopardy. Remember, technology-based content that is vi-

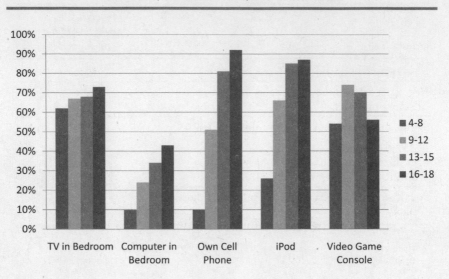

FIGURE 6.3. PERSONAL TECHNOLOGIES AVAILABLE TO CHILDREN,
PRE-TEENS, YOUNGER TEENS, AND OLDER TEENS

sually stimulating and has variable sound levels makes these devices more appealing and more distracting than non-technology objects that might be in a child's room, such as books or non-electronic toys. Regardless, having media available in the location where children and teens spend most of their time at home can only contribute to this form of iDisorder.

HOW TO HELP AVOID AN ATTENTION-DEFICIT iDISORDER

In this chapter I have discussed the problems people have attending to one thing as the technological world around them screams for their attention. And those screams are quite alluring, with moving images (high definition and even three-dimensional), high-quality sounds, and gratifying emotional rewards that draw attention from a primary task to something distracting. I have also talked about psychological research surrounding multitasking, or perceived multitasking, which is actually just task switching. We know that it is not good for a person to switch focus often, and we also know that it is better for us to stay connected to one task at a time, but with such a veritable array of competing stimuli how can we possibly avoid continually having our focus challenged? In essence, how can I teach you to focus when you need to focus *and freely* task switch in a way that won't negatively impact what you are doing. Here is my step-by-step plan:

- Step 1: *Start with a prioritized task list.* We all lead exceptionally busy lives and at any given time we *could* be doing one of many tasks. Right now I could be writing, but I also could be cooking dinner, getting dressed to go to the movies, washing today's lunch dishes, doing some laundry . . . and the list could go on and on. Take a sheet of paper and make a list of everything that you think you need to do or could be doing at this time. Make sure you list work-related items as well as recreational items and don't forget to include chores and family obligations. Now, next to each item put a number to indicate how important it is that you do this activity *right now*. I use just 1, 2, and 3 to indicate three levels of importance, but you will find your own system. Now, I know this seems like a lot of work, but rewrite the lists with all of the "1"s on a separate page, followed by a page with the others in order of importance. This keeps the potential distracting tasks to a minimum since you are only looking at the top, most important tasks.

- Step 2: *Carefully select a work area that will minimize potential distractions.* Recall that in the study where we observed students studying we found that they were most distracted when more computer windows were open, and Gloria Mark and others have found that e-mail and other computer activities are distracting, so set up your work environment with minimal distractors. Turn off the TV, shut off the computer screen, move the cell phone out of range. Don't worry, you will be able to check in at the next step.

- Step 3: *Establish tech breaks.* The brain is a wonderful organ but it is limited in its ability to juggle multiple tasks. Certainly we are capable of task switching among several tasks but consider what must be going on in the brain of a person who is steeped in technology, particularly those vehicles for connection and communication. An fMRI measures oxygen flow—which is linked directly to neural activity—so imagine a brain that is constantly thinking, "I wonder who might have sent me a text in the last few minutes" or "I wonder if anyone commented on my social network post." Oxygen is rushing to areas that are concerned with these communications and since there is only a finite amount of oxygen (and activity) at any one time, the brain is constantly switching from worrying about what the person is missing, to the task at hand, and then back again. This means less brainpower for doing your work, be it studying for school, paying attention in class, or even concentrating during a work meeting. By the way, this process is way more difficult for a young person, as the decisions that their brain makes as to which areas to activate and which to ignore come from the prefrontal cortex, which does not completely develop until sometime in their twenties. That teen can't concentrate on his studies because he is thinking about his social networks. This was shockingly clear when we found out that if our students checked Facebook just once during their 15-minute study period they had worse grades. There is a solution for this task-switching craziness: "tech breaks." Since the mind is going to wander, particularly in our world of highly engaging, sensory experiences offered by technology and media, plan for them. Start with a clean work area. Turn off or remove all technology. In 15 minutes give yourself a one-minute tech break to check your social networks, your phone, or whatever else you think you should be attending to. Set a clock to remind you of your break's beginning and end. Set it again for your second break. I will talk more about this concept in the final chapter of the book, but it works!

- Step 4: *Learn what distracts* your *mind*. Everyone has his or her own distractors, and it is important that you identify exactly what keeps pulling your attention away. It is important to note that you will find different things distracting at different times and while doing different tasks. When I was in college I found food to be an amazing distractor. I would settle in to study for an exam and my stomach would start grumbling and that leftover pizza would start calling to me from the refrigerator. When teens study, their technology calls to them. People need to know how they best learn and how they are most likely to be distracted. Then they can focus on removing those distractors and using them specifically for tech breaks. This is a form of what psychologists call "metacognition," or knowing how your brain works (and what makes it not work as well).

- Step 5: *Pay attention to your stress level.* Distractions cause us to switch focus and switching focus often leads to stress from uncompleted work. Reduce stress by preventing interruptions.[43] Research shows that reducing stress leads to longer and happier lives. For an overwhelmed task-switcher, preventing interruptions may be the best way to alleviate stress. Tell people you communicate with regularly that you are not available for a certain time frame. Put a message on your e-mail or voice mail explaining that you are away for an hour, several hours, or even a (gasp) full day. In the last chapter of this book I will talk more about the role of nature in preventing or reducing stress, but, in brief, research has shown that just getting into a more peaceful environment for 15 minutes can reset your brain and reduce stress. Even just looking at photos of nature can do the same. Keep a set of your favorite nature photos and use them to calm your brain and stop it from incessant task switching.

Not everyone who shows signs of ADHD has the disorder. But I firmly believe that frantic task switching due to technology overload is another form of iDisorder that you can, if you work at it, eliminate from your life.

SEVEN

Communication 101

Safety (and Training) behind the Screen

You're not looking at them and they can't see your facial expressions on an e-mail. Talking face-to-face is harder because you have to keep eye contact and give them your attention . . . and [then you only get to] talk yourself when there's a proper break.

—Ryan, age 23, when asked about why he prefers communicating electronically rather than face to face[1]

When I started high school I had just moved from back east and I was totally shy. If I tried to talk to someone during lunchtime or during passing periods I would stammer and turn red and sweat and sound like an idiot. I ended up eating alone and walking home alone. Then I discovered MySpace. I found out that even though I couldn't talk to someone when they were standing right in front of me I was able to chat with that same person online. I made four friends this way and now eat lunch with them every day and hang out with them on the weekends. Thank God for MySpace!

—Yolanda, age 14

My husband and I used to go to the movies and out to dinner with friends every weekend. Now he says that he doesn't really like going out and would rather stay home and "be with me." But he's not really doing anything with the kids or me. Instead, he's always on the computer updating his status and commenting on articles he reads or in one of the dozens of online groups he follows. In just a short time he has gone from Mr. Social to Mr. Online.

—Jan, a 42-year-old mother of two teenagers

There are many people who prefer to "talk" electronically rather than do so in person, such as Ryan, who is quoted above. Some are shy and socially awkward and hide behind their computer and smartphone screens, and some may, in fact, not learn how to truly communicate with people in the real world. Others, like Yolanda, make use of the safety of being behind the screen to develop their face-to-face communication skills. And then still others, like Jan's husband, retreat from real-world connections and become preoccupied with communicating in the cyber world, withdrawing into their own "TechnoCocoons."[2]

When the first one-to-one technological communication device—the telephone—arrived, it certainly changed the way we communicated. However, it took that device 20 years to penetrate society.[3] That gave people a substantial amount of time to learn and understand how to use the telephone, including how to integrate it into their lives effectively. Now consider some of the new media forms of e-communication and how quickly they penetrated society. Cell phones took 12 years while the World Wide Web took four. Instant messaging took the same four years but blogging emerged in three, and social networking took even less time to become a normal part of our communication arsenal. When a technology such as social networking explodes on the scene and becomes a major communication vehicle there is little time to learn how to integrate it effectively. This is even more problematic when that communication tool is highly engaging. It is these new modalities that are appearing and penetrating our world rapidly that are, I believe, leading many of us to exhibit signs and symptoms of psychiatric communication disorders.

There are several psychiatric disorders that involve, as the major symptom, problems with communication, and one of them has signs and symptoms that fit people such as Ryan and Yolanda. Named "social phobia" in the *DSM,* or in its more extreme form, "social anxiety disorder," this problem is characterized by intense fear in social situations, which causes distress and a reduced ability to function in daily life. Social phobes are those people who are constantly on guard; they fear being judged by others and worry about being embarrassed or even humiliated by their own actions. Social phobes exhibit mild-to-severe reactions to their anxiety, including, if the anxiety becomes high, panic attacks.

Although these problems may not appear severe to the casual observer, they can have significant ramifications for the afflicted person. People with social phobia find it difficult to interact with others in a face-to-face environment and often prefer the sanctuary of their home and their technology. Someone with antisocial personality disorder uses the same technology to verbally harm people. Let's first take a look at people with social phobia and see how they might be manifesting symptoms of a communication iDisorder.

John is a 27-year-old graphic designer who makes a great living working for a video game development company. John is exceedingly shy and, if given the opportunity, would prefer to work out of his home rather than in the office. His company allows some flexibility in his schedule but requires John to be in their physical office at least two days a week. On the days that John is home he communicates via e-mail, and his e-mails are clear, precisely written, and even funny. At least via e-mail there are no signs of either shyness or that "inability to relate" that permeates communication disorders. When John is at the office he hides in his cubicle, rarely talking to anyone. In meetings he fidgets by tapping his finger on the table rhythmically, constantly checking his phone, and rarely making eye contact even when asked to speak. His speech is halting and full of "uhs" and long pauses. John is not alone. Many people have difficulty relating to others whether they have an official diagnosis or not. And our over-reliance on technology can possibly trigger some of these classic symptoms or exacerbate those that already exist. Is John just painfully shy or is he suffering from a communication iDisorder?

EMPATHY 2.0: VIRTUAL EMPATHY

Along with a profound lack of social skills, poor communication skills, and repetitive behaviors, one of the most common symptoms in communication disorders is the inability to demonstrate empathy. Imagine a parent and child are playing happily—a phone call interrupts the two, and the call ends with the parent sad and crying. If the child is, say, three or four years old, he/she might immediately come up, sit on the parent's lap, and offer a favorite toy as a way of soothing the parent. This is an early demonstration of empathy. That same toddler, just two years earlier, would have likely either ignored the parent or tried to hit them to get their attention.

This is what psychologists refer to as the Theory of Mind (ToM) or the ability to understand other people's reactions and emotions. When someone attains their ToM they can mimic those feelings as well as begin to empathize with them. Children with communication disorders often have substantially delayed maturation of the ToM compared with normal children.[4]

Empathy has three major components: (1) a cognitive mechanism that allows people to imagine the internal mental state of another person; (2) an affective part where someone can match the emotions of another person; and (3) a neurological part that includes two components: (a) where the brain reacts with appropriate neuronal activity through what are known as "mirror neurons,"[5] and (b) the "empathy circuit," which consists of activity in the orbital-frontal cortex and the amygdala.[6] Each component is considered to be necessary in developing the ability to understand others' motives, emotions, and feelings.

Several authors have speculated that technology is reducing our ability to be empathic to others. For example, Dr. Sara Konrath and her colleagues at the University of Michigan examined 72 studies that measured empathy of more than 13,700 university students between 1979 and 2009—real-world empathy, not online empathy—and found major decreases in "empathic concern" (e.g., "I often have tender concerned feelings for people less fortunate than me") and "perspective taking" (e.g., "I sometimes try to understand my friends better by imagining how things look from their perspective"). Strikingly, those decreases were of a larger magnitude than both the relationship between the impact of violent video games on aggression and long-term increases in narcissism among young adults, both of which are considered to represent strong longitudinal trends.[7] Konrath and her colleagues concluded,

> As a result, we speculate that one likely contributor to declining empathy is the rising prominence of personal technology and media use in everyday life. Clearly, these changes have fundamentally affected the lives of everyone who has access to them. With so much time spent interacting with others online rather than in reality, interpersonal dynamics such as empathy might certainly be altered. For example, perhaps it is easier to establish friends and relationships online, but these skills might not trans-

late into smooth social relations in real life. There have been significant declines in the number of organizations and meetings people are involved in as well as in the number of average family dinners and friendly visits. Indeed, people today have a significantly lower number of close others to whom they can express their private thoughts and feelings. Alternatively, the ease and speed of such technology may lead people to become more readily frustrated or bored when things do not go as planned, resulting in less empathic interactions. Furthermore, people simply might not have time to reach out to others and express empathy in a world filled with rampant technology revolving around personal needs and self-expression.[8]

Konrath and her colleagues also pointed to the rise of reality television shows, where role models are most often depicted as being profoundly less empathic than one might want in a friend. Other technologies may also play a role in restricting empathic responses, as seen in a 2007 study by Dr. Steven Kirsh, who found that young people are faster at identifying a happy face compared to an angry face, but if they play a violent video game prior to looking at the facial expression task they are much slower at recognizing the happy faces.[9]

In Chapter 5, I described how in my own research lab we have studied what we call "virtual empathy" in an attempt to assess the conditions under which these understanding responses to other people's feelings might take place.[10] Spearheaded by our students Alexander Spradlin and John Bunce, my colleagues and I found that indeed virtual empathy is real and does have real impacts on relationships. Interestingly, out of a range of potential predictors of those who might show more of this form of caring, two Internet activities rose to the forefront: social networking and instant messaging.[11] In addition, in this same study, we measured real-world empathy and found that those who are better able to express virtual empathy were also better able to express real world empathy. Employing a statistical model, we showed that practicing virtual empathy actually led to people being better at expressing empathy face to face. With these results in mind, let's take a look at the emerging role of social networking in helping people with communication difficulties to learn socialization and communication skills.

ON THE INTERNET NOBODY KNOWS YOU'RE A DOG

There is a famous comic strip from a 1993 issue of the *New Yorker* magazine[12] that shows a dog typing on a computer while he tells his fellow canine, "On the Internet nobody knows you're a dog." The comic strip is telling us that the Internet is a great place to communicate no matter who you are, what you look like, and even whether you have difficulties relating to people. As we discussed previously, a key component of the Internet is its anonymity and the safety one feels behind one of many glass screens. You can text from your phone without seeing the person at the other end just as you can e-mail, instant message, post on a social networking site, blog, or use any form of communication that isolates your physical being from the communication partner or partners (in the case of social networking posts, for example). In a classic study, Paul Brunet and Louis Schmidt of McMaster University paired young women and asked them to engage in a ten-minute free chat conversation under one of two conditions: either they used a text-based chat such as AIM or they used a live webcam. In front of a webcam shy women were less self-disclosing than those women who were not shy; in the text-based environment, where they could not see each other, shyness was not related to self-disclosure. Shy people and extroverted people disclosed just as much as long as they didn't actually see each other.[13] This result has been replicated over and over with the same result: The more "anonymous" you feel online, the more you are willing to share information about yourself.

This ability to shield yourself behind a screen may prove valuable to those who are unable to communicate effectively in person. Sometimes called the Strangers on a Train Effect[14]—where people find it easy to share information with a stranger whom they will never see again—this phenomenon has been extended to show that people will disclose more personal information online than face to face.[15] How strong is this effect? It turns out that even if you know the person at the other end of the screen you still feel more disinhibited and willing to share. And communicating through technology has great promise for making it easier for anyone to talk about his or her feelings to another person.

Internet researcher Jeffrey Hancock and his colleagues have shown that this effect even goes deeper into the expression of one's personal identity: "Research has demonstrated that Internet users take advantage of technological affordances to present idealized versions of the self in their online self-presentation." Extrapolating their research, Hancock said, "Our findings suggest that the idealized versions of the self presented online may reinforce 'actual' self perceptions unrelated to the mediated interactions. In other words, not only can people take advantage of online anonymity to explore new aspects of the self, they also can take advantage of the public nature of the Internet to help realize idealized concepts of self."[16] Hancock described perfectly what happened to Yolanda. Given the aid of communicating behind the screen, Yolanda was able to practice "talking" to her peers, solidify her sense of self, and emerge in the real world as a person who knows how to communicate face to face.

Social networks are, by their Internet-based nature, played out behind screens. As the relative "new kids in town," Facebook and GooglePlus are now receiving attention from psychologists who are discovering their strengths and weaknesses from a mental health perspective. For example, Emily Orr and her colleagues from the University of Windsor found that shy university students spent more time on Facebook but had fewer friends than students who were not shy.[17] Add to this the research by Tracii Ryan and Sophia Xenos from RMIT University in Melbourne, Australia, who used the Big Five Inventory—a psychological instrument that measures five personality factors: extraversion, agreeableness, conscientiousness, neuroticism, and openness to experience—to query 1,158 Facebook users and 166 non-users concerning their personality characteristics.[18] As I mentioned in an earlier chapter, Ryan and Xenos found that social media users tended to be more narcissistic. More important, they also tended to be less socially lonely, which, coupled with Orr's work, suggests that social networks may be the perfect places for shy people to converse with friends and develop communication skills to help them conquer their social communication difficulties.

Tim Blumer, a lecturer at the Berlin University of the Arts, provided an interesting model depicting why shy people might make great strides in communicating in a mediated environment such as a social network. The model, depicted in Figure 7.1[19] below, suggests that based on psychological gratifications theory, social networking sites allow shy people to control their environment and the information they wish to share, to stay anonymous even if they know their online partners in the real world, and to make the friends and acquaintances who are important to their social sense of self. Although Blumer suggests that social networking may not provide the best environment for shy people due to the *potential* loss of privacy, control, and anonymity, he does admit that it is too early to tell and that perhaps the increased options of finding friendship on a social networking site may transcend the loss of control over presenting oneself. In a recent published study, Levi Baker of the University of Tennessee noted: "Given that learning about others and disclosing personal information often leads to greater intimacy, using social networking services that allow personal information exchanges may facilitate relational development."[20]

Interestingly, a series of earlier studies, performed in the mid- to late 2000s in both the United States and other countries, helps us understand what exactly shy, socially lonely people might get from social networking. The study helps explain how social networking enhances their abilities and self-esteem to a level that affords further real-world opportunities for development and communication success. In one study Patti Valkenburg and her colleagues at the University of Amsterdam examined pre-adolescents' and adolescents' patterns and reasons for online communication and con-

FIGURE 7.1. MODEL SHOWING HOW PERSONALITY CHARACTERISTICS IMPACT THE CHOICE OF COMPUTER-MEDIATED COMMUNICATION (CMC) THROUGH PSYCHOLOGICAL GRATIFICATIONS[21]

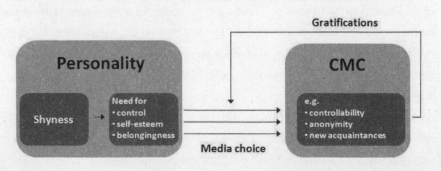

cluded that there was support for the social compensation hypothesis, where those shy and lonely individuals use mediated (behind the screen) communication tools as a way of compensating for their shyness and anxiety when they have to communicate with someone face to face. In their study, more than one in three pre-adolescents and adolescents believed that the Internet is more effective than face-to-face communication for talking about intimate topics.[22]

In several follow-up studies (all performed prior to the current social networking craze), Valkenburg and her colleagues found that because of social compensation, and the fact that online communication tools promoted more self-disclosure than face-to-face communications for shy people, these socially anxious pre-adolescents and adolescents were more likely to engage in identity experiments—pretending to be someone else—where they were able to demonstrate parts of their personality online that would remain hidden if they were to communicate in the real world.[23] Add to these results findings by Israeli scholars[24] that online self-disclosure increased reciprocal disclosure from others, and you have a perfect environment for the shy, lonely, socially anxious adolescent and young adult to discuss their feelings and have those feelings reflected back empathically.

One final thought on social networking as an emerging option for those with communication difficulties concerns what is known as the pragmatics of communication. I introduced this concept when I talked about the fact that people behind screens are not as aware of each other's reactions and feelings. Pragmatics also poses a problem for people with communication issues, but for a different reason. When you have difficulties communicating—regardless of whether you have a psychiatric disorder or are just shy—you lack the understanding of elements of communication that are normally learned as an infant and a toddler (remember the child giving his mom his favorite toy to soothe her tears?). For example, while most children, teens, and young adults learn the subtle nuances of communication, such as taking turns when you talk, pacing normal conversations, and even making small talk with people, those who have social phobia or social anxiety often do not tend to internalize those strategies. Being on a social network, where there is time to consider responses in a simulated turn-taking environment, almost provides a level playing field for those with communication disorders.

One study out of Carnegie Mellon University by Robert Kraut, who performed the classic HomeNet Study referred to in the chapter on technologically induced depression,[25] looked at the social use of computers by adults on the autism spectrum. One subject, 24-year-old John, had the following to report about communicating online: "One guy, I was talking to online said, 'This is not John. John stutters and talks fast. This can't be John.' I talked so intelligently, articulately online that he couldn't believe it was me."[26] It seems John is capable, at least online, of changing his entire way of communicating, to the extent that those who know him can't identify him as the one writing the material. This is someone who has learned some linguistic pragmatics. And one-on-one environments are only augmented by group sites, where people communicate on topics that are interesting to them, including movies, rock groups, TV shows, etc. Shared interests can help teach those pragmatics that should have been learned as a toddler.

THE "REAL" PAIN OF SOCIAL REJECTION

Before I talk about ways to escape or avoid having a communication disorder, it is important to mention an interesting study published recently in the *Proceedings of the National Academy of Sciences*.[27] In this study Professor Ethan Kross obtained a sample of people who had broken up recently with a mate and were emotionally upset by the experience. While monitoring their brain activity in an MRI chamber, he asked them to view a photo of a positive experience in their life as well as a picture of their ex. He also exposed them to a thermal device that delivered pain equivalent to holding a hot cup of coffee without the sleeve. According to the study's conclusions, ". . . powerfully inducing feelings of social rejection activate regions of the brain that are involved in physical pain sensation, which are rarely activated in neuroimaging studies of emotion. These findings are consistent with the idea that the experience of social rejection, or social loss more generally, may represent a distinct emotional experience that is uniquely associated with physical pain." This study demonstrates clearly the extent to which emotional pain of these communication disorders can be rather strong and harmful.

HELPING THE COMMUNICATION CHALLENGED

The disorders that involve communication issues range from social phobia and antisocial personality disorder to people who are just shy and
have difficulty connecting with others. Regardless of the reason, all of
these involve difficulties in communicating in a face-to-face environment.
There are many ways to assess your ability to successfully communicate.
The most common tool that psychologists use is called the Interpersonal
Communication Test, which is available in two versions: a full 25-item
quiz and an abridged 10-item quiz. Both are available online, and most
websites will give you a short report based on your answers and then offer you an extended report for a small charge. I have found that often the
short report is sufficient, though the full 25-item version is the best way to
assess your communication skills.[28]

When someone suffers from a communication disorder the most important task is to get him or her to "relearn how to communicate." This
means that they need to first understand the pragmatics of communication, which includes all of those niceties that we learn in childhood, and
second, they need a place to practice those newly acquired skills. The practicing part has been made much easier now that we have so many communication devices that help people feel more comfortable behind a screen.
Along these lines, I view communication as being represented as a two-
dimensional model in terms of the number of cues available to the communicators—words, sounds, facial expressions—and the synchronicity of
the conversation, defined as the time between when a message is sent and
when it is read or heard.

In terms of cues, think about receiving an old-fashioned letter from a
friend or relative. What cues do you have in the letter that will help you
understand not just the words and message but the "feeling" and "context"
behind those words? For example, imagine that your friend wrote in the
letter, "I am feeling sad today." Do you have a sense of her level of sadness? If she were standing in front of you and told you that she felt sad,
you would have other cues to indicate the depth of her angst, including
her facial expressions, tears, body language, and even the cadence of her
words. On the piece of stationery you have literally no cues other than her

two-dimensional words (and maybe a smudge from tears or writing that is shakier than normal, but those are difficult to infer).

The second communication dimension is called synchronicity, or the time lapse between when a message is received and a response is sent *and* received *and* read. Suppose you look at the postmark on the letter and realize that it was mailed a week ago. Is your friend still upset? Perhaps, but the passage of time may have changed those feelings and emotions. This is often what happens in communications that are asynchronous.

The diagram in Figure 7.2 on the next page shows a variety of communication tools along these two dimensions. Communication modalities that afford more essential cues to the receiver are shown toward the top of the chart while those with fewer cues are at the bottom. The second dimension, synchronicity, indicates how rapid a "typical" response is proffered on that dimension. For example, at the top right you will find face-to-face communication. This communication modality has the most cues (closest to the top of the chart) and the most synchronicity (closest to the right side of the chart). On the bottom left you see a handwritten letter, which has the fewest cues (closest to the bottom) and the least synchronicity (closest to the left). This makes sense because if I am talking to you face to face I get all of your cues (auditory, visual, tactile, kinesthetic, olfactory) and I am getting your message synchronously, right at the exact instant that you are transmitting it. In contrast, that letter has only those two-dimensional words and it was mailed a week ago.

In the upper right corner of the chart you see three communication modalities: face to face (the most cues and the most synchronicity), video chat (which removes the cues that you gain when you are physically in the same location with someone but maintains the synchronicity), and talking on the telephone (which now removes all visual cues but maintains the auditory cues and the synchronicity). In the upper left quadrant you see two communication techniques—audio podcast and voice mail—that provide only those two-dimensional words in an auditory format. They have a moderate level of cues but less synchronicity. Of course, if a person leaves you a voice mail and you listen to it immediately then the synchronicity improves, since the message is almost being transmitted in real time. Note that the video podcast is slightly above the audio podcast because it adds

FIGURE 7.2. TWO-DIMENSIONAL MODEL OF COMMUNICATION MODALITIES

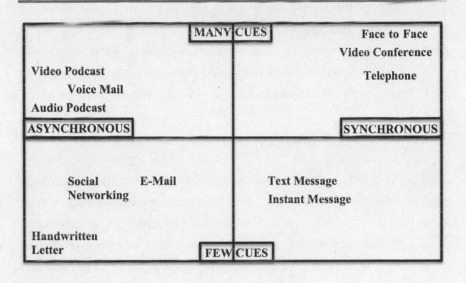

a visual cue to the communication along with the same auditory and word cues. In the lower right and lower left you see the more common communication tools, including texting and IMing, which both are more synchronous (unless you are like certain friends of mine to whom I send a text and get a reply four hours later!), and, to the left, social networking and e-mail, both of which can be more or less synchronous depending on the lag between communication and response but which provide, in their typical use, two-dimensional word cues.

We know that people who have communication problems—whether they are just shy or even more severely impacted by social phobia—have difficulty finding the correct words and need more time to think before responding. This means that those tools that are more asynchronous—precisely those tools on the left side of the chart—would be the best for them to use when practicing communicating with others. This allows time to think and edit one's words before sharing them with the other person or even the world. My advice is to encourage someone who has a communication disorder to make use of several aspects of the Internet, including all of those tools that allow for more asynchronous communication. However, after getting to know someone, it then becomes important to transition those communications to the tools on the right side of the chart, those with a faster response time and more synchronicity. The ultimate goal, of course, is to develop friendships where the bulk of the communication is firmly planted in the upper right corner. Note that using these tools requires some-one to learn all of the pragmatics of conversation, which includes precisely those that present difficulties to sufferers of a communication disorder.

SOME OTHER INTERESTING STRATEGIES

One of the difficulties that people with communication disorders have is sharing information with others. A clever experiment by Jonah Berger, a professor at the Wharton School at the University of Pennsylvania, looked at what the impact of both physical and emotional arousal had on sharing information. In one of his studies he divided his participants into four groups. Two groups watched a highly arousing movie clip, either funny or anxiety provoking, while the other two watched a low-arousing clip, designed to induce contentment or mild sadness. Immediately after viewing the clips the participants were told they were to be in a second study where they then immediately read an article and saw a video and were asked how willing they would be to share each with their friends. His results showed that those in the high arousal conditions were more interested in sharing. He replicated this result but replaced the arousing movies with jogging in place, which induced the same results. Either emo-tional or physical arousal made people more willing to share with friends. Although Berger's interest is in marketing and he is really looking at what will help companies get their products shared, these results suggest that communication-disordered people could increase their physical or emotional arousal level in order to begin sharing with others.[29]

There are numerous other tools to help people with communication disorders. Some researchers suggest that affective (emotionally charged) video games might be used to support teens with these types of disorders,[30] while others have tested a variety of cognitive-behavior therapy tools both online and offline and found that the online versions were at least as effec-tive if not more effective than in-person treatments.[31] Finally, there have been a few studies looking at unique ways of using online Web 2.0 facilities to enhance communication skills. One study used a virtual conversation partner for simulated, live conversations.[32] Another found that if a person used an avatar during a negotiation task, say on a video game or in a 3-D immersive environment such as *Second Life,* they were more socially intimate and self-disclosing if they were assigned an attractive avatar and more confident if they were assigned a tall avatar.[33] Although most people do not use avatars as a representation in cyberspace, this study suggests that using a tall, attractive avatar has psychological benefits that might assist people with communication disorders.

I would like to make two final notes about this form of iDisorder. First, as we find ourselves using more technology to communicate and as we spend less time doing so face to face, it becomes critical that we aren't drawn into a completely online world. The case of communicating online entices people such as Jan's husband, who was described at the top of this chapter, into a world where online communication becomes more important than real-world exchanges. As with Jan's husband, this can promote isolation and present a serious problem for the rest of the family. The strategies provided here and elsewhere in the book can be implemented with people who are choosing to remove themselves from the real world.

Second, for people who are hiding behind the screen because of their shyness, it is great that they can practice communicating online, but they need opportunities to practice connecting with people both online and offline. It is most certainly one thing to be able to hold up your end of a conversation in a cue-deprived, asynchronous environment where you have time to measure your words and edit yourself before completing a communication. It is quite another set of skills to be able to communicate face to face. Both forms of connection are important. It is not sufficient to hide behind a screen and become an excellent cyber communicator. Learning the skills online in a safe environment is a fine idea, but the iDisorder will still remain until you practice and perfect those skills in the real world.

EIGHT

You Only Think You're Dying

When Pain Is Just Pain

My co-worker Tammy is always telling me about these health problems she has. It seems like every time I talk to her she has something new. Her latest ailment is restless leg syndrome, which makes it hard for her to sleep. Now she's taking one drug that makes her sleep, and another one to calm her legs down. She also believes she has fibromyalgia, and ADD, which she claims is making her unable to concentrate at work. She takes a lot of sick days and when she is here she spends way too much time looking up her symptoms on those health websites. Personally I think she's a hypochondriac—she just needs to eat better and exercise, and stay off the computer!

—Jan, 35, Torrance, CA

Tammy is one of millions of people worldwide who turn to media to find answers about everything relating to their health.[1] Whether it is a health-related website such as WebMD or a late-night television commercial for prescription drugs, Tammy is part of a twenty-first-century trend of seeking advice and answers to physical ailments through media channels rather than in person with health professionals. Some of this information can be helpful and offer talking points for doctor visits, but much of it only triggers anxieties and fears that we are actually much sicker than we really are. Tammy, for example, felt a pain in her side one day and immediately determined it was fibromyalgia, a nerve-related condition that causes body aches and pains through nerve channels. Tammy learned about fibromyalgia from a television commercial for Lyrica, in which a woman her age is seen rubbing her neck, arms, and side and describes an unbearable, persistent pain. Instead of calling her doctor right away, Tammy instead visited a website to determine whether the pain was indeed fibromyalgia or a more serious health problem. Since her symptoms didn't match the description for the condition, she ended up with the erroneous diagnosis of appendicitis. The website said appendicitis can be life-threatening if not treated immediately, so Tammy called her doctor for an emergency appointment. During the doctor visit Tammy found out she didn't have appendicitis but had simply strained a muscle picking up a heavy box. But Tammy wasn't convinced and her online behavior continued. Over time this led to the belief that there was something seriously wrong with her.

Hypochondriasis, or health anxiety, is a psychological disorder that causes people to believe they are ill when they aren't. According to the *DSM,* the symptoms of hypochondriasis are:[2]

1.   A persistent non-delusional belief you have a serious illness, despite medical reassurance that you do not, a lack of physical findings to support your belief, and failure to develop the disease.
2.   You do not recognize the concern is excessive.

People who have hypochondriasis truly believe they are physically ill, yet there is no evidence to support this. Even when a doctor has found nothing physically wrong, the individual continues to have this belief. To be diagnosed with hypochondriasis, one of the somatoform disorders classified by the *DSM,* people must hold this belief for more than six months. Somatoform disorders—or the expression of psychological pain through physical symptoms—are a major problem in healthcare.[3] Up to 26 percent of patients who visit their primary care physician show some somatoform symptoms, most commonly through complaints about aches and pains that diminish their moods and alter their thoughts and behaviors; further, the physical symptoms are often brought on by the worrisome thoughts.[4]

With the Internet boom and the availability of information about our health in today's media environment, it is easy to see how someone could hold these beliefs and have them reinforced by the information they seek. Hypochondriasis has been around a very long time, yet the ease and speed at which we obtain information is a recent phenomenon. When people experienced physical symptoms in the past, they sought the advice of their doctor; today, people seek the advice of Internet websites, peers in chat rooms, or celebrity doctors on television. This can have profound consequences, especially when people take advice from unauthorized sources to try some remedy that could ultimately harm them or prevent them from getting the correct medical advice. With the high cost of healthcare and the large numbers of uninsured, more people are choosing not to see a doctor and seeking free advice and diagnoses over the Internet.

According to a study about treatment for health anxiety by researchers at the University of Manitoba in Canada,[5] the disorder "may be triggered by experiences such as everyday symptoms (a skipped heartbeat, a headache, or the illness associated with common cold and gastrointestinal viruses), a threatening experience such as finding a breast lump or by hearing stories about health issues in the community or media." The health worries may be mild to severe depending on the symptoms the person has. The authors write:

> Some individuals may worry about a specific illness or body symptom, while others worry about many. Conviction about actually having a serious disease may be part of the picture. Health anxiety is often associated with high levels of worry, excessive focus on bodily symptoms, checking for symptoms and signs related to health concerns, and frequent efforts to obtain reassurance.

In a large-scale German study of hypochondriasis,[6] researchers discovered that medically unexplained symptoms were extremely common, particularly pain, where 30 percent reported back pain, 25 percent reported joint pain, 20 percent reported some pain in their extremities, 19 percent reported headaches, and 5 percent reported chest pain. Gastrointestinal symptoms were also very common, with 13 percent of their sample reporting bloating, 11 percent reporting some food intolerances, and 11 percent reporting abdominal pain and other stomach discomforts. The last category was cardiovascular symptoms, with about 11 percent reporting some heart palpitations. The symptoms were more common in people over 45. Many participants also reported health anxiety, with 17 percent saying they often worry about having a serious illness, and 29 percent reporting they often worry about their health. Studies in the United States have found similarly high levels of health anxiety.[7]

Further, researchers have discovered that people who have this disorder believe that healthy people have absolutely no aches and pains. They tend to be hyper aware of their bodies[8] and to consult their doctor as soon as any symptoms arise. They also tend to believe that physical exercise exacerbates physical illness; therefore many people with this disorder avoid physical activity altogether, which, in many cases, is exactly the opposite of what a doctor would advise.

It is possible that hypochondriasis can be triggered by media use and media content, specifically by excessively visiting health websites, watching certain television programming, and viewing television commercials pushing prescriptions drugs. This chapter will explore how these media-related activities trigger or exacerbate existing health anxiety.

CYBERCHONDRIACS

A former neighbor of mine was sure her ten-month-old baby boy had autism, a very dangerous condition for a child. He didn't smile and laugh as much as other babies she knew, and he was cranky and pouting most of the time. She told me she had input his symptoms on an Internet website, and they matched the diagnosis of autism. She was frantic. She had seen the media reports of certain vaccines being linked to autism, and since she had just taken the baby in for his last round of shots she was convinced that this is what caused his odd behavior. She took him to the doctor, who said he probably had a gastrointestinal problem that made him look unhappy. She wasn't convinced. Now, autism is a serious disorder and early identification can help raise a happier, healthier child. What she didn't know, however, is that autism is impossible to diagnose in babies because it is marked by social behavioral deficiencies and learning disabilities that are not evident in such a young infant. Her doctor told her to wait a couple of years and then take him to a specialist.

The Pew Internet & American Life Project reports research statistics, articles, and general information about people's technology use. According to the Pew Center, searching for health information on the Internet is more popular than any other specific Internet activity, with 80–89 percent of all people using health websites.[9] In fact the study shows it as the third most popular media activity, after sending e-mail and doing basic Internet searches. Looking for health information is just as popular as reading blogs, looking up an address or phone number, or paying a bill online. In fact, on a typical day more people seek health information online than visit doctors.[10]

The good news is that people's use of online health material is less pronounced than it used to be. In a recent study published in the *New England Journal of Medicine*,[11] a survey of 16,000 people over seven years also found that people's trust in their doctors has increased with the ascent of the Internet. The study found that people tend to seek information on the Internet first and then take that information to their doctor visits. Susannah Fox, an associate director of the Pew Research Center's Internet & American Life Project, says "the study dovetails with previous research showing that the Internet is not replacing the role of doctors in people's health."[12] The problem, though, is that there is still a large group of individuals who do not seek help from their doctors and would rather believe what websites tell them. Dr. Marc Feldman, an expert on somatoform disorders, calls these people "cyberchondriacs," those who constantly check their symptoms on health websites for diagnoses.

Interestingly, those in the higher income brackets seek health information online more than those with lower incomes,[13] probably because they have more access to computers and may be more educated, creating greater confidence in their decision making. Results from the Pew Center indicate these individuals are also more likely to seek treatment information and obtain data regarding their test results online as well.

DR. OZ SAID SO

Besides going online, people get ideas about their health from watching voluminous medical dramas, documentaries, and talk shows. Shows such as *House, The Dr. Oz Show,* and *Grey's Anatomy* depict medical procedures and various diseases and ailments in an overly dramatic, easily explainable, and over-simplified manner. It is possible that people who view a lot of these shows get ideas about their own health by watching operations, diagnoses, and other health-related issues. Research has supported this from the cultivation perspective—which posits our views of the world and ourselves are based on an accumulation of what we see on television over time—and other related theories. Cultivation explains why people who view these television programs could apply what they see to their own lives or believe that what they see represents reality.

Jan Van den Bulck, a professor of media studies at Leuven School for Mass Communication Research in Belgium, is a leading researcher on how television influences people's thoughts and expectations. In a study published in the *European Journal of Emergency Medicine,* Van den Bulck looked at the relationship between people's estimates of surviving a heart attack with cardiopulmonary resuscitation by doctors and nurses and their medical drama viewing. Van den Bulck gave a questionnaire to a random sample of 820 third- and fifth-year college students in which they reported their (fictional) medical television viewing behaviors, their knowledge of cardiopulmonary resuscitation (CPR), and their estimates of the survival rate after in-hospital CPR. The results were staggering: People who view large amounts of medical television dramas have higher estimates of CPR survival. Van den Bulck concluded that, "the consumption of medical television drama is related to overestimating survival chances after in-hospital resuscitation by physicians and nurses following cardiopulmonary arrest. A practical knowledge of basic cardiopulmonary resuscitation techniques moderates but does not eliminate the television effect."[14]

The number of television programs devoted to health-related issues is unprecedented.[15] On the daily *The Dr. Oz Show,* one or more health-related topics are examined, summarized, and neatly wrapped into a one-hour talk show. He offers solutions and advice for everything from what supplements you should be taking to the advantages of losing ten pounds. His website alone is a dizzying array of medical, psychological, biological, and psycho-sexual information and advice. A recent visit offered topics ranging from "Concerned about Ovarian Cancer" to "Suffering from Fibroids" and "Anti-Cancer Superfoods." Most of the website's content revolves around topics that consume many Americans' thoughts. He offers so much advice that it would be impossible for someone to follow all of it. But this is precisely why so many Americans may develop hypochondriasis: because if Dr. Oz says you should do something and you don't, that little pain in your chest turns into a major concern. People may feel guilty that they aren't following this expert advice, and, rather than seeking real knowledge from their own doctor, they rely on the summarizations and blanket statements made by a TV personality. To be fair, one positive aspect of these programs is that they shed light on health problems that may have gone overlooked in the past.

In addition to television programming, the past 15 years have seen a dramatic increase in the prevalence of advertisements for prescription drugs and other supplements. According to the FDA, drug advertising has never been outlawed or banned in the United States, but in the mid-1980s, drug companies started taking their pitch from the doctor's office to the airwaves in the form of direct-to-consumer advertising. Drug advertising is now on television, the Internet, magazines, newspapers, and billboards. The FDA does not review these ads; however, drug companies are encouraged to be truthful in their advertising. Further, in a meta-analysis of studies regarding prescription drugs and doctors' use of name-brand drugs, 75 percent of the studies showed that prescription drug companies influence doctors to prescribe their medications.[16] And if doctors with advanced years of education react so strongly to drug company influence, what chance do people without medical training have against this onslaught of medical advice?

Bob is a late-night television junkie who likes to watch crime dramas. A bit socially isolated after his wife of 30 years died in 2009, Bob tends to spend a lot of time alone and suffers from mild depression associated with grief. During his late-night TV viewing he is exposed to dozens of advertisements for prescription drugs, all asking him if he has certain symptoms and telling him that he should take this or that medication. Bob visits his local health clinic about once a month, each time complaining about a new health problem and asking for a specific medication to help it go away. Since his clinic is associated with a teaching hospital, the doctors rotate shifts, so it is rare that Bob sees the same doctor twice. After a year and a half of this behavior, the head nurse at the clinic recognized Bob's pattern and alerted the doctors. The next time he came in with back pain, instead of giving him yet another prescription, his doctor referred him to a psychotherapist.

So why do people listen to late-night TV ads and believe the Internet will give them sound medical advice? The answer is because they trust them.

IT'S ALL ABOUT TRUST

People may exhibit the symptoms of hypochondriasis because the information they find reinforces a belief they have about their health. One important component of believing in something is trust. We studied people who search the Internet for advice and found that people who already had high levels of trust also tended to trust the information they read on the Internet.[17] We also found that those who used the Internet more often tended to use unverified material.

After observing our students using non-credible websites and other marginal information in their research papers, we decided to do a study to determine how and why people turn to websites for information, and how much people trust the information they seek. We also wanted to determine under what conditions people use peer advice or expert advice when seeking information on the Internet. We concluded that "the context of the decision (in this case, the website) influences the weight given to expert versus peer reviews in the decision-making process. Expert reviews are given more weight when objective information is being sought about a product or service, whereas peer reviews are given more weight when subjective information is sought."[18] Other scholars have discovered that people trust online health-related material more than they do user-generated material such as Wikipedia, social networks, and peer reviews.[19] Since health-related website content is thought to be objective information written by experts rather than peers, it is easy to understand why people use it to seek answers about their health.

Research has shown that trust is positively associated with online source use,[20] that trust is a key issue for maintaining a successful long-term online relationship with a website,[21] and that people who are more trusting tend to trust Internet information more. Since many of these websites have been around a long time and employ real doctors, it is understandable that they gain the trust of people seeking answers to their health questions. Luis Casalo and his colleagues at the University of Zaragoza, Spain, developed this definition of trust: honesty, benevolence, and competence. Honesty is the belief that one will keep one's word while benevolence "reflects the belief that one of the parties is interested in the well-being of the other."[22] Competence is related to the perceptions of the website contents, specifically whether they are true. Further, to trust a website one must believe in the reliability or strength of that site.[23] Casalo and his colleagues[24] found that people's levels of trust predicted their commitment level to a website. Therefore, people with more trust in the site had a longer relationship with it.

Oxford Professor William Dutton says Internet trust—or what he calls "cybertrust"—is influenced by several factors, including experience and education. Dutton and his colleague Adrian Shepherd discovered that people discontinue using websites because of a perceived risk or lack of trust. Those who perceive a risk involved in using a website will turn to other sites.[25]

But what about accuracy? Don't people care that the information they seek may not be accurate? A credible online source has been defined as one that provides correct information without bias and contains material written by experts who are trustworthy.[26] In our peer vs. expert advice study discussed earlier in this chapter, we found that people tend to give more weight to experts rather than peers, but the perception of a website's credibility by its placement and appearance—called "source credibility"—can have just as much of an effect on our decisions. Jennifer Greer from the Reynolds School of Journalism at the University of Nevada-Reno conducted a study about Internet source credibility. She writes, "Information from sources rated as high in expertise leads to the greatest attitude change among those receiving the message; low-expertise sources typically produce no changes in attitude."[27] Audiences find online information has varying levels of credibility. People who feel that a source is credible will also believe the information from that source is credible. Because medical websites have source credibility, people may trust the information contained in it and look to it for accurate information despite the varying levels of accuracy its contents may possess.

The perception of information is also important in understanding whether people believe a website has high or low credibility. In their study of Iraq War-related information, Junho Choi of Kwangwoon University in Seoul, along with James Watt and Michael Lynch of Rensselaer Polytechnic Institute, found that opponents of the Iraq War believed the Internet sources to be more credible than did pro-war or neutral respondents. The diversity of information was cited most often as why the group perceived high credibility of Internet sources about the war.[28]

Other reasons for turning to websites instead of doctors to seek medical advice are:

- Immediacy: You don't have to wait for a doctor's appointment to get an answer. Websites offer immediate information.
- Comfort of Home: You can look up your symptoms in your pajamas if you'd like. You can avoid having to wait in a doctor's office, especially if you are uncomfortable.
- Cost: Most online health websites offer free information.
- Ease of use: Using online health websites is extremely easy, with many of them offering "symptom checkers" where you can type in your symptoms and the website will give you a variety of diagnoses from which to choose.

AN INNER NEED

One explanation for exhibited hypochondriasis symptoms is what communications scholars call the Uses and Gratifications (U&G) Theory. U&G explains our connection to media and media content as an inner need that we satisfy. It says people choose to use certain media or technology because those systems and their content match their feelings, desires, values, or beliefs. Nupur Tustin, a doctoral student at the Annenberg School for Communication at the University of Southern California, conducted a study on the uses and gratifications of using health websites.[29] In her research with more than 150 cancer patients she discovered that those who were dissatisfied with their physician's care and diagnoses were more likely to use online health information rather than the information from their doctor. Doctors' empathy levels and the time they spent with the patient were negative predictors of this online behavior. In other words, patients whose doctors have poor bedside manners are more likely to turn to the Internet for information.

Another explanation for people exhibiting hypochondriasis through media is a concept from behaviorism called "reinforcement contingencies," which are secondary gains that reinforce or maintain the disorder. These contingencies could allow people to receive support from loved ones and acquaintances, get out of undesirable working conditions or work in general, avoid physical exercise, or explain another condition, such as obesity. In health psychology this is called the "sick role," whereby individuals play the role of a sick person—whether or not they are actually ill—to reap the benefits of being sick. I have a friend who is always posting online about her various ailments, and each post gets at least one empathic comment from her friends, which undoubtedly then reinforces her disclosure, making it all the more likely that she will continue. It is a vicious cycle, and technology certainly makes it easier to find an audience that will listen to a litany of one's ailments.

During an interview, Janice, a 38-year-old single working mother of two, told us about her belief that her doctors had misdiagnosed a lump in her neck. Janice was convinced that the lump was cancerous despite lab tests that had determined the lump was a benign cyst. Her doctor had even offered to remove the cyst to alleviate her concerns, but Janice refused the treatment. Janice was overwhelmed with caring for her two children and not having any time for herself, and the pretend illness seemed to take her mind off her worries. One day a co-worker at her medical supply office mentioned something about the lump. Janice lied and told her it was a tumor and that doctors were unsure how long she had to live. This drew much support from her supervisors and office mates, and Janice reveled in it. She continued to perpetuate the lie and took time off work for "doctor visits" and "radiation therapy." Over time Janice had to admit she didn't have the disease and eventually quit the company after her co-workers stopped trusting her.

Like Janice, people who fake being ill are not classic hypochondriacs, though the fakers' behavior may have begun this way. Dr. Marc Feldman is a clinical professor of psychiatry and adjunct professor of psychology at the

University of Alabama and an expert in a phenomenon called Munchausen by Internet (MBI), whereby individuals pretend to have diseases and other conditions and seek support in chat rooms and virtual support groups.[30] People use their fictitious illnesses to gain attention and sympathy, or to control others. He told us that individuals engaging in MBI "differ in an important way" from cyberchondriacs—those who constantly check their symptoms on websites—in that the person with the fake illness understands they are not ill, while the cyberchondriac believes they are ill.

> In MBI cases, the person knows that he or she is not actually facing the claimed ailment or crisis; in contrast, the cyberchondriac does believe— wrongly—that he or she is ill and in need of formal diagnosis or treatment. When confronted with inconsistencies, most MBI patients/perpetrators abruptly disappear from the boards or groups to which they have been posting. Few of them have openly explored their own online behavior, but those that have describe a deep need for validation, attention, and concern that they have felt unable to meet in any other way. Often they have personality disorders which render them likely to use self-defeating behaviors in an effort to meet their needs, rather than prosocial behaviors that will serve them well in the end.

So what we see is two similar yet distinct conditions born from media use—one in which people use the Internet to bolster and reinforce their somatoform disorder, and another in which people use Internet sources to maintain and gain feedback on a false condition.

"TREATING" CYBERCHONDRIACS AND MUNCHAUSEN BY INTERNET SUFFERERS

Hypochondriasis can be psychologically damaging, causing depression and persistent anxiety. Body-focused anxiety and other somatoform conditions can be caused by ideal media images,[31] media and technology overuse, and substandard healthcare providers. It can also be caused by an over-reliance on and trust in websites and television content. The most widely accepted and preferred treatment for this disorder is cognitive-behavioral therapy, whereby patients are trained (usually by an empathic therapist) to confront their condition through discussion and education.[32] Several related approaches have shown excellent results as well, including:[33]

- Psychoeducation, where people attend lectures, watch demonstrations and videos, and engage in focused group discussions. They also complete brief exercises that can: (1) monitor and challenge thoughts, (2) identify avoidance behaviors, and (3) monitor daily hassles. This form of therapy tends to work well with those who have mild symptoms of health anxiety rather than full-blown hypochondriasis.
- Explanatory therapy, where patients are persuaded there is nothing physically wrong with them by having doctors test them for their perceived ailments and show them the results. Doctors may possibly provide medication for anxiety if the belief persists.
- Exposure and response prevention, which includes *in vivo* exposure, where the patient is exposed to hospitals and doctors; interoceptive exposure, such as "exposure to naturally occurring somatic sensations such as physical exercise to induce rapid heartbeat"; and imaginal exposure, where the patient imagines that he or she has developed a disease. "Exposure is often combined with response prevention, to encourage the patient to delay or refrain from bodily checking and from seeking medical reassurance."[34]

Long-term cognitive-behavioral therapy tends to work best with people who have been diagnosed with hypochondriasis because they usually also have mild to severe depression. There is no indication that one treatment works faster than the others. If you think you or someone you know has hypochondriasis, the Whiteley Index,[35] a widely used test to find hypochondria, can be used to find out. As with all tests the result must be interpreted cautiously. A high score is an indication that you could profit from talking this over with your doctor. Here are strategies on how to assuage the symptoms of a hypochondriasis iDisorder:

1. The first step is recognizing that you have (or someone you know has) the disorder. The best way is to see a licensed clinical psychologist or psychiatrist and have them determine whether you have the condition. Or, to see whether you may have symptoms related to the disorder, take the Whiteley Index. Recognizing that you may have hypochondriasis sometimes helps people understand that their physical symptoms are not real medical problems.

2. Seek advice from your doctor rather than health-related websites. WebMD and other medical websites are useful tools to understand conditions that have already been diagnosed by your physician but less effective in initially diagnosing the problem. It is always best to see a medical doctor to determine whether you have a physical ailment. If you don't like your doctor's diagnosis, get a second opinion.

3. Understand how to assess the credibility of health websites. If you do use health-related websites, learn how to filter out information written by peers and others who are not experts or doctors from information that is trustworthy, factual, and well researched. Always be sure to look up the credentials of the person writing the information.[36]

4. Avoid "buying in" to commercial claims. Pharmaceutical companies prey on hypochondriacs, and if you believe what an advertisement tells you over the advice of your doctor, you could end up taking harmful drugs that have little to no effect on your condition and may cause further stress, anxiety, and other, real, health problems.

5. Reduce general anxiety. Often general anxiety will exacerbate our physical ailments to the point where people believe they are sick when they are not. By reducing anxiety—through pursuing therapy, taking meditation, reducing your workload, and, most importantly, avoiding the urge to constantly check out your physical symptoms on the Internet—the acuteness of the physical pain should diminish.

6. Exercise. Physical exercise is one of the best ways to reduce stress, and the time spent exercising will take the place of your online and other media-related activities.

7. Unplug. As we have discussed in other chapters, getting away from your daily routine and into nature for a while is probably the best way to alleviate the symptoms of psychological disorders brought on by media use. Purposely avoid checking your phone, going online, and being exposed to television and other media that contain commercial advertisements and other distractions.

The symptoms of somatoform disorders, conditions that create internal psychological warfare through perceived physical symptoms, show up in a quarter of people worldwide. The prevalence of these disorders is surely exacerbated by technology and media use and can result in millions of dollars spent on unneeded doctor visits and an exorbitant amount of time wasted worrying about illnesses or other conditions that simply are not real. In our lab study we discovered that certain activities are related to somatoform disorders such as hypochondriasis, including preferring to multitask, getting anxious about missing cell phone calls, using Facebook, and instant messaging.[37] In the next chapter we will examine another somatoform disorder, body dysmorphic disorder, whose sufferers believe they have a deficit in their appearance while in general others do not concur.

NINE

Does My Profile Pic Make Me Look Fat?

New Media and Our Relationship with Our Appearance

I'd Rather Die Than Be Fat.

—Unnamed actress

People don't see me. No one sees me. It's like being fat. No one takes you seriously. You just don't exist—you're so big, you're not even there.

—Anonymous person with an eating disorder[1]

We turn skeletons into goddesses and look to them as if they might teach us how not to need.

—Laurie Halse Anderson, author of *Wintergirls*[2]

Brittany is a typical 21-year-old college student: She averages about 12 semester units working toward her criminal justice degree, works part-time as a server, lives with a roommate in a small, two-bedroom apartment, and often stays up late to finish papers and study for exams. Brittany is also a media junkie. She walks around with her iPod earbuds in place all day; spends countless hours on Facebook, You-Tube, and her smartphone; and always has the TV on when she's home.

Shayna, Brittany's roommate, often overhears Brittany talking to her friends about how she wants to look like a character on the drama *Criminal Minds,* a blonde FBI agent who also happens to have the shape of a Barbie doll—and that she needs to "lose a few pounds" before going home for the holidays to make her ex-boyfriend want her back. Brittany is clearly obsessed with the show and her favorite character. Not only does she record all the episodes and watch them repeatedly, she is also following the show online through discussion groups, logging onto the television network's website, and even following the actress's Twitter feed, where she talks about how difficult it is to maintain her weight.

One night when Shayna returns from work, she notices the trash can full of snack wrappers. When she asks Brittany about them, she says she had a craving for junk food while studying for a midterm. About a week later Shayna comes home and finds a green industrial trash bag full of empty containers and wrappers in their kitchen, and the cabinets void of the snack items. As she walks toward her bedroom she hears what sounds like vomiting coming from Brittany's bathroom. Not wanting to be nosy, Shayna decides not to ask Brittany about it. Instead, Shayna calls a nurse at the university to see what she should do to help. The nurse tells her Brittany should seek help for an eating disorder.

Brittany has what the American Psychiatric Association calls bulimia nervosa, one of the disorders defined in the *DSM* that can have crippling effects on its sufferers. Bulimia mainly affects young women but is found in men and women of all ages and, along with the closely related disorder, anorexia nervosa, affects nearly 70 million people worldwide and up to 25 million in the United States alone.[3] Eating disorders are the primary cause of death in teen girls, and 20 percent of anorexics will die from complications associated with the disorder. Since the 1950s we have seen a marked increase in eating disorders among 15- to 24-year-old females, with recent studies showing rates as high as 300 in 100,000.[4]

The rise in these disorders, especially among young women, goes hand in hand with the increase of media and technology use, as research on eating disorders began just 30 years ago,[5] about the same time we began investigating the psychological, physiological, and sociological effects of technology.[6] As most scholars in this area agree, the advancement of technology and the media's persistent focus on beauty and thinness has contributed to these conditions in profound ways. Television has traditionally been seen as the main culprit, including its advertisements for beauty products and other reminders of why our body may not be acceptable in its present state. However, the Internet and other technologies (what industry professionals call "new media") burst onto the scene, presenting beauty images 24/7 on all of our devices, and this is undoubtedly exacerbating this problem. It is likely that Brittany's daily and perhaps unhealthy relationship with media and technology, and her strong desire to look like one of the characters on television, led to her binging and purging behavior, one of the classic symptoms of an eating disorder.

EATING DISORDERS

People with eating disorders worry obsessively about becoming fat or overweight, have a distorted body image, are unable to control their food intake to maintain a healthy weight, and widely fluctuate in their body image depending on their current size, shape, or weight.[7] The *DSM* defines three characteristics of eating disorders:

1. *Anorexia,* which is a "loss of appetite accompanied by inability to eat."
2. *Binge eating,* which is "excessive eating beyond the amount necessary to satisfy normal appetite."
3. *Purging,* which is "emptying the stomach by induced vomiting or the bowels by induced evacuation with enemas or laxatives."[8]

There are two main types of eating disorders, anorexia nervosa and bulimia nervosa (which is what Brittany suffers from). People with anorexia nervosa abstain from eating and keep their body weight lower than the minimum healthy weight for their height and age. Anorexics also achieve this goal by binging and purging—where they overeat and then vomit or excrete the food with laxatives or enemas—or by restricting, where they simply avoid eating. Bulimia nervosa is characterized by frequent episodes of extreme binge eating, where a person eats a considerably larger amount of food than most people would in a discrete time period and lack self-control during the episode. This is normally followed by purging.

Eating and self-image disorders don't only affect the individuals who have them. According to the National Institute of Mental Health, and every other major health organization investigating this problem, the prevalence of eating disorders and their association with disease, suicidal thinking, depression, and other psychological disorders suggests they represent a major public health concern that needs to be addressed. This is particularly important since most people who have an eating disorder do not receive treatment, either because they hide the problem from their loved ones, they are ashamed, or it goes unnoticed.[9] Here are some further statistics on what we do know from research across the globe:

- Only 1 in 10 people with eating disorders receives treatment.[10]
- Just 35 percent of the people with eating disorders who do receive treatment do so at a specialized facility for eating disorders.[11]
- Women who have a mother or sister with an eating disorder are two to three times more likely to also develop one.[12]
- Eating disorders were first diagnosed in the 1970s, about the same time television became a staple in American homes.[13]
- People with eating disorders and body dysmorphic disorder have lower self-esteem.[14]

Our society's increasing reliance on media and technology, and the permeation of media images through all the various devices we use on a daily basis, are all part of the mix in creating and maintaining these disorders.

MEDIA CAN CAUSE AN EATING DISORDER

In a famous study that illustrates how media can cause eating disorders, researcher Anne Becker studied girls in a remote island in the South Pacific to see how they acted before and after the introduction of television. Becker visited the small hamlet of Nadroga, Fiji, in 1995, just before television was introduced and again three years later. In her 2004 article,[15] Becker explained that she picked Fiji for its socially accepting views that supported "robust appetites and body shapes"—the people on the island believed that a larger body indicated a woman had social support and was capable of hard work.

Before Becker's initial visit, eating disorders were virtually non-existent in Fiji, and no *DSM* eating disorder was recognized there. Prior to the introduction of television, only 3 percent of Fijian teenage girls had reported they had vomited to keep their weight down. Amazingly, Becker discovered that after television was introduced 15 percent of the girls reported this behavior. That's not all that Becker found. About three quarters of the island girls said they felt "too big or fat" on her second visit. Of the girls who watched television at least three nights per week, 50 percent were more likely to feel fat after viewing TV and a third were more likely to diet. Clearly the introduction of the television, with all of its skinny actresses, influenced Fijian girls to pay more attention to their shape, and, extrapolating Becker's research, television made some of those girls anorexic. The Fiji experiment in the mid-1990s was a harbinger of things to come as society saw an accelerating wave of new media and technologies.

No single cause of eating disorders has been identified, but researchers have shown a strong connection between media consumption and these behaviors. The symptoms and severity differ widely among individuals, but in all cases, eating disorders are marked by negative self-evaluative behaviors and a persistent focus on weight and body shape.[16] Viewing large amounts of media images—such as female actresses' Barbie-like, impossibly thin bodies—can cause people to want to look or act like the characters they see. And these images show up again and again in all visual media—from traditional forms such as television and movies to new technologies such as social networks and online video sites.

Three decades ago, when television was the major form of media, a person could change the image bombardment by changing viewing habits. Now, however, as we can view television on multiple devices, anywhere, and at any time, the problem has spiraled out of control. But still, it is not just televised images that are the cause. Messages that invade our space are omnipresent. Say, for example, you Google the words "weight loss" to see what new diets people are discussing on the Internet. The next time you start a search by typing a "W"—even if you are looking for something else completely—Google's drop-down menu will suggest that you look at "weight loss" searches again. Even worse, the advertisements on web pages will change as a function of your searching habits. Search for diets and you will start to see advertisements for diet aids pop up on the screen. Type the word "diet" in an app store and you will be provided with literally hundreds of cell phone apps to help you accomplish your goals, regardless of how unhealthy they might be. Make a comment on an online discussion about weight loss and you will receive e-mail updates when someone adds a comment to the discussion. How can you resist all of these reminders that literally arrive with a trumpeted call to pay attention to your body and what you eat? If you are able to ignore those suggestions, as soon as you start your car the GPS displays an advertisement with a coupon for a fast food restaurant. Targeted images are pervasive and alluring, as they grab our attention through media that we access all day long. We are being hounded, and we can't simply turn off the television anymore.

BODY DYSMORPHIC DISORDER

Related to anorexia and bulimia is body dysmorphic disorder (BDD), a less severe condition that generally doesn't cause physical ailments. However, its impact on psychological health can be profound. This disorder affects both women and men: Women usually feel they need to lose weight or "fix" some defect, while men tend to believe they are too small and need to bulk up or have some other physical deficit. While some self-examination is normal, people with BDD excessively check their appearance and worry constantly that they are not "good enough."

According to the *DSM,* symptoms of BDD include:

1. A preoccupation with an imagined defect in appearance.
2. Significant distress or impairment in occupational, social, or other important areas of functioning.
3. Obsession about one's looks.
4. Social and family withdrawal.
5. Delusional thoughts and beliefs.

6. Suicidal thoughts.
7. Low self-esteem.
8. Self-consciousness in social situations.
9. Belief that others are mocking their defect.
10. Self-medication with alcohol.
11. Repetitive behavior (applying makeup, checking appearance in mirror, exercising).
12. Perfectionism.

Body dysmorphic disorder causes people to over-identify with their appearance; in other words their identity is tied too closely with how they look and not enough on other factors such as personality, intelligence, and other traits that most people value more than appearance alone. In study after study, people who have body dysmorphic disorder judge their body image negatively while over-valuing the importance of appearance, perfectionism, social acceptance, youthfulness, and symmetry.[17] These values reinforce the idea that they are aesthetic objects and, in social situations, a social object.[18] These idealized values differentiate a person with BDD from, say, a disfigured person who accepts their appearance and has high self-esteem.

June has a master's degree, owns a public relations (PR) firm, and lives in a cottage by the beach. June's life is the envy of her friends. In her field, a fashionable and attractive appearance is important; at least that's the perception among many PR professionals. June also maintains a Facebook page to attract potential clients and promote the ones she already works with. June's body image issues began way back in middle school when a mean kid at school teased her about her slightly protruding chin, calling her "Wicked Witch." She would stare at her chin for hours in the mirror, trying to find a head position that would make her look less like the *Wizard of Oz* villainess. As she grew into a teenager her chin became even more pronounced. She complained about this to her mother, who told June it was nothing to worry about and that she would eventually grow into it. And she did. But June still sees it as a gross, pointy protrusion that is a severe deficit, and she does everything she can to cover it up. In all her Facebook photos, June's head is tilted upward so her chin appears rounder.

Last summer June attended a networking event where she posed for pictures—making sure to keep her head in a position to best hide her chin—with the leaders of several non-profit agencies, her company's main clientele. The next day someone tagged her in a candid photo taken the night before. June was mortified. The photo showed her with her head down, laughing with one of the agency heads. Her chin, she thought, looked enormous. She immediately untagged herself and removed the photo from her page, then posted a nasty message on the Facebook page of the person who took the photo. No one else even noticed her chin, but June was so obsessed with it she acted uncharacteristically. Eventually her obsession became so great she went to a cosmetic surgeon to fix her chin.

Sadly, there is no way that June would have ever been able to remove every Internet photo that showed her imagined Wicked Witch chin. After all, more than three billion photos are uploaded to Facebook every month.[19] If you add in the next four most popular photo sharing websites—Flickr, Picasa, ImageShack, and Photobucket—it is estimated that there are more than 30 billion images on the Internet. How can anyone hope to find and remove all unflattering pictures? There are even websites that accumulate and display many of your photos from various sites across the Internet. But the bottom line is that once a photo of you—no matter how unflattering it might be—is posted, it may be reposted and appear in numerous locations. Unfortunately for June and others who have BDD—especially those who have high-profile jobs where picture taking is a common occurrence—the prevalence of such websites will only fuel their disorder.

THE "THIN IDEAL"

One of the most dramatic areas of research in the past decade has focused on the connection between the rise of an idealized female form in the media and the marked increase in anorexia and bulimia among young women. In general, constructed media—that is, media content produced by someone—portray thinness as an ideal measure of beauty.[20] In the past we saw these images appear on scripted television, reality programming, talk shows, and advertising, as thin women and toned, handsome men were heralded as closer to perfect than the average person. And now we see these images appear in new media technologies such as YouTube and social network advertising. In most new video games, for instance, users are able to choose an avatar, a digital, simulated representation of a person. In all cases (except Wii, where the user can create their own avatar) the digitized person is attractive and thin.

Seeing these images can have destructive consequences. While American women have generally become larger over the past 30 years—with a current average clothing size of 14 and one-third wearing a 16 or larger—the image of women portrayed in the media does not mirror this reality.[21] According to the American Medical Association the average woman's body is slightly larger than the recommended healthy level; however, according to the same standards, actresses' and models' bodies are often 20 percent or more underweight. On the one hand, we see skinny, successful, happy women on our screens and ultra-thin representations of ourselves in avatars, while on the other hand, more than half of the female species looks nowhere near that ideal.[22] Females who want to achieve these ideal beauty norms are more likely to exercise and diet but are also unlikely to succeed,[23] causing them to feel depressed, anxious, and self-conscious.

THERE'S NO ESCAPE FROM YOUR SOCIAL SELF

Humans are social beings whose identities are tied to a host of qualities, groups, people, situations, and ideas. As part of our humanness, we tend to compare ourselves to the rest of the world, whether it is done at a conscious level or not. And while sometimes we may feel like we want to crawl under a rock, no one actually lives there. Instead, we live in a social world filled with pressures to fit in, to be liked, and to belong. Psychologists and media experts have proposed and tested several theories to explain why we act this way. Social identity theory[24] explains that this yearning to belong drives us to behave and think in ways that represent the values and norms of whatever group we identify with. It is easy to understand, then, why we would be drawn to images of socialized people and situations and try to change ourselves in the process. Consider the power of social networking. Looking at your friends' posted daily activity logs and pictures, seeing their fun and exciting lives when you feel yours is dull and mundane, can create an inner dialog that goes something like: "Dan has so many friends . . . his friends are so nice to him . . . he is always having people over . . . he is so happy in all his photos . . . Dan looks so great, so tan, so fit . . . why doesn't he ask me over . . . I wish I had as many friends as Dan . . . I wish I looked like Dan. I wish my life was like Dan's." Clearly Dan portrays a healthy and fit image, which induces envy from his acquaintances and makes them examine and compare themselves to him. With the perception that Dan has such an exciting and fun life, his friends may desire to be part of his social group so they, too, can reap those benefits. Also, since physical attractiveness usually leads to rewards, it is clear that seeing Dan's Facebook page can drastically change their views about themselves.

Another theory that explains the desire to fit in is Social Learning, developed by Stanford Professor Albert Bandura. Social Learning Theory explains that individuals are socialized by watching positively or negatively reinforced behaviors demonstrated by others.[25] When positive behaviors are rewarded, people become successful members of a group. Those who view this action in turn want to emulate the behavior so they, too, can be accepted and ultimately satisfied.[26] Through social learning, people model the behaviors of fictional characters that they see on the screen as well as "real" characters, including reality stars, people on social networks, and singers and musicians in music videos. Without counterbalancing the images with a separate strong influence—such as a parent or peer—or strong self-identification, this altered reality may become what people believe about themselves.[27]

UNKNOWN CAUSE IS A *CAUSE FOR CONCERN*

In this chapter we have explored the idea that viewing certain images in the media can cause people to have eating disorders and BDD. Ideal beauty, in the form of symmetry, ultra-fit men and ultra-thin actresses and models, airbrushing, and scripted realities can all crush our self-esteem and lead us to make self-evaluations that cause severe psychological damage. Without other major positive influences and a strong sense of self, we can start to believe that because the people in the media gain rewards for looking "perfect," we must also strive to attain this. Unfortunately we usually can't measure up to the media's ideals and therefore become depressed, anxious, and self-conscious. Research on eating disorders alone shows the potential negative influence of repetitive and idealized images. The fact that eating disorders were not diagnosed until the 1970s reveals a connection between the rise of the perfect form—idealized by characters in the media—and self-image-related disorders.

While we know the traits, thoughts, and behaviors of people who have BDD and eating disorders, the causes have baffled researchers for the last half century. Some hope may be found in new brain research, however. In one experiment, researchers found that women with bulimia nervosa have different brain functions than "normal" women. Rachel Marsh and her colleagues at Columbia University discovered that women with the disorder tended to be more impulsive and made more mistakes than a group without bulimia nervosa when given the task to identify arrow direction on a computer screen.[28] Their brain activity patterns were also different. Through a functional magnetic resonance imaging (fMRI) scan (a type of scanning device used to detect brain functioning) the women with bulimia nervosa showed little brain activity in areas involved in self-regulation, which suggests these patterns are associated with impulse control problems and could possibly explain binge eating behaviors and other impulses The author writes, "Altered patterns of brain activity may underlie impaired self-regulation and impulse control problems in women with [bulimia nervosa]. These findings increase the understanding of causes of binge eating and other impulsive behaviors associated with BN and may help researchers to develop better targeted treatments."[29]

HOW YOU CAN PREVENT MEDIA FROM CAUSING BDD AND EATING DISORDERS

Let's start with our children. What can you do to alleviate the impact of media on them and help them avoid eating disorders? Obviously we need to make sure that, at a minimum, we monitor their eating and their exercise. How do we do that amid the massive media messages that scream for them to get thin and yet eat junk food? Here are some strategies:

1. Make sure that your young children (up to ten years old) rarely consume media on their own without parental supervision. Practice "co-viewing,"[30] where you spend time with your children while they are playing video games, watching television, and even surfing the Internet. Co-viewing allows you to talk to your children about the advertisements they see and the comments that people make on social networking sites about the way people look. Use these opportunities to start teaching your children that they should look to positive sources for their social learning and not focus on those negatives that may lead to an eating disorder.

2. Young children play with toys and dolls. As we have seen, those dolls most often represent an overly accentuated—and largely impossible—body type. Show your daughters how Barbie would look if she were life size and how Ken's muscles are unrealistic. One nice trick is to tape a large piece of paper on the wall and ask your child to draw what they think their body looks like on the paper. Then have your child stand against the paper and trace their actual body. Do this as they grow and use it as a guideline for talking about the diversity of body shapes and how they are all "normal" and not in need of "repair."

3. When it comes to your pre-teens, it is important to recognize that video gaming increases dramatically starting at about nine years of age[31] and that the images in video games can lead to eating disorders.[32] Female game characters are nearly always depicted as impossibly thin and voluptuous while male characters are idealized and overly muscular. Make sure that you are aware of the games your pre-teens play and talk with them about the impossible bodies they might see. And don't forget that the use of more media of all types was related to worse health, which makes frequent media users prime candidates for an eating disorder.

4. Body image issues are particularly profound in teenagers. The subtle and often hidden pressure to look good and have a beautiful or buff body is found across all media and teens are affected by these messages. Spend time with your teen and monitor the

media that they use daily. Remember that both video gaming and spending time online were related to health issues, so focus on those first, with other media coming later. Make sure that they understand the messages that are being sent though the television shows they love, the gaming characters they guide, and the chatter online and point out the inconsistencies between those images and reality. Start talking about bodies and healthy eating at a young age and by the time they are teens they will likely point out to you the subliminal messages in their media.

5. Regardless of the age of your children, consider the following:

- Encourage a positive body image by not making fun of or teasing about appearances and by avoiding comments about people's weight or body type.

- Monitor websites that they visit. Many Internet sites discuss anorexia and other eating disorders. Some are excellent while others may cause more problems by actually encouraging teens to modify their lives to look better.[33]

- Self-esteem is fragile in childhood, and, as we said earlier, poor self-concept can increase the odds of an eating disorder. Practice good parenting by using positive reinforcement with your young children for their behaviors and by not emphasizing their looks. As they grow they may get negative messages about their body and a solid self-concept will help control the impact of those hurtful messages.

6. If your child or teen does exhibit signs of an eating disorder, then it is important to seek medical and psychological treatment. Eating disorders can be deadly and there are excellent programs that treat these disorders and focus behaviors toward health. Contact your local medical association or psychological association for referrals to established programs.

Now, on to you. The first step is to evaluate your relationship with media. Ask yourself the following questions:

1. Do you sometimes feel you are consuming too much media?

2. Do you feel guilty for watching too much television or spending too much time on social networks?

3. Do the images you see and the dialog you hear on television and in advertisements make you feel bad about yourself?

4. Do you often compare yourself to the people you see on television, in the movies, on social networks, or on YouTube?

5. Do you worry about not looking as attractive as the characters you see?

6. Is your identity primarily tied to your appearance?

If you answered yes to any of these questions, the next step is to recognize that what you are feeling is probably a result of what you are viewing. Simply having the knowledge that you are reacting to these images is a powerful step in assuaging their impact. If you feel you are being manipulated by media messages or images, and they are causing you to change your eating or self-evaluative behaviors and you can't stop, you need to seek help.

TREATMENTS

Eating disorders are serious conditions that require treatment. Most experts agree that a multi-disciplinary approach is needed to treat anorexia and bulimia, and in severe cases people may need hospitalization. Cognitive-behavioral therapy is a common treatment for these disorders, along with group therapy and support groups, culinary therapy, and Dialectical Behavior Therapy, which teaches the sufferer new strategies to cope with the disorders' associated emotions and triggers.[34]

As we have discussed in this book, the media's ability to create cultural norms and artificial ideals can have damaging effects on those who view them most, especially among the most impressionable populations. The most pervasive images that contribute to eating disorders and BDD come from television, but magazines, Internet advertisements, and social networking contribute as well. Among all the iDisorders discussed in this book, eating disorders are perhaps the most damaging because they can lead to severe physical and psychological problems, including death.

TEN

Delusions, Hallucinations, and Social Avoidance

Is Technology Making Us Appear "Schizo"?

I keep hearing my phone ring and when I go to check it nobody's there. I hate it when other people have the same ringtone as me. I think somebody's trying to reach me. It drives me nuts!!

—Salvador, 18

One of the most severe forms of psychological pathology is schizophrenia. You may be more familiar with this disorder than some of the others described in this book because schizophrenia is often associated with the crazed or psychotic characters in films, books, television programs, and other popular media. The exaggerated behaviors of typical schizophrenics are so pronounced they make for great visual images on the screen. Consider these notable characters: Jack Nicholson's portrayal of Jack Torrance in *The Shining,* whose delusions led him to attempt to murder his family; Edward Norton's unnamed protagonist in *Fight Club,* who struggles with sleeplessness and hallucinations while his alter ego commands him to start an underground fighting club; and Russell Crowe's portrayal of Nobel prize–winning mathematician John Nash, whose schizophrenia caused him to think he was secretly working for the government in *A Beautiful Mind.* But schizophrenia is a real and quite debilitating disorder that varies in severity and almost always requires medication and therapy to alleviate its symptoms.

People who suffer from schizophrenia have trouble working and interacting with others, and they often rely on their families or a facility to take care of them. Classic symptoms are delusional thoughts and hallucinations, disorganized behavior and speech, and social withdrawal. Unlike other psychological disorders such as anxiety, the symptoms of schizophrenia do not normally appear in healthy individuals.[1] However, some associated personality disorders have symptoms that are far less debilitating and allow their sufferers to maintain jobs and have semi-normal social lives. Schizoid personality disorder, defined by emotional coldness and extreme social withdrawal, and schizotypal personality disorder, in which the person exhibits odd speech and thought patterns, magical thinking, and delusions, are two of the more common disorders. I believe our complete reliance on technology can make us look like we have these disorders or even cause brief episodes in which we experience them. Rather than looking at each disorder individually, I will examine how technology use relates to the various overlapping symptoms of the "schizo" group; therefore, I often use the term *schizo-disorder* as a general term to describe the related symptoms. Below are the symptoms associated with schizoid personality disorder and schizotypal personality disorder.

Symptoms of schizoid personality disorder:[2]
- Almost always chooses solitary activities.
- Has little, if any, interest in having physical relationships with others.
- Takes pleasure in few activities.
- Lacks close friends or confidants other than first-degree relatives.
- Displays emotional coldness and detachment from others.

Symptoms of schizotypal personality disorder:[3]
- Believes in odd things or magical thinking that influences behavior and is inconsistent with subcultural norms such as being telepathic, superstitious, or clairvoyant.

- Undergoes unusual perceptual experiences, such as appearances by others who are not there.
- Has odd thinking and speech.
- Shows suspiciousness or paranoid thinking.
- Behaves or appears in ways that are odd, eccentric, or peculiar.
- Lacks close friends or confidants other than first-degree relatives.
- Experiences excessive social anxiety that does not diminish with familiarity and tends to be associated with paranoid fears rather than negative judgments about the self.
- Appears indifferent to the praise or criticism of others.

SOCIAL WITHDRAWAL

Alan is a 48-year-old computer programmer who has worked from home for more than 20 years. When Alan was a boy he had lots of friends, loved to hang out with the neighborhood kids playing kickball in the cul de sac, and was sociable at school. In high school he became slightly more withdrawn and chose to be alone a lot. He rarely signed up for after-school programs, sports, or group projects, and he always sat in the back of the classroom. In his second year of college he was introduced to computers and found he had a knack for fixing them. After college he started working for a major computer company, and then he discovered the Internet. Alan was one of the first to join online bulletin boards and chat rooms, discussing computer issues with other programmers through a worldwide network of people who devoted their lives to creating new ways to make computers work faster, communicate more effectively, and function better. Years later he discovered the world of online gaming, specifically *World of Warcraft*, which consumed most of his time when he wasn't at work. He purchased a comfortable chair and a massive, wall-length table where he put his computers, monitors, keyboards, wireless mice, and volumes of computer manuals. His computer use was so enveloping he rarely slept or ate, and after a few years, Alan could no longer tolerate going to the office. He found being around other people annoying and asked his supervisor if he could work from home. His company agreed, hooked up a network and server at his apartment, and Alan has worked from his "station" ever since.

Because of the nature of his job, Alan eventually became socially withdrawn, so that now his only communication is through the computer. He has direct-deposit checks and orders his home-delivered meals over the Internet, so there is no reason to leave his cavernous dwelling. His mother and two sisters call once in a while, but Alan usually ignores their attempts to reach him. He deals with co-workers only through e-mail and rarely goes to the office unless there is a mandatory meeting. When he does go into work, people whisper about his increasingly strange appearance: His long, straggly, unwashed hair has the odor of dirt; his thick glasses sit oddly on his face; and his Pink Floyd t-shirt is from his boyhood days. He doesn't seem to even notice or care that people are talking about him. Alan's only friends are other online gamers and programmers who are just as socially isolated.

Alan is also a virgin—he has no interest in women, and he ignored the only girl who gave him attention in college. Alan is a classic example of someone who has developed schizoid personality disorder with symptoms of other schizo-disorders. The least severe of the schizo-related disorders discussed in this chapter, people with schizoid personality disorder seek isolation, exhibit coldness, and lack interest in being with other people. It is clear in Alan's case that Internet and computer use have exacerbated his problem and may have caused some of his odd behavior and desire to be alone.

According to the Bureau of Labor Studies, on an average day 60 percent of self-employed people, and 20 percent of those who work for others, work from home.[4] Our reliance on computers and other devices to "keep us connected" may also be doing psychological harm if we rely too much on them and not enough on maintaining healthy lifestyles, including face-to-face interactions that give us the needed context and cues that socialize us. Even though some research suggests that Internet use helps bolster social connections,[5] our research shows the opposite—that media and technology use is highly correlated with social withdrawal and isolation.[6]

TROUBLE CONNECTING

It's not only the social withdrawal of high technology users that makes them seem as if they have schizo-disorders. People with schizoid personality disorder describe themselves as "empty" or "without a self." They struggle with identity issues and often appear icy and withdrawn to others.[7] The more distance they put between themselves and others, or hide behind their "screens," the more they exhibit emotional coldness.

Through our research lab at California State University, Dominguez Hills,[8] we have conducted dozens of studies on the relationship among technology, media, and psychology. In our recent study on media use and psychological disorders, we found that higher media use was significantly correlated with schizoid personality disorder, especially in the younger generations. We discovered that the total daily use of media and technology, as well as, more specifically, hours spent online and playing video games, were all associated with schizoid disorders in both the iGeneration (those born in the 1990s) and the Net Generation (those born in the 1980s). Those teens and young adults who used more media and technology and also those who played more video games and spent more time online were more likely to evidence the signs and symptoms of schizoid disorders. This shows possible support for the notion that media and technology are making us more socially isolated and causing us to be emotionally distant.

Another interesting result from our study was that younger people who feel anxious when they can't check their e-mail or text messages as often as they want to also show higher levels of schizoid personality. This could indicate that when we can't connect with our friends and family through an artificial device we feel isolated. According to Adam Smith in *The Psychological Record*:

> People with schizoid personality disorder have been described as unable
> to experience social warmth or to have deep feelings for others. They seem
> to be indifferent to the praise and criticism of others. People with schizoid
> personality disorder have difficulty understanding social interaction and
> they unintentionally disregard social conventions. They tend not to com-

municate their thoughts and emotions. They may struggle to understand morality and they may sometimes harm others. . . . People with schizoid personality disorder do have an empathic impairment.[9]

In our recent study on empathy and media use, we discovered that among all forms of media that we tested, playing video games was the only one that was directly related to lower real-world empathy.[10] In other words, people who play video games a lot show less empathy toward others than those who do not play video games or play very little. It is possible that the desensitization process of the first-person shooter game creates an emotional distance between the user and those portrayed on the screen.

DELUSIONAL THINKING, HALLUCINATIONS, AND ODD BEHAVIORS: "SHE TOLD ME TO!"

One of the more pronounced symptoms of people with schizotypal disorder is odd speech or thinking. People with this disorder often talk to imaginary people who they believe are commanding them to do something. Every time I go shopping I see people exhibiting this behavior. They walk down the aisles talking to themselves, gesturing, laughing, and speaking louder than they would if there was a real person next to them. And they act as if no one else is around them, seeming oblivious to the actions of others. Of course we know they are simply talking on their cell phones through their hands-free device, but they exhibit the same symptoms of someone with schizotypal personality disorder. You see people doing this all the time—in their cars, at the mall, at the post office, and on university campuses—and it makes them appear disordered.

Another symptom of schizotypal personality disorder is delusions, or beliefs that people are relating to you in ways that are not real (e.g., others are trying to contact you for an important task, someone is in love with you when they really aren't).[11] One piece of technology that makes us *look* as if we're a bit delusional is our navigation systems. I am lost without my GPS. Unless I know exactly where I'm going, every time I get into the car I plug in the address of my destination and the GPS tells me how to get there. I am so reliant on the system that even if I know the way I still listen for that soothing British voice to tell me where to turn next. We rely so much on computers and other systems to be accurate that we no longer trust our instincts and our experiences ... we have become over-reliant on the instrument, the voice if you will, that tells us what to do and how to do it. Someone speaks to us from our car's dashboard, telling us exactly where to turn, and we believe them. Even when the system is wrong, we still believe it will get us to our destination. And when it doesn't, we blame the "voice," saying, "she told me to!" For more evidence that we have total trust in our computer systems, look at these three accidents that all occurred less than two months apart in 2011:

- On April 25, a GPS system directed a woman to turn into oncoming highway traffic in Dunmore, Pennsylvania. The woman, who ignored a "DO NOT ENTER" sign, said she was following the GPS's instructions when she turned north in the southbound lanes, hitting another car.[12]
- On May 10, 44-year-old Amy Macchiarelli's white Corolla was struck by a train after her GPS told her to turn onto the train tracks in Delaware. Luckily she was able to get out of the car before the train hit it. She was cited for "inattentive driving."[13]
- On June 14, three women visiting Bellevue, Washington, ended up in the waters of Mercer Slough after their GPS directed them down a boat ramp. They said they were just doing what the GPS told them to do.[14]

SOMEONE'S TRYING TO REACH ME!

Sometimes we exhibit delusional thinking about our cell phones. *Vibranxiety,* or *phantom vibration syndrome,* is the result of being so tightly connected to our wireless mobile devices that we begin to check for messages or even answer the phone when it hasn't actually rung or vibrated. The phantom vibrations or sounds, according to Tom Irvine of Vibrationdata, may be triggered by similar sounds or may occur with no external stimuli.[15] Irvine interviewed Jeffrey Janata, director of behavioral medicine at University Hospitals in Cleveland, who explained:

You come armed with this template that leads you to be attentive to sensations that represent a cell phone vibrating. And it leads you to over-incorporate non-vibratory sensations and attribute them to the idea that you're receiving a phone call. When cell phone users regularly experience sensations, such as vibrating, their brains become wired to those sensations. Neurological connections that have been used or formed by the sensation of vibrating are easily activated. They're oversolidified, and similar sensations are incorporated into that template. They become a habit of the brain.

Janata says this syndrome is a result of neuroplasticity, in which the brain forms new connections in response to environmental changes. Of course this phenomenon is most likely caused by our constant need to feel connected. Brian, who works at a plastics manufacturing plant, is a father of three young boys. On the weekends Brian is active in his kids' sports, coaching Little League and cheering them on in soccer. Brian gets so many phone calls and text messages from his co-workers and family that he leaves his phone on all day and all night. Recently, Brian has felt his phone vibrating in his pocket and when he goes to check it, nobody has tried to reach him. Confused, Brian first thought the vibration was real and there was a problem with his phone. When he took it in for service and they found nothing wrong with the device, he concluded that it was all in his head. His obsessive checking has become so frequent that his family jokingly calls him the "answer man."

I AM ENGAGED TO BRAD PITT

Delusional people also fixate on people in the media. With images of famous faces flashing at us thousands of times per day, people who already have fantastical thinking may start to believe the people they see are real, that they have a personal connection with an actor or actress, or that a celebrity or sports figure is in love with them.[16] People with this type of delusion, called *erotomania,* feel such a deep connection that they believe they have a romantic and spiritual relationship with the object of their delusion. People with schizo-disordered delusions usually attempt to contact the celebrity by sending letters, e-mails, and gifts; calling them on the phone; or following them around. Some, especially males, may get arrested for their behavior, trying to "rescue" the objects of their delusions from some sort of "danger."[17]

Consider these cases of celebrity stalking where the person was clearly delusional:[18]

1. In 1981, John Hinckley, Jr. was so obsessed with actress Jodie Foster that he moved to New York to be near her. He called and sent messages that were not returned. To gain her attention, Hinckley attempted to assassinate then-president Ronald Reagan to re-enact the plot of Foster's film *Taxi Driver,* in which she portrays a child prostitute. At his trial Hinckley was found not guilty by reason of insanity. In 2005 he was granted a conditional release from Saint Elizabeth's Hospital in Washington, D.C.

2. Religious zealot Zack Sinclair was convinced that God ordered him to pray with actor Mel Gibson. The Idaho drifter once interrupted Gibson while he was at church, insisting that Gibson pray with him. Sinclair was sentenced to three years in prison for stalking Gibson. It is clear that Sinclair also suffered from hallucinations.

3. Schizophrenic felon Gary Benson stalked comedian Jerry Lewis, at one point going to Lewis's Las Vegas home and threatening his life with a gun. Benson was sent to prison for six years and when released he sent Lewis a letter saying *"Dear Jerry, Your Dead. Your friend, Gary Benson."* In 2001 Benson died in jail of heart disease while awaiting trial for again stalking Lewis.

4. Emily Leatherman was so delusional that she listed John Cusack's address as her own. In her numerous attempts to meet him, Leatherman visited the offices of the actor's colleagues and threw love letters over the fence of his home. He now has a restraining order against her.

5. Greg Broussard stalked actress Halle Berry, believing he was engaged to her. A California judge ordered the Navy Seal to keep at least 100 yards away from the actress and to stay away from her bodyguards.

Media images of celebrities can be very powerful to delusional people. There are even websites devoted to stalking celebrities that can bolster these behaviors. But delusional thinking can also appear in those who have real interactions with people. Take the example of Greg, a 42-year-old socially awkward account manager at a paper company. Greg was lonely and desperately wanted to be in a relationship. He was tired of the traditional dating scene—striking out every time he tried to even talk to a woman at a bar—and after some egging on by a co-worker, he decided to try online dating. He started with Match.com, where you can look at people's profiles initially without a paid membership. Greg's idea was to contact as many women as possible, hoping at least one would be interested and want to date him. Greg posted a photo of himself that was taken in college 20 years earlier, and with the help of his co-worker posted a quite flattering—and completely inaccurate—profile of himself.

As predicted, Greg had several online interactions with the women he found, which made him even more determined to find someone. When faced with synchronous conversation, though, Greg was unable to keep up his online persona and the women would eventually stop contacting him. Because of his desperation, Greg would continue to contact the women, believing that they really did like him. Without a clear explanation for why they stopped contacting him, Greg believed the women were just playing "hard to get."

One such woman was Natalie, a 28-year-old brunette hairstylist. Greg had initially contacted her with a cavalier "What's Up?" posting on her profile page. Natalie was intrigued by his flattering photo and positive profile[19] and sent back a message that read, "Not much. How are you? Want to chat?" Greg was so excited that Natalie contacted him that he began asking personal questions about her looks: "What size jeans do you wear? Do you like to wear belts? I like women who wear belts. I like it when women wear white T-shirts and jeans. Do you wear that stuff?" These were just some of the comments and questions he posted. At first Natalie continued to be intrigued and answered his questions. The next day Greg posted even more personal comments, as he began to believe that Natalie was interested in him and wanted to date him. Natalie was instantly turned off by his focus on appearance and the personal nature of his questions and stopped responding to him. Even though they had no other interaction, Greg had the delusional belief he was dating Natalie and started showing her photo to his co-workers. Had this been a live meeting, Greg would have understood through Natalie's behavior that she was not interested in dating him. Without the social cues of face-to-face interactions, Greg was unaware that Natalie had moved on and was no longer interested.

SOMEONE'S OUT TO GET ME

Paranoia and paranoid delusions are another acute symptom of the schizo-disorders. Paranoid individuals tend to believe that others are "out to get them," or they are suspicious of others' actions. They also may believe that outside forces are hurting them or want to do harm to them. There is also a psychiatric diagnostic category called delusional disorder, in which the person experiences "non-bizarre" delusions (e.g., involving situations that actually occur) whereby someone else's actions trigger a delusional belief.[20] For instance, we know from past research that people who use social networking sites are more jealous in their romantic relationships.[21] Others claim social networking causes jealousy in relationships because people witness and analyze the communication between their current partners and their partners' former lovers[22] or other people believed to be a threat. When people have these jealous ideas or, worse, act on them, it makes them seem as if they have schizotypal personality disorder.

Amy Muise and her colleagues at the University of Guelph in Ontario, Canada, looked at young people's jealousy levels related to social networking use and found a strong positive relationship. Muise concluded that:

> For all of the positive aspects of the increased social connection that Facebook enables, there may also be some costs for those individuals involved in romantic and sexual relationships. Our data showed a significant association between time spent on Facebook and jealousy-related feelings and behaviors experienced on Facebook.

Look at these stories from the United Kingdom in which Facebook users went beyond being jealous and exhibited a delusional disorder that led to violent acts:

- Brian Lewis, of Wales, strangled his girlfriend Hayley Jones to death in the home they shared with their four children. Lewis allegedly told police that Jones had become secretive about her Facebook use by turning off the computer when he was around and preventing him from accessing the site. Ten days before her death, Jones had changed her Facebook profile status from "in a relationship" to "single."[23]
- Paul Bristol, 25, was sent to prison for life for stabbing his ex-lover to death after seeing a Facebook photo of her with a new boyfriend. Camille Mathurasingh, 27, was killed by Bristol in April 2009 after the IT technician, who lived in Trinidad and Tobago, flew to London within two weeks of seeing the picture. The judge in the case apparently told him, "Clearly you were eaten up by jealousy."[24]

Of course these are extreme cases of paranoia and rage, but these behaviors are also exhibited by people who may not act out in a violent way. A Facebook user relayed a story to me about a friend of hers from high school who became enraged because she thought her friends on the site were getting together without her.

> The other day Terry posted this on my wall: "What, are you guys all having fun without me? I know you and Candy and Kim are doing something this weekend. Why aren't you inviting me? I'm fun!!" I have some photos of me and Candy and Kim from last year . . . she must think those are recent. It's so sad.

In our lab research I discovered some interesting findings in a study on media use and schizotypal personality. We found an inverse relationship among Baby Boomers (those born between 1946 and 1964) between the disorder and computer use, meaning the more Baby Boomers used computers and e-mail the less they exhibited schizotypal symptoms.[25] However, we found a disturbing trend: In most technology-use categories, higher use equaled more schizotypal behaviors, signs, and symptoms, regardless of age.[26] From being online and using social networking, to texting and instant messaging, to playing video games and listening to music, the more people engage in technology-related activities, the more they exhibit schizotypal behaviors.

Remember, the symptoms of schizotypal personality disorder are odd thought and speech patterns, magical thinking, and delusions. Is technology making us crazy? Well, if you are in your teens and 20s it certainly may be linked to symptoms of a serious disorder. In our study we discovered that delusional thinking was positively correlated with instant messaging, text messaging, playing video games, being online, and total daily media use. So, younger people, with their higher total media use, are showing much more delusional thinking than older people as a result of using technology. This is problematic and needs to be addressed, especially since media use is just going to increase as it becomes a 24/7 mainstay in our lives.

HELP FOR PEOPLE WITH SYMPTOMS OF SCHIZO-DISORDERS

In this chapter we have discussed how technology and media use can cause symptoms and signs of schizo-disorders. We know that these symptoms exist more in younger people and those who use more media. So what can we do to help?

People who do not get treatment for schizo-disorders tend to lead very lonely lives and have trouble doing regular activities such as attending school or work. It is common for people with these disorders to rely on their families for financial support, though many end up in psychiatric group homes.[27] Treatment can help manage symptoms and improve quality of life, but early detection is important. Schizophrenia and its associated disorders affect approximately 1.4 to 4.6 out of 1,000 people worldwide,[28] and if you consider the short episodes associated with technology use, that number greatly increases. Remember, people with technology-induced symptoms of schizo-disorders usually have not been diagnosed with the psychiatric disorder but only exhibit the symptoms associated with it. Within the past two decades researchers have become increasingly interested in preventing these disorders by uncovering risk factors for psychoses and developing useful assessment tools for early detection.

Since young people are the ones showing more schizo-disorder symptoms, it is important to understand how to detect them early in life. When a person is at risk for developing a mental disorder they are in what psychiatrists call a "prodromal phase" or an "at-risk mental state," which is a period of altered functioning when they may exhibit some symptoms before the onset of a schizo-disorder.[29] Because most scholars agree there are no specific symptoms that characterize the prodromal stage,[30] it is difficult to detect. However, the prodromal stage is important because if the illness is detected early, it may not become as severe. Some of the symptoms exhibited by individuals who are at risk for a mental disorder include anxiety, irritability, apathy, social and interpersonal isolation, brief psychotic episodes (delusions and hallucinations), poor concentration, suspiciousness or paranoid ideation, thought disorders, and eccentricity, all of which can be brought on by excessive technology and media use. Not all people who exhibit these symptoms will develop schizophrenia or other psychotic disorders, which makes diagnosis tricky. Instead of making predictions about the severity of the disorder, psychiatrists have determined that these people are instead simply at risk of developing the psychosis.

The major difference between full-onset psychosis and the prodromal stage is the intensity, duration, and frequency of the delusions.[31] For instance, if a person has a delusion for an hour or so, and then it goes away and the person realizes the belief was false, then this may be seen as a subthreshold form of a psychotic disorder. If the person has the belief for just one hour twice a month, even that may be considered below the threshold for diagnosis. In other words, the episodes did not happen long enough or frequently enough to be considered at risk. Once these delusions reach a certain level of intensity, frequency, or duration, a diagnosis of psychosis can be made. Most people who are high media and technology users and exhibit the symptoms of a schizo-disorder probably do not have the disorder; rather, the symptoms occur once in a while, or infrequently, which could indicate that they are in the prodromal stages.

There are a variety of scales used to detect at-risk mental states, all of which should be administered by a psychiatrist.[32] If you feel you are experiencing one or more symptoms of schizo-disorders, seek help immediately. Sometimes these symptoms occur rarely and are the result of other factors.

Remember, people who exhibit the symptoms of schizo-disorders as a result of technology or media interactions probably do not have full-blown schizophrenia but may be headed toward a schizoid personality disorder or schizotypal personality disorder. If you or someone you know is experiencing hallucinations or severe delusional thinking, it is best to seek professional help immediately. Here are some ways to help people who exhibit some of the milder symptoms of schizo-disorders brought on by technology:

1. If you feel someone close to you pulling away or lacking empathy, check to see whether they are playing a lot of video games, specifically first-person shooter games. These tend to diminish empathy in people. If it is a child or teenager, you may want to talk to them about their media use, their social networking activities, and whether they may feel emotionally withdrawn.

2. Withdrawal from social situations could be part of one's personality, but extreme withdrawal usually indicates depression, and you should encourage the sufferer to seek therapy and psychiatric help. Medication is usually prescribed for people with this condition.

3. Suspicious or paranoid thinking or superstitions could indicate too much time watching television, looking at Facebook pages, or seeking information on the Internet. Encourage the person to talk to people about their feelings, and help them to avoid being cynical, so that they can see people's true intentions rather than those created by their suspicious mind.

4. If they are not taking pleasure in activities, this could also indicate depression, or simple boredom in creative people. Talking to the person about what he or she likes to do and then incorporating

those activities into their lives is important. If you feel the person is depressed, suggest they see a therapist or psychiatrist.

Ultimately, the best way to assuage the symptoms of media-induced schizo-disorders is to "unplug" for a while. Get outside in nature, spend live, face-to-face time with others, and take a break from technology.

ELEVEN

We Like to Watch

There are plenty of people who don't have an issue at all. They can look at pornography and it's not an issue for them; it's not a problem. . . . But those for whom it is an issue for them, and who have the addictive tendencies that come with it, voyeurism can be very, very dangerous. Even if it's just going onto a Web site and looking at pictures, and they're not out there, actively trying to participate in it . . . that can set the stage for increasing their behaviors.

—John O'Neill, director of addiction services
center, Menninger Clinic, Houston[1]

Social voyeurism is the culture that the Internet has recently developed where people are looking into the social lives of others without necessarily participating. It's similar to cyberstalking, but perhaps more socially acceptable. It's basically watching people broadcast their lives to the world.

—Dan Levcille, Quora admin[2]

This past year, my friend Ben, who is a high school math teacher in southern California, had a very surprising event happen to him. During a routine exam at school, he was collecting and holding the cell phones and smartphones of students who were being administered a test. As he organized the batch of phones that he had collected, he casually glanced down at the screen of one female student's phone. He was shocked by what he saw: the lines of text messages sent to and from this 14-year-old student and another male student were intensely graphic and sexual in nature. Ben found himself suddenly and involuntarily thrust into a national debate over "sexting," the use of text messages and attached photos to engage in virtual sex with another individual.

What Ben didn't know at the time was that researchers are learning what motivates young people to text intimate sexual fantasies. The Pew Research Center's Internet & American Life Project study found that 4 percent of cell phone–owning teens ages 12 to 17 say they have sent nude or nearly nude images of themselves through text messages and that 15 percent have received one. When they looked at just the oldest kids, they found that 8 percent of 17-year-olds have sent one, and a whopping 30 percent have received one. The Pew study also found that teenagers who pay their own cell phone bills are more likely to sext than teens not paying their own bills. (Perhaps those teens who can earn their own money to pay their bills are given a lot of autonomy by their parents.)

According to this national study, there appear to be three main scenarios for sexting: sexting between two romantic partners; exchanges between two uninvolved people, one of whom wants to be involved; and—most relevant to our current discussion—exchanges shared with others outside the relationship.[3]

Ben approached me about a week after the event happened, and he asked me what I thought he should do. Should he share what he found with the parents of the two teens involved? Or should he let the whole issue go, assuming that the sexting represented the normal expression of feelings associated with puberty? I raised several key issues with him. I reminded him of the serious legal implications of sexting, namely, that sexting involving underage participants is legally equivalent to child pornography. In some cases, teens sending sexts and teens receiving sexts have been arrested and accused of illegal behavior.[4] I also described how, yes, sending nude or nearly nude photos of oneself to a romantic partner—at any age—can be part of sexual play that enhances the intimacy of a relationship. The legal fact that teens are "underage" is irrelevant to the psychological processes related to mating that are occurring in their brains. In many ways, our society encourages teens and pre-teens to engage in this form of behavior. Shannon Shafron-Perez, at the time a J.D. Candidate at the University of La Verne Law School, provided a powerful description of this:

Play "Name That Curve." Using your cell camera, take shots that show just a hint of different curves on your body— your hips, breasts, butt, etc.—and then send them to your guy. Type a little note, and ask him to guess what part of your anatomy is in each photo. This tip explaining how to use an ordinary camera phone as a sex toy is readily available at www.cosmopolitan.com, the website for one of America's top selling magazines. Women of all ages (including underage teenage girls) turn to Cosmopolitan for advice on fashion, sex, and dating.[5]

Finally, I asked Ben if he had considered the tremendous damage that might be done to these two individuals if the exchanges were shared with others. You probably have heard the stories of graphic photos or videos of unsuspecting individuals getting posted online and then being distributed and viewed by large numbers of people. Most people remember the private sex video of wealthy hotel heiress Paris Hilton and her then-boyfriend that became an Internet "sensation." That video, or parts of it, is posted on websites, some for pay, attesting to the strong public demand. Recently, U.S. Congressman Anthony Weiner had to retire his position after photos of his pelvic area surfaced on the Internet. Although it was revealed that he had voluntarily sent these photos through tweets to his followers, I don't think he ever expected most of the United States would want to see, as well. When the news story first broke—after one of his Twitter followers blew the whistle on him— the image was displayed on national television. It was also available online at numerous websites, and news stations re-broadcast the images for weeks.

Not everyone's secret graphic content goes "viral" online, but it is quite possible that your material will still be uncovered by someone snooping around. William A. Herbert, a lawyer for the New York State Public Employment Relations Board, outlined a growing conflict between electronic exhibitionism (e.g., employees posting on blogs and social networks) and electronic voyeurism (e.g., the negative consequences of employers searching for the posted personal information). Interestingly, he infers that much of what happens when people post private material online falls under the "toilet assumption," in which a culture ignores a social problem by placing it out of view.[6] Herbert applies the assumption to electronic exhibitionism in which people think, for example, that by deleting something online it is permanently deleted or, in his words, "in the toilet." He describes many ways to resolve the conflict: To prevent e-mail voyeurism at work he suggests employers allow employees to encrypt personal communications and create self-destructing messages.[7]

A few days after I consulted with Ben about the situation, he called and told me that he had come to a decision. In the end, my friend Ben decided to let the situation go despite his initial inclination to contact the parents of the students and share what happened. Although I respect Ben's decision, as it was based on a careful reflection, I worry that those racy text messages and/or the photos that were attached to them will be shared with a third party who will then share them with another person, and so on.

IT'S NOT JUST "CLINICAL" VOYEURISM

Traditionally, voyeurism is described with reference to sexual content and sexual arousal in the psychology literature. However, it is clear that there are many other ways that voyeurism can manifest itself online and in the media. People like to see not only photos of unsuspecting individuals that show nudity or sex-related content, but also photos and videos of individuals engaged in their private lives: having arguments, emotional breakdowns, and moments of joy. Modern computer-based technology allows for a drastic increase in the opportunities for these lesser types of voyeurism. So, although most individuals are not voyeurs in the clinical sense as defined in the American Psychiatric Association's Diagnostic and Statistical Manual of Mental Disorders, many of us are engaging in other types of voyeuristic behaviors.

For example, I met a young woman, Christine, who told me about her obsession with reality TV stars and soap opera actors. Although Christine has two young sons, two dogs, a husband, and a large home that requires regular attention, she opts instead to spend most of her day watching her favorite shows on television, re-watching her favorite episodes online, and engaging in Internet-based discussions at reality TV and soap opera fan websites. Her obsession is so consuming that she sometimes forgets about important family events. Earlier this year, she booked a trip for her and her friend to a soap opera fan weekend event in Las Vegas. Her husband normally is supportive of her activities, but when he found out about this particular trip, he got very upset. Christine had planned her trip for the weekend of Father's Day and had not even realized it. When voyeuristic behaviors and the activities surrounding them interfere with your daily life—working, spending time with family, and running the household—then they qualify as an iDisorder.

Graphic materials are available online to virtually anyone. In a recent study, Ronald M. Holmes at the University of Louisville and his colleagues conducted a detailed content analysis of available digital photographs posted and traded online in voyeur-related activities. The authors generated ten categories of photographs: (1) true voyeurs (pictures taken of someone from afar), (2) accidental voyeurs (accidental exposure or photos taken for other reasons that coincidentally have voyeuristic content), (3) panties/buttocks/genitals, (4) sex acts (taken mostly with hidden cameras), (5) group sex shots (again, using hidden cameras), (6) bathroom scenarios, (7) dressing, (8) sunbathing, (9) cheerleaders, and (10) incest.[8] These types of images are available to virtually anyone and provide material for potentially disruptive, voyeuristic behavior.

Voyeuristic behavior is an example of a psychological disorder known as "paraphilia"—arousal by what is considered an abnormal or unusual stimulus, in this case, sexual arousal in response to observing someone who is not aware they are being observed. In the *DSM,* the definition of voyeurism is that, over a period of six months, there is a history of recurrent, intensive, sexually arousing fantasies, sexual urges, or behaviors involving the act of observing an unsuspecting person who is naked, in the process of disrobing, or engaged in sexual activity. Further, the individual acts on the desires and urges, or the desires and urges cause marked distress or interpersonal difficulty.[9]

I had a difficult time finding information about the rates of this kind of voyeurism in America, but I did come across a study done in a Scandinavian country that could provide an estimate of the rates in the United States. Niklas Långström at the Karolinska Institutet in Stockholm and Michael Seto at the Centre for Addiction and Mental Health in Ontario, Canada, analyzed data from a large-scale survey of sexual attitudes and behaviors in Sweden. They found that the self-reported rates of engaging in a voyeuristic behavior were 11.5 percent for men and 3.9 percent for women. Relatively high socioeconomic status males were the most likely to be voyeurs, and, further, those males and females having more psychological problems, lower life satisfaction, and more signs of a current mental disorder were also more likely to act voyeuristically.[10] Another hint at the prevalence of voyeurism in the population comes indirectly from a study by Patrick Marsh at the University of South Florida and his colleagues. These researchers looked at the rates of paraphilia (including voyeurism) in a voluntarily admitted group of men in a psychiatric facility. They found that 8 percent of the men could be classified as exhibiting a form of voyeurism.[11]

Recent research suggests that voyeurism might start at a young age, particularly in this era of omnipresent online sexual images. Michele Ybarra and Kimberly Mitchell at the University of New Hampshire completed a study of youth in which they focused on intentional pornography-seeking behavior both online and offline. The study, based on nationally sampled data from the Youth Internet Safety Survey of 10- to 17-year-olds, found that pornography seekers are more likely to be male than female and that older youth are twice as likely as younger youth to seek pornography. Additionally, online pornography seekers were 3.5 times more likely compared with offline seekers to also report features of major depression and 2.4 times more likely to report a poor emotional bond with their caregiver. The authors said that they believe it is unlikely that exposure to pornography is a direct cause of these problems.

Finally, the researchers asked whether parental controls on access to pornography would affect kids' intentional pornography-seeking behavior. The researchers looked at three types of parental controls: having home rules against viewing pornography, installing blocking or filtering software on the computer, and checking the browser history for visits to pornographic websites. Surprisingly, there was no difference between pornography-seeking and non-seeking youth for any of the parental safeguards studied.[12] Although only a small percentage of the population might suffer from the clinical aspect of voyeurism—viewing "hidden" photos, watching voyeuristic pornography, or having associated psychological problems—many more of us might suffer from lesser forms of voyeurism that are supported and enabled by modern technology.

THE LESSER SIDE OF VOYEURISM

Voyeurism can serve as a motivator for technology use. In a study of college students, Mun-Young Chung at Kansas State University and Hyang Sook Kim at Pennsylvania State University found there were six main motivations for podcast use, one of which was a social interaction factor that included voyeuristic intentions related to peeking in on other people's lives (the other five motivations were entertainment, education, escape, habit, and convenience). In fact, social interaction was statistically the most important of all six of the motivations. In looking at the comments from the college students, Chung and Kim also learned that students use podcasts as fashion statements, much like they do cell phones. It's as if, for some students, viewing podcasts fulfills the same need to watch others without interaction that is also fulfilled by browsing social network sites and watching reality television.[13]

Despite being highly touted as a key interactive feature of the Web 2.0, even blogging provides opportunities for voyeurism. A two-part study by Youngbo Jung and colleagues at the University of Southern California looked at users of a Korean blogging site. In the first part of the study, the researchers found that one of the two main motivations for reading blogs was voyeurism, with users higher in voyeuristic intentions being more likely to read other people's blogs. The other main motivation for reading (and posting) blogs was impression management, which is people's desire to present a coherent and meaningful representation of themselves online that might or might not match their personality offline. In the second part of the study, the researchers discovered that the desire to compare oneself to others (social comparison) can drive voyeurism (and impression management). In other words, people who want to compare themselves to others—perhaps a form of "keeping up with the Joneses"—do so by anonymously viewing other individuals' blogs and by planning how they will modify their online presence to maximize their online reputations. The results also showed that feeling anonymous online (e.g., perceived anonymity) contributes to voy-euristic surveillance of blogs.[14]

So, the desire to spy or eavesdrop on others in an anonymous way is not just related to sexual content but can occur in settings in which participants seek social, emotional, or political information about others (e.g., through monitoring social networking profiles or blogs). You can try to see for yourself if you might suffer from this lesser, non-clinical, form of voyeurism. Lemi Baruh at Kadir Has University in Istanbul developed a scale that can be used to assess your personal inclination toward voy-eurism, shown in Figure 11.1.[15] The scale contains several hypothetical scenarios in which you are given the opportunity to be a voyeur or not be a voyeur. Read each scenario and indicate your probable response on the seven-point scale, which ranges from immediately stopping the voyeuris-tic activities to trying to increase those activities. Of course, no scale like this will accurately assess your voyeuristic personality tendencies unless you answer honestly to each item, carefully weighing your past reactions to similar situations. Responding in a way that makes you look good to others—what psychologists call social desirability—will defeat the useful-ness of the measure.

The voyeurism scale in Figure 11.1 might best be used to identify some-one with a voyeuristic personality that might or might not fall into the clini-cal definition of having a disorder. Baruh published data representing the typical responses of participants in his study (Figure 11.2). This allows us to compare our own responses to a reference sample. There is no cutoff for being considered "voyeuristic," but you might consider yourself to have a voyeuristic tendency if you responded above the median level on a major-ity of the items. In other words, total up your score and compare it to 19 points. If your score is higher than 19 points, then you might be engaging in and have an inclination to engage in problematic voyeuristic behaviors. Importantly, Baruh's voyeurism scale is not the way that a professional cli-nician would diagnose voyeurism. That would be done using the definition of voyeurism from the *DSM* described above, along with a detailed series of interactions with a person to learn as much as possible about their psy-chological background.

FIGURE 11.1. PERSONAL INCLINATION TOWARD VOYEURISM SCALE

How Would You React to These Situations?	Immediately Stop Looking/Listening/ Reading (1)	(2)	(3)	(4)	(5)	(6)	Try to See/ Hear/Read All You Can (7)
			Your Reaction				
If you realized that you could see inside the bedroom of your neighbors because they forgot to close their curtains.	1	2	3	4	5	6	7
If you were to overhear your next door neighbors discussing their sexual lives.	1	2	3	4	5	6	7
If you were to read a message that was sent to somebody else.	1	2	3	4	5	6	7
If you were part of a conversation where your friends were gossiping about the sexual life of a person you're familiar with.	1	2	3	4	5	6	7
You realized that instead of giving you your own photograph prints, the photo lab gave you a set of photographs showing a couple skinny-dipping in a pool.	1	2	3	4	5	6	7
While shopping in a clothing store, you see a gap through which you can see inside a dressing room.	1	2	3	4	5	6	7
If you were to overhear a husband and wife discussing problems that they are having with their kids and/or other family members.	1	2	3	4	5	6	7
If you were to witness someone having an emotional breakdown and displaying extreme anger or sadness.	1	2	3	4	5	6	7

FIGURE 11.2. MEDIAN RESPONSES TO "PERSONAL INCLINATION TOWARD VOYEURISM SCALE" REACTION ITEMS

How Would You React to These Situations?	Typical (Median) Response
If you realized that you could see inside the bedroom of your neighbors because they forgot to close their curtains.	2
If you were to overhear your next door neighbors discussing their sexual lives.	2
If you were to read a message that was sent to somebody else.	3
If you were part of a conversation where your friends were gossiping about the sexual life of a person you're familiar with.	3
You realized that instead of giving you your own photograph prints, the photo lab gave you a set of photographs showing a couple skinny-dipping in a pool.	3
While shopping in a clothing store, you see a gap through which you can see inside a dressing room.	1
If you were to overhear a husband and wife discussing problems that they are having with their kids and/or other family members.	2
If you were to witness someone having an emotional breakdown and displaying extreme anger or sadness.	3

THE RISE OF REALITY TELEVISION

Voyeuristic content is not just the purview of the Internet. The nature of television is changing in a way that provides more and more voyeuristic content through the spate of reality television programming. Although not all studies agree on the exact role of voyeurism in the appeal of reality TV, there is a consistent link between reality TV viewing and a voyeuristic profile. Zhanna Bagdasarov at Rutgers University and her colleagues carried out a television study with two parts, one a content analysis of TV shows from various genres (reality TV, situation comedies, and night-time soaps), another a survey of students' TV viewing habits. The results showed that persons who score higher on a general voyeurism scale view more voyeuristic television content.[16] In another study of reality television, Zizi Papacharissi and Andrew Mendelson at Temple University found that passing time and deriving entertainment were the two most powerful reasons for reality TV viewing; however, voyeurism was a significant, albeit smaller, factor. More specifically, using a complex statistical analysis of their survey data, the authors identified two types of reality TV viewers motivated by different factors. The first type of viewer was entertained by reality TV in their free time and had the perception that reality TV was indeed real. In contrast, a second type of viewer was found to be externally controlled (they perceived that factors outside themselves steered their lives), was not very mobile, and did not have much social interaction. It was this type of viewer for whom voyeurism (and companionship) was a motivation for watching reality television. The authors of the study described this second type of viewer this way: "For viewers who used the medium for its voyeuristic appeal and companion value, reality TV substituted for other activities that could not be experienced due to lower mobility and lower interpersonal interaction levels."[17] I imagine that shy or depressed individuals would fall into this second category, as they would be less likely to seek out physical interactions with other individuals in their daily activities.

Another study by Lemi Baruh discovered that those people who viewed more reality TV also had higher voyeurism scores, and this relationship held even after taking into account potentially confounding factors such as desire for social comparison, self-monitoring, and total television viewing hours. Expanding on their work, the researchers analyzed a set of reality TV shows, searching for elements that might contribute to their voyeuristic appeal. For example, Dr. Baruh analyzed segments of the TV show *The Amazing Race,* in which teams of "regular" people race around the world for clues to a large cash prize. Viewers of this show watch teammates argue about their plans for success and see team members have emotional breakdowns. An analysis of the correlations between voyeurism and reality TV watching revealed that scenes that allowed for a "fly on the wall" perspective, as with *The Amazing Race*; scenes in private or semi-private settings; scenes containing gossip; and scenes containing nudity all contributed to the voyeuristic appeal of the TV shows.[18]

CHECKLIST FOR KNOWING IF YOU HAVE A PROBLEM

I have synthesized the literature on voyeurism in electronic formats and have compiled below a list of possible tip-offs that you might have a problem that is interfering with your everyday functioning. Remember that none of these behaviors is a real problem unless it is disturbing your social interactions, your family functioning, your work life, your productivity, or your emotional and mental states. In those situations, you should consider seeking professional advice about how to control your behaviors and thoughts if you feel that you cannot make changes on your own.

1. I spend a lot of time viewing people's posts and profiles online.
2. I highly enjoy watching reality television.
3. The time that I spend viewing other people's information online or watching reality television gets in the way of doing other things, like housework or socializing with family and friends.
4. I scored very high on my reactions to viewing other people's personal and private information in Figure 11.1 (above 19 points).
5. I have sent and/or received "sexts."
6. I have strong urges to go online and view pictures of unsuspecting persons who are naked, in the process of disrobing, or engaged in sexual activity.
7. I like to view online content containing gossip, nudity, and/or private or semi-private settings of individuals.

Of course, not all of these checklist items are equal. Some items—particularly items 3, 4, 5, and 6—are more worrisome than others and you should pay more attention to those items than the others. If you experience just one of these items, then you should consider how your everyday life and activities might be affected by your voyeuristic behaviors.

Earlier, I mentioned statistics and studies regarding how teens access pornography on the Internet. There is no doubt that teens are hooked on reality television shows and on using social networking sites, both of which are prime grounds for viewing voyeuristic content. Many parents find it tempting to employ home safeguards to prevent their kids from seeing pornographic content, but don't forget that Ybarra and Mitchell's study of kids going online found that these home solutions did not affect pornography-seeking behavior.[19] It is almost certain that savvy pre-teens and teenagers—who make up almost all kids in that age range—find ways around home rules and safeguards. Having open communication with kids, as well as a hands-on but affectionate "authoritative" parenting style, could be a key to controlling problematic Internet exposure to voyeuristic material.[20]

WHAT TO DO TO CHANGE

The best available data show that voyeuristic content on TV is centered on reality television shows, evening soap operas, and situation comedies. Of course, these shows also are available online as instant downloads on popular media hosting websites such as Netflix and directly from the television networks' websites. It might seem surprising that television sitcoms have voyeuristic content, but it is quite true that part of the appeal of these types of shows is the viewer's anonymous access to the private lives of the show's characters. Susan Sontag described this concept well in her description of the appeal of the classic 1950s American sitcom *I Love Lucy*:

> The creators of "I Love Lucy" seemed also to understand that the serialized television show had a unique effect on its viewers, that it fostered an illusion of intimacy unknown in previous entertainments. . . . The sitcom invited the audience to observe Desi's exasperated mutterings or Lucy's whines with an amused sense of superiority. This sanctioned voyeurism couldn't help but flatter the viewer it entertained.[21]

Many persons who find themselves in this position might also find it difficult to voluntarily reduce their exposure to these types of shows. A potentially powerful deterrent to watching such shows is to read about the downside of the production of voyeuristic content. More specifically, it might pay off to become sensitized to the negative ramifications of a voyeuristic production upon its participants. It's easy enough to find out about the real "private" lives of reality TV stars, for example, by reading entertainment magazines or newspaper accounts of their lives off of the shows. In many cases, the actors' brushes with the entertainment industry have had negative consequences in their lives.

Beth Montemurro at Pennsylvania State University at Abington studied viewers' reactions to reality television through an analysis of postings on websites that focused on one of the popular summer television shows, *Big Brother.* By a careful consideration of the themes that ran through the posts, she suggested that part of the pleasure of watching reality television involved the lack of power of the actors, in that the actors have consented to having their every move recorded and potentially shown to the audience. In other words, the actors have no control over the use of their imagery. In contrast, the producers of the TV show have complete control over the actors. This scenario with actors as the victims of the producers benefits the viewers, who also get to experience this sense of control over the powerless actors.[22] You might find this thought that you are taking pleasure in other people's loss of control repulsive enough to stop you from watching reality television so much.

Awareness of the lives of the people behind the shows or voyeuristic content could also provide sobering information to help those who feel that they have a problem with viewing online or offline pornography. Donna M. Hughes from the University of Rhode Island made a very compelling counterargument to viewing online pornography with her essay entitled "Prostitution Online." In that essay, Professor Hughes makes three important points. First, Internet technology allows increased exploitation of women and children (including voyeurism). Second, Internet technology also allows increased privacy by men who exploit women. Third, exploitation damages the dignity and images of women and, of course, is illegal with children.[23] Awareness of those three points may help someone break from a voyeuristic iDisorder.

What should you do instead of watching reality TV, YouTube videos, or online pornography? One possibility is to take a nature break. As defined in earlier chapters, nature breaks don't have to mean literally going out into a highly natural environment. Rather, taking a nature break can simply involve turning off your devices and doing something away from the computer and television—reading a book or newspaper might work. No doubt, however, you can have your nature breaks do double-duty for you by using the break to engage in some physical exercise. Then, your break will keep your mind away from the troubling media content and contribute to your physical fitness at the same time. You might also consider distracting yourself with non-voyeuristic content, such as documentaries, other types of fiction (on television or online), and other media formats (such as radio). Doing so ought to reduce your exposure to potentially problematic content.

Several research studies on voyeuristic behavior found connections between what is called "social comparison" and voyeurism. It may be that observing how other people behave in their natural (and hence spied upon) environments provides a reference point for us to see how we match up to others. Doing less social comparison by worrying less about how you compare to other people might reduce your need for viewing voyeuristic media content. Avoiding these voyeuristic situations might also have the positive side effect of making you more comfortable with who you are.

I like to take a different approach to altering my own behavior. I operate through rewards; psychologists refer to these as "positive reinforcements." I can find many objects and activities that I find rewarding enough to serve as a replacement for the behaviors that I want to eliminate. For me, food is a powerful reward. When I've been really good at avoiding my problem behaviors, I will indulge a little at my workplace and visit the campus coffeehouse to enjoy a chocolate chocolate-chip muffin. My friend Patrick likes to reward himself with some blocked-out free time to read books for pleasure. Of course, rewarding yourself is a general strategy for changing your behavior, and other general strategies mentioned throughout this book might serve as well.

TWELVE
It's All in Your Mind

What I've been doing over the last few months is attempting to convince people that we're facing an issue that's as important and unprecedented as climate change. And I call it "mind change" because I think there are certain parallels. With mind change the issue is how the new technologies, the new environment of two dimensions, might be impacting on the human mind, and changing the way especially young generations may be thinking or feeling.

—Andrew Maynard, director, Risk Science Center[1]

The quote above is not from a Luddite who is railing against the evils of technology, but rather from Baroness Susan Greenfield, a respected professor of synaptic pharmacology at Oxford University and a member of the UK House of Lords. Professor Greenfield studies the science of the mind and has argued passionately that our growing use of social media—particularly Facebook, Twitter, YouTube, and video gaming—is changing our brains. In an interview with the *Daily Telegraph* she argued that although some "very good things" were emerging from our experiences with information technology—including a higher IQ, a better memory, and faster processing of information—she insisted that, "Rather than sleepwalking into this we should be the masters and not the slaves of technology and harnessing it in ways that we could do exciting and fulfilling things with."[2]

I agree with Baroness Greenfield. As I have shown in this book, many of us are on the verge of an iDisorder as our daily interactions with media technologies may be imbuing us with signs and symptoms of one of many psychological disorders, including narcissism, obsessive-compulsive disorder, addiction, depression, attention-deficit disorder, social phobia, antisocial personality disorder, hypochondriasis, body dysmorphic disorder, schizo-disorders, and voyeurism. As Baroness Greenfield insists, avoiding an iDisorder is an issue of "mind change." Luckily for us our brains are constantly changing. Neuroscientists call this "neuroplasticity," which is basically a constant process of strengthening and weakening neuronal (nerve cell) connections in the brain as a function of our experiences.[3] It is definitely a plus that our brains continue to change in response to both external and internal stimuli. This helps us create new memories, revisit old memories, and continually integrate our experiences in the real world with our representation of those events in our inner world. Given that our brains are inundated by stimuli all day long and that the digital content currently available in our world is the equivalent to everyone in the world tweeting or blogging constantly for a century,[4] neuroplasticity is a brain saver.

We have even started to see research showing how our brains have adapted to having so much available information through what researcher Betsy Sparrow of Columbia University calls the "Google Effect." In a series of four laboratory studies, Professor Sparrow and her colleagues discovered that our constant habit of checking Google for any tidbit of information that strikes our fancy "has trained us to use the Internet as a specialized external memory" (e.g., "What movie did that actress that we just saw star in a few years ago with that guy with the beard?" is a question that can be answered with just a few mouse clicks or smartphone touches). In her studies, Sparrow found that if someone knows they will have future access to information on the Internet or on their computer, they won't remember information as well as if they are told that it will not be available. But they do recall exactly where to find it quite well, even down to the folder on the computer where the information is stored.[5]

In this chapter I will outline a plan that will help you avoid getting an iDisorder or, if you are already showing symptoms of this new millennium malady, rid yourself of the problem. The plan is not complicated but will take some thinking and planning to execute. It combines what scientists have learned from fields such as neuroscience, biology, psychology, and education. The plan integrates the latest research about the brain as well as the most recent psychological science.

RESETTING YOUR BRAIN

People spend their days perched in front of many different screens, and it is important to recognize how that impacts the way their brains work. I have found it best to think about the brain by using an analogy created by years of viewing functional magnetic resonance imaging (fMRI) brain scans. If you have never seen such a scan, it includes a colorful representation of the areas of the brain that are active at any given moment. For example, one such fMRI[6] compared the brain scans of women with bulimia nervosa and healthy women while they completed a task that required self-regulation. The task was simple: identify the direction that an arrow on a computer screen is pointing. The trick was that sometimes the arrow would point right and be shown on the right side of the screen so that the information matched. Other times the arrow might be pointing right but placed on the left side of the screen so that the information did not match or was considered conflicting. On the fMRI, red areas showed increases in activity while answering the questions correctly when provided with conflicting information, and blue areas showed brain activity increases when answering correctly given matching information. The scan for the bulimic women showed much less red but more blue, indicating that brain activity scans are a powerful tool that can be used to understand how information is represented in the brain and how this correlates with mental disorders.

Scanning machines that use the fMRI technique measure oxygen flow in the brain's blood vessels. The oxygen flow indicates which neural areas in the brain are activated and processing information. Following this argument my analogy involves understanding that there is only a limited amount of blood available in your brain, which correlates with a limited amount of neuronal processing at any given time. This is important when considering how technology use impacts our brains.

Although fMRI research is fairly new—and expensive, though much less so than it was when these machines were originally introduced—we are now seeing some fascinating research that tells us how the brain reacts to technology. For example, the brain scan research by Dr. Gary Small, a professor at the Semel Institute for Neuroscience and Human Behavior at

UCLA, revealed that older adults who had never used the Internet showed less brain activation during Internet searches than those older adults who had already mastered the Internet. He discovered that, as seen in Figure 12.1 below, when they surfed the Internet these older adults showed more brain activity than when they simply read a book. Other scientists have found similar manifestations of differential brain activity by Internet addicts,[7] video game players,[8] movie viewers,[9] and television viewers.[10]

We know that each technology a person uses engages their brain. When a person multitasks with several technologies the brain is even more engaged, perhaps with a near maximal amount of neuronal activity. So, what happens when that activity ceases? Studies are now starting to demonstrate that technological activities such as video game playing have residual neurological effects on the brain for some period of time after the game is completed.[12] Now imagine someone who plays video games, surfs the Internet, sends and receives text messages, sends e-mail, and listens to music—all at the same time. This person's brain must be literally buzzing with neurological activity, and stopping the use of technology most likely won't eliminate the overload.

According to research on "Attention Restoration Theory (ART),"[13] when someone interacts with a natural environment their attention is captured in what is referred to as a "bottom-up" process, meaning that it is

FIGURE 12.1. BRAIN SCAN OF AN OLDER ADULT READING A BOOK
(LEFT) COMPARED WITH SURFING THE INTERNET (RIGHT)[11]

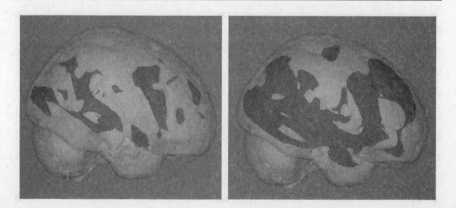

driven by calming external stimuli seen in nature, allowing the parts of the brain that are overworked to recover. In contrast, according to this theory, urban environments contain stimuli that capture our attention dramatically with sights, odors, and sounds, which requires attention to overcome the aversive stimuli and leads to less calmness and more residual brain activity at the attention level.

What does this mean for resetting your brain? Research has shown that spending more time with nature—taking a nature break for just a few minutes—can decrease stress and increase our brain's ability to process information. Interestingly, this can be taking a short walk in nature, viewing nature photos, or even using an avatar to maneuver through a virtual nature setting.[14] Although the original research compared memory for people who either walked through a nature setting or downtown Ann Arbor, Michigan, recent work by a team at the University of Michigan found the same restorative effects from just ten minutes of viewing pictures of nature.[15]

Experiencing nature requires focusing on the natural environment with all of your senses so that brain activation can die down. On a recent vacation I drove out to see a blowhole on the island of Kauai that not only spouted water but also made a sound like a horn if it got up enough steam and water and, as we discovered, sometimes produced single and double rainbows. While I was observing nature at it's most amazing, a family arrived with a mother, father, and three children all under the age of six. I watched the mom snapping pictures with her digital camera while the dad used his handheld video camera to capture the moment. At the same time the three kids were shouting with glee every time the water blew, and the littlest one giggled every time the rainbows appeared. "Look mommy," she squealed, "A rainbow! A pretty rainbow!" Her mom's response was, "Shhh . . . I am trying to get a picture of it." The little girl tried to talk to her dad and he didn't even respond as the video camera recorded the moment. I am assuming that the parents were recording the event to enjoy later, but can someone really enjoy nature when viewed through a tiny aperture? Can we get full enjoyment later when we only get to reminisce about our photo opportunity? If we have to keep our camera steady and carefully record the event are we really enjoying it? I would say that the kids who actually watched the entire performance by the ocean truly enjoyed it while the parents may or may not even look at their photos later and likely will not be able to re-create the full enjoyment because they never really saw the complete picture nor did they process it with areas of their brain that respond solely to these nature scenes. If you are going to use nature as a restorative cure for technologically induced brain overload, it is best to remove all technology from the scene.

What other activities restore your brain to its pre-technology settings? One study found that music and art rated as "beautiful" showed brain activation in areas associated with pleasure. However, art and music rated as "ugly" showed activation in a totally different area that is most likely not restorative at all.[16] It turns out that music activates the same reward circuits in the brain that react to food and sex, and brain scans have shown that just listening to music for a short time can help reset the brain.[17] Other research has found that brief exercise—a ten-minute walk at a brisk pace in one study—can keep the brain fit[18] and even hot baths can do the same.[19] In addition, several studies have shown that your brain functions better if you expose it to youthful environments,[20] and laughing aloud also has similar restorative benefits.[21] Here are some other activities that have been linked to changes in the brain:[22]

- Having a rich social life.
- Learning multiple languages.
- Learning to play a musical instrument.
- Practicing yoga.
- Consuming omega–3 fatty acids.
- Doing puzzles, including Sudoku and crosswords.

One final note on brain functioning concerns children, teens, and young adults. When babies are born, most of their neurons lack an outer covering called myelin that is required for successful transmission of nerve impulses between nerve cells and also between the body and the brain. Myelin ensures rapid transmission of information at a rate 50 times faster than through unmyelinated fibers.[23] This process of gaining myelin is not completed until a young person reaches his or her mid- to late twenties, and before then the myelin is particularly lacking in the prefrontal cortex, which is the seat of reasoning and decision making as well as the area that controls multitasking. This means that the brain is even more distractible in children, teens, and young adults, which means they need more frequent brain resetting than adults.

REMOVING DISTRACTIONS FROM YOUR ENVIRONMENT

Several researchers, including David Levy, a professor at the University of Washington, have suggested that we are manifesting "popcorn brains"—a brain so used to the constant stimulation from multitasking with electronic devices that it can't deal with life in the real world, which is much less stimulating. Other researchers concur with Levy that excessive multitasking is harmful to your brain, showing that those who multitask more are less able to identify human emotions and those who are online more than ten hours a day have less brain "gray matter" than those who are online less than two hours a day.[24] What this suggests is that it is important to consider how much you are multitasking and structure your environment to limit those distracters.

Research is fairly clear that performing one task at a time is much better than performing multiple tasks simultaneously (which is really just rapid task switching). With such engaging technologies in our workspace we are all subject to these distractions. As I pointed out in Chapter 6, even those people, such as computer programmers, who should focus on their work are not able to maintain their focus for more than a few minutes. And the major distracter is TECHNOLOGY. In our own study we found that students who glanced at their Facebook page just once during a 15-minute study period performed worse than those who never looked at that page, and students who had more windows open on their computer lost more focus on their studying.

Suggestions for clearing your workspace of distractions vary from creating your own "digital diet"[25] to "information fasting" or taking technology sabbaticals varying from a few hours to days or even weeks.[26] All of this is fine, but impossible for most people. Face it: We are connected and we have created a cyber world that requires us to be connected. With that in mind, you can do things to restructure your environment to make it less prone to interruptions and more conducive to focus.

Each of us operates differently and is impacted differently by distractions. For instance, I cannot have the television on when I am reading a book, but I can have the television on in the background while I write, as long as it is adjusted to a fairly low volume level. In a study from my research lab we found that while younger generations claimed to be able to multitask with more technologies—and did so on a routine basis—there were certain technologies that everyone found difficult to do in tandem with others, including reading a book and playing video games. While younger generations self-interrupt often, older ones do so less often and with a more restricted range of technologies.[27] The solution involves what psychologists call "metacognition" or knowing how your brain works.

Metacognition is defined as being aware of your own mental processes and understanding your brain and how you handle incoming information. This means that someone who has strong metacognition is a person who knows which tasks are easy or difficult and which learning strategies work best under which settings. One study, for example, found that those computer science students who were aware of their metacognitive processes chose to turn off a distracting instant messaging screen in order to complete their work. They did better than those students who were less aware of their metacognitive abilities and left the interrupting IM screen visible.[28] In a study from my research lab we flooded students with text messages during a videotaped lecture and found that those who chose to ignore the text messages until a time when the lecture material seemed less important showed enhanced memory for the material.[29]

So it is up to you to decide which technologies induce task switching and also when that process is harmful to learning. My daughter, for example, finds that having the television on when she is checking her social networks for messages is just fine and not distracting, but having her smartphone by her side is extremely distracting when she is studying for an exam. If she is just doing what she calls "mindless" school work she has no trouble switching back and forth to incoming text messages. If you find yourself easily distracted the first step is to determine what distracts you under what conditions. Then eliminate those distractions from your work environment.

This sounds reasonable, but what about your brain? Sure, you can turn off your smartphone, music, television, e-mail, and other distractions, but is "out of sight" the same as "out of mind?" As you might suspect, they are not. In fact, many technological actions are firmly ensconced in the brain and are stealing valuable resources needed for actual attention. In fact, these "internal" interruptions are just as brain activating as external interruptions, such as responding to a phone call or text message.[30]

GIVE YOURSELF TECHNOLOGY BREAKS

If you constantly use your smartphone and computer you are flirting with an iDisorder and, I think, are guaranteed to have problems removing all distractions from your work environment for any period of time. If you are like most children, teens, and young adults who have grown up in a technologically immersive world, you are unlikely to be able to even ponder a life without your phone by your side for even a moment. Consider, for example, an interesting study done with children and pre-teens who ran what the authors called the "Marshmallow Test." In this study, 6- to 13-year-old students were asked to delay gratification during a paper-folding task and not eat marshmallows that were prominently displayed in front of them. The children folded fewer papers if they were asked to delay gratification, compared with a control group that had no such limitations and ate marshmallows before folding papers. Similar results have been shown with adults who were on a diet and asked to ignore a snack close by.[31] Another study showed the same results for adults who were either allowed to watch a funny video before doing a counting task or asked to simply wait to watch the video (and listen to the laughter of those watching the video) until after completing their very simple task. Not surprisingly, the tempted group made more counting mistakes as their brains were undoubtedly distracted by the thought that they were missing out.[32]

If you fit into this category of someone for whom "out of sight" is not "out of mind," then you might consider using *technology breaks* to keep you from having a brain that is constantly activated and thinking about the Internet, social networking, and other highly engaging daily activities. A tech break is similar to that late afternoon coffee break when you are feeling low on energy and need a dose of caffeine to feel more motivated or energized. In this case, however, you set a time period when you remove all technology and focus on your work. Set a timer to alert you when that period has elapsed—then you grab your phone or your laptop, check in with your cyber world, and put it all away and go back to your work.

I have invited teachers to try this in the classroom and parents to use this at the dinner table; start with a 15-minute focus time, followed by a one-minute tech break.[33] After a visit to a school, where I talked about tech breaks, one teacher e-mailed me:

> My French 3 students and I had a blast on Wednesday. The 90-minute class went smoothly and fast. We had 2 cell phone breaks and students were able to go back to business. The next day, some students who had heard about this opportunity asked me if they would also be able to use their cell phone and I said yes. I explained to my classes your research findings and I also talked about procedures and rules. Basically, they were told that after important activities and if they were focused, on-task, and attentive they could use it. Disruption was for example a no cell phone privilege. Students want to check their Facebook page every 15 minutes. So they will behave and stay focused if they know they can do that.

How do you know if you need a tech break? Just notice how long you are able to focus on a single task before switching to another and note what tasks appear to draw your attention more strongly. Consider the obvious distractions: smartphones, laptops or desktops, television, and music, and pay close attention to when you are humming along with a song as you are supposed to be focusing on a task or glancing at the laptop to check your e-mail. If any of these are distracting, turn them off, remove them from your sight, and give yourself a tech break every 15 minutes. Do know that the older you are the more likely you are to be distracted by those chimes and flashing reminders.[34] But then again, if you are younger you may not have your prefrontal cortex completely myelinated and you may be at risk for distractions, also.

IMPRESSION MANAGEMENT 2.0

When we meet someone we make an impression based on the way we dress, how we act, our body language, the words we say, our vocal inflections, and other salient cues. Communications online are limited to words and pictures, which means you have to help people fill in the blanks that are missing from face-to-face encounters. In 1959, Erving Goffman, an esteemed professor of sociology at the University of California and the University of Pennsylvania, coined the term "impression management" as a way of describing this process.[35] In his famous book, *The Presentation of Self in Everyday Life,* Goffman talked about how people control or guide the impression that others get of them by directing the flow of information. Like a theater production, there is a front stage area where the person is presenting the self that he or she wants others to see—often referred to as the "ought self"—that reflects how the person feels others expect him or her to act. Then there is the back stage area where individuals can be themselves and present their "true self." To Goffman, and others, managing one's impression is a full-time "dramaturgical" acting job.

Given that we are now communicating often with people who do not see us face to face, it is critical that you manage the impression that people glean from your writing and other online activities. For example, in Chapter 2, I talked about narcissism and how your writing style—particularly your use of personal pronouns such as "I" and "me"—as well as your choice of social networking photos (mostly individual or posed) can give people the impression that you are all about you. Contrast that with the use of "virtual empathy," where you understand and share others' feelings. Which self do you want to put on the front stage? Research by Nicole Krämer and Stephan Winter of the University of Duisburg-Essen in Germany found that online social networking sites help you manage your online personality impression. Krämer and Winter found that you feel better about yourself (called "self-efficacy" by psychologists) if you have more online friends, more details in your profile—particularly more humorous details—and more personal photos expressing your fun side, such as you at events, at parties, and with other people.

While you are managing the impression that you make on people, it is also important to manage what you get back from those people, or your "social capital" in the online and offline worlds. Social capital—resources available to people through social interactions—can be obtained both online and offline, but with the hours that we spend online it is helpful to maximize social capital in your virtual worlds. Healthy people need to gain social capital from friends—old and new, real and virtual—and family. Social networking provides a simple way of doing that through "friending." In one study of nearly 2,500 Facebook users, researchers at the University of Texas found that social networking use was indeed related to social capital.[36] A study at the Massachusetts Institute of Technology found that this form of social capital, however, was comprised of "weak ties" rather than "strong ties" because the former are quite easy to maintain on a social network.[37] Additional research has discovered that social networking both maintains and solidifies existing offline relationships and also is strongly related to social capital.[38]

To maximize your social capital, should you gobble up as many friends as you can, indiscriminately adding anyone who asks to be part of your social network? Should you try talking to as many of your "friends" as you can? The answer to the first question is most likely "no," given what is known as "Dunbar's Number," which asserts that, based on the size of the neocortex in primates and humans, a person can only maintain between 100 and 200 stable relationships in their online and offline worlds.[39] The answer to the second question was answered in several studies that directly linked online communication and subjective well-being.[40] So, the key is to use your social networks to build up social capital but recognize that online communication and connection do not produce ties that are nearly as strong as offline, real-world communication. You need social capital including both weak and strong ties. They serve different functions and will provide options for staying emotionally and mentally healthy.

PAY HEED TO CONTEXT

When I discussed the two-dimensional model of communication, I indicated that one of the major components of communication is being able to understand someone's context or the mental, physical, geographical, and emotional state that someone is in when they receive your message. Remember that although you cannot see the person at the other end of an electronic communication he or she is real and made of flesh, blood, and feelings. Develop a five-minute "e-waiting period" between the time you write any message (text, social network post, e-mail) and the time you press "send" or "post." Five minutes is enough time to rethink your message and decide if it may need to be softened or changed in any way to make it potentially less harmful. If you feel that you are not capable of determining whether you should send a message, perhaps you might want to try Google Goggles, a tool that requires you to do some math problems before allowing you to send an e-mail message. This was created as a sobriety test, but I actually think that it provides a brain break from thinking about the content of the message and allows you time to reset your brain and view the message in a new light.

Your real social capital is most likely going to come from people you know in the physical world rather than through your virtual social networks. Knowing that, as well as knowing that you may get interrupted by communications from your electronic world, you should develop rules about how to deal with intrusive e-connections when you are actually face to face with friends. Too often you see people with their smartphones lined up on a restaurant table, willing to interrupt themselves to respond to whoever has just sent a text, called, or even posted on a social network. This doesn't mean that you can't respond to these interruptions if they are important; it just means that you have to define an "important" message in advance and then leave the rest alone for after your social get together. In Erving Goffman's terms, you are facing a double front stage when you are both in someone's physical presence but also connected electronically to others. You need to take your local audience—your dinner companions—into account while understanding the needs of your remote audience.[41]

TO SLEEP, PERCHANCE TO RESET YOUR BRAIN

There is no denying that technology and media are highly entertaining, are highly engaging, and can lead to a loss of sleep, particularly when you use interactive technologies at night, right before bedtime. A recent study by the National Sleep Foundation[42] uncovered some startling observations on the negative impact of technology on sleep. Here is a sampling of their findings:

- While experts recommend nine hours of sleep for teenagers, the average teen gets just shy of seven and a half hours of nightly sleep.
- Experts recommend eight hours of sleep for adults, but 77 percent of young adults (19–29) get less than seven hours.
- Just before closing their eyes, 95 percent of people use some sort of electronic device at least a few nights during the week. Older people are more likely to be watching television, while younger people are more likely to be on their computer or playing video games.
- Within the last hour before sleep, 61 percent of people use their computer (36 percent in the bedroom), including 77 percent of teens and 73 percent of young adults.
- Within the last hour before sleep, 38 percent of people are on a social networking site, including 70 percent of teens and 63 percent of young adults.
- Thirty-nine percent of people bring their cell phones into the bedroom and leave them on while they are sleeping or trying to sleep. This includes 56 percent of teens and 67 percent of young adults. Twenty-two percent of people leave their cell phone ringer on while they sleep, and between one in ten and one in twenty are awakened at least a few nights a week by calls or texts.
- Within the last hour before bedtime, more than half of teens are texting, while slightly less than half of young adults are sending those short texts.

The bottom line is that most teens and adults are not getting enough sleep, and sleep is absolutely essential. The brain needs that time to consolidate important memories and knowledge and to prune brain connections that are deemed to be unimportant. The problem in getting the required sleep lies in the technological activities that precede sleep and that are likely to cause an iDisorder. According to Dr. Charles Czeisler of Harvard Medical School, "Artificial light exposure between dusk and the time we go to bed at night suppresses release of the sleep promoting hormone melatonin, enhances alertness and shifts circadian rhythms to a later hour—making it more difficult to fall asleep. This study reveals that light-emitting screens are in heavy use within the pivotal hour before sleep. Invasion of such alerting technologies into the bedroom may contribute to the high proportion of respondents who reported that they routinely get less sleep than they need."[43] According to recent research it is active technologies—computers, Internet, cell phones—that are more alerting than passive technologies, such as television and music.[44] Here is excellent advice from the National Sleep Foundation:[45]

- Have a regular time that you plan to go to sleep every night and when you plan to awaken in the morning to make sure you get the recommended amount of sleep.
- Avoid bright lights after sunset.
- Exercise regularly but not in late afternoon or evening.
- Relax before going to bed.
- Avoid caffeinated beverages, alcohol, and large meals as much as possible, but most certainly in the few hours before you plan to go to sleep.
- Have no distractions in your sleeping area. That means no technology in the bedroom (television is a passive activity and is an exception)!
- Keep the lights dim in the bedroom and interact only with passive technologies, including television and music, in the hour before sleep.

MINDFULNESS AND POSITIVE PSYCHOLOGY

Two relatively new fields of psychology offer suggestions for avoiding or eliminating an iDisorder. Mindfulness is derived from Buddhist philosophy and has to do with being positive, in the moment, non-judgmental, and non-reactive. A wealth of data shows that simple techniques to achieve mindfulness are available and useful in keeping free of stress. For example, one study found that people who flourish in life have three positive emotional events for every negative one,[46] while another found that when you are stressed, you have increased activity in the right prefrontal cortex of the brain but when you are feeling great you have increased activity in the left prefrontal cortex. Certain activities will increase this left-side advantage, including doing nothing, taking a long shower, walking a dog, and meditating.[47] There are many excellent books on mindfulness, including Jan Chozen Bays's *How to Train a Wild Elephant & Other Adventures in Mindfulness* and Jan Kabat-Zinn's *Mindfulness-Based Stress Reduction.* Pick up either or try the following simple tasks:

- Consciously identify often during your day what you appreciate at the moment. It can be another person, yourself, or something in your environment.
- Be aware of nature by paying attention to all the things that your senses perceive and learning which ones reduce your stress.
- Reminisce about good times in your life.[48]
- Learn to meditate (experts recommend mental silence meditation, sometimes also called Sahaja yoga); it changes your brain for the good,[49] and it makes you laugh more and even not use the word "I" as much.[50]

Traditional psychology deals primarily with how the mind works, what can go wrong with it, and how to fix it. A new field known as positive psychology focuses instead on what goes right and how to maintain that path. According to the Positive Psychology Center at the University of Pennsylvania and its director Dr. Martin Seligman, the developer of this new field of psychology, "Positive Psychology has three central concerns: positive experiences, positive individual traits, and positive institutions. We can't do much about those institutions but the center offers educational programs and resources for teachers and families to change our life experiences in favor of positives and against the negatives."[51] Positive psychology is not about being Pollyannaish or seeing life through rose-colored glasses. It is about moving your focus from everyday problems to everyday successes.

BEING A NEW MILLENNIUM PARENT

In *Me, MySpace, and I: Parenting the Net Generation,* I wrote about a model I developed to help "digital immigrant" parents deal with their "digital native" children. The model is called TALK, which stands for trust-assess-learn-"k"ommunicate. (I know that communicate starts with a "C," but TALC is not a great acronym as it reminds people of babies and talcum powder.) The key area is trust, and it can only be generated through communication. Here's my recommendation. As soon as you give your child that first smartphone to play with or a tablet for entertainment or sit her down in front of a computer or even a television set, you should start having weekly discussions about the role of technology in the family and in the world. These are basic and simple. They last for 15 minutes, no longer, and start with everyone sitting down on the floor, which somewhat equalizes the power structure, with taller people perceived as having more power than shorter people. Ask your child, using developmentally appropriate language, questions about technology, such as, "How did you like playing with my phone? What was fun about it?" and then let your child talk. As they grow, the questions should get more focused, such as, "I heard something about cyberbullying. Have you or a friend ever been cyberbullied? What happened? How did it feel?" Then you sit back with a smile on your face (trust is engendered more by nonjudgmental communications) and let your child talk. The rule is for every one minute that the parent talks, he or she listens to the child talk for five minutes.

A second way of developing trust is through family meals. Research has shown that having at least three to four family meals a week leads to major benefits for both physical and psychological health for children, teens, and families.[52] Have a set time for family meals and insist that everyone come to the table when called (with perhaps a small penalty if they don't). In order to ensure that the family uses this time for discussion instead of television or e-mail and text messages, use tech breaks at the table. Everyone turns off his or her phones, puts away all technology, and after, say, 15 minutes, everyone gets a one-minute tech break. Then, it is back to discussion and family time. The discussions at dinner are similar to those during family meetings, but now the parents get to talk more. Still, the balance should be tipped in favor of the kids talking and the parents listening. This is a time for parents to be non-judgmental and to assess what technology their kids are using by asking questions such as, "Have you tried any new websites recently?" and "Can you show me how to do such-and-such after dinner?" These two activities comprise the "A" and "L" of the TALK module.

What I am proposing is being a proactive, authoritative parent who anticipates problems before they occur through both the family meetings and family meals. The authoritative part includes setting limits on your children's technology-related behaviors, but doing so in consultation with the children and in a warm, non-judgmental manner. Again, this is part of both the meetings and meals. What do you do if you discover that your children are already having problems with technology? When you swing into reactive parenting the tendency is to set stiff penalties, such as yanking the Wii console away for a week or taking the cell phone and not returning it for a month. This is too harsh for a first infraction. You should adhere to the rule of using the "least restrictive alternative" as an initial penalty and then spell out in a written, posted behavioral contract how those penalties will escalate. So, if your teen has trouble stopping his video game when called to dinner and you get upset, first restrict its use for the rest of the day. Then set up a contract that says the next time it will be 24 hours, and the next (if there is one) will be 48 hours, and then keep doubling the penalty. Usually the first few small penalties are sufficient, particularly if the contract is made in a non-judgmental manner and set up in conjunction with the teen's contributions to the discussion and penalties.

CLOSING THOUGHTS

As you read through the chapters in this book, hopefully you realized that many of us are using technology and media in ways that either produce symptoms that match those of a variety of psychological disorders or exacerbate already existing signs of a disorder. I have tried to approach this topic in a neutral manner because I don't feel that technology is inherently bad. I have many different tech products and relish learning something new all the time. What does concern me is how we use those technologies and how that might impinge on our emotional well-being. In each chapter I provided you with a rationale of why psychologists believe you are facing many potential iDisorders and how mental health professionals suggest you keep yourself healthy. The strategies that I suggest are not difficult to implement nor are they complex or convoluted. Most of them are simple and rely mainly on paying attention to what drives the signs and symptoms of your iDisorder. Some, such as tech breaks and e-waiting periods, simply require setting up time constraints on checking in with your technology and waiting to send or post messages. Most are equally straightforward and require equally little effort.

Now it is time for you to avoid your own iDisorder. Paying attention is half the battle. Watch how you interact behind the screen. Pay attention to the words you use, the pictures you post, and the interactions you have with people. Pay attention to websites you visit and technologies that you use to see if they might be causing symptoms of an iDisorder. Notice how you interact with other people in public. Do you keep your cell phone on the table at a restaurant? Do you answer calls or respond to text messages while you are with other people? Think about spending time interacting with the people who are right in front of you rather than those who are elsewhere. It's all about being aware of and monitoring your behavior around all of these marvelous technological inventions.

Notes

CHAPTER 1

1. Other dictionaries select words of the year and many of them are also technological in nature. For example, Merriam-Webster selected *woot*—a gaming term meaning triumph or joy—in 2007 and *Facebook* was a top ten member. The American Dialect Society selected *app* as number one in 2010, *tweet* in 2009, and their word of the 2000-2009 decade was *Google*. Their word of the 1990s was *web*.
2. http://www.nimh.nih.gov/statistics/index.shtml
3. American Psychiatric Association. (2000). *Diagnostic and Statistical Manual of Mental Disorders* (Revised 4th ed., text revision). Washington, DC: Author. NOTE: The DSM-IV-TR will be referred to as the *DSM* throughout the rest of the book.
4. Weil, M. M., & Rosen, L. D. (1998). *TechnoStress: Coping with Technology @Work @Home @Play*. New York: John Wiley and Sons.
5. Ibid.
6. All of my work is done in the George Marsh Applied Cognition (GMAC) Laboratory at California State University, Dominguez Hills. This lab includes four Ph.D. faculty and eight to ten undergraduate and graduate research assistants. At any given time, the GMAC Lab, as it is known, has ten to 15 active research projects, some using survey research tools and some using laboratory experimental psychological procedures.
7. Millon, T., Davis, R., & Millon, C. (1997). *Manual for the Millon Clinical Multiaxial Inventory—III (MCMI-III)* (3rd ed.). Minneapolis: National Computer Systems.
8. Rosen, L. D., Carrier, L. M., Cheever, N. A., Rab, S., Arikan, M., & Whaling, K. (unpublished manuscript). *iDisorder: The Relationship between Media Use and Signs and Symptoms of Psychiatric Disorders*. NOTE: The *MCMI-III* was developed for use with adults who are seeking mental health treatment and, as such, may not be completely interpretable for our general population in this study. All conclusions from this study were validated by other research carried out by psychologists and psychiatrists with normal and clinical populations.
9. Carrier, L. M., Cheever, N. A., Rosen, L. D., Benitez, S., & Chang, J. (2009). Multitasking across generations: Multitasking choices and difficulty ratings in three generations of Americans. *Computers in Human Behavior, 25*, 483-489.
10. The *MCMI-III* cautions that it is not appropriate for adolescent populations. With this in mind, any conclusions that we draw from teenagers' data will be compared with and validated by additional research by other scholars.
11. Lenninghan, M. (November 17, 2010). *Global mobile penetration on track for 100%*. Retrieved from http://www.totaltele.com/view.aspx?ID=460322.
12. The iPass Global Mobile Workforce Report. Understanding enterprise mobility trends and mobile usage. iPass, Inc. May 24, 2011.
13. Rosen, L. D. (2010). *Rewired: Understanding the iGeneration and the Way They Learn*. New York: Palgrave Macmillan.
14. Rosen, L. D. (2008). *Me, MySpace, and I: Parenting the Net Generation*. New York: Palgrave Macmillan.
15. Turkle, S. (1995). *Life on the Screen: Identity in the Age of the Internet*. New York: Simon & Schuster.

16. www.scottevest.com.

17. In both *Me, MySpace, and I* and *Rewired* I discuss the concept of generational differences and how experts believe that most people in a generation fit most of the characteristics. However there is no cause to assume that everyone in a generation will behave and feel the same. In our work we find remarkable consistency in values, attitudes, and beliefs within a generation and strong differences across generations. It is important to note that all generational research combines people born within a certain time span into one group and then looking at "average" behaviors, feelings, and attitudes for that group. Averages entail simply combining a set of scores and finding the typical or middle point for that measure. This does not mean that everyone acts or feels the same way but that, on the whole, the group appears to show a systematic trend.

18. My blog postings can be found at http://www.psychologytoday.com/blog/rewired-the -psychology-technology.

19. http://www.psychologytoday.com/blog/rewired-the-psychology-technology/201010/ taking-virtual-break-can-you-survive-without-your-tech.

CHAPTER 2

1. American Psychiatric Association. (2000). *Diagnostic and Statistical Manual of Mental Disorders* (Revised 4th ed., text revision). Washington, DC.

2. Paulhus, D. L. (1998). Interpersonal and intrapsychic adaptiveness of trait self-enhancement: A mixed blessing? *Journal of Personality and Social Psychology, 74(5),* 1197-1208.

3. Kaufman, S. B. (January 22, 2010). Why are narcissists (initially) so popular? *Psychology Today.* Retrieved from http://www.psychologytoday.com/blog/beautiful-minds/201001/ why-are-narcissists-initially-so-popular.

4. Kohut, H. (1972). Thoughts on narcissism and narcissistic rage. *Psychoanalytic Studies, 27,* 360-400.

5. Turkle, S. (1995). *Life on the Screen: Identity in the Age of the Internet.* New York: Simon and Schuster.

6. Cross, P. (1977). Not can but will college teachers be improved? *New Directions for Higher Education, 17,* 1-15.

7. Raskin, R., & Shaw, R. (1988). Narcissism and the use of personal pronouns. *Journal of Personality, 56(2),* 393-404.

8. DeWall, C. N., Buffardi, L. E., Bonser, I., & Campbell, W. K. (2011). Narcissism and implicit attention seeking: Evidence from linguistic analyses of social networking and online presentation. *Personality and Individual Differences.* In press.

9. Twenge, J. M., & Campbell, W. K. (2009). *The Narcissism Epidemic: Living in the Age of Entitlement.* New York: Free Press.

10. Twenge and Campbell's research is controversial. For further information see the following articles: Trzesniewski, K. H., & Donnellan, M. B. (2010). Rethinking "Generation Me": A study of cohort effects from 1976-2006. *Psychological Science, 5(2),* 58-75; Twenge, J. M., & Foster, J. D. (2010). Birth cohort increases in narcissistic personality traits among American college students, 1982-2009. *Social Psychological and Personality Science, 1(1),* 99-106; Donnellan, M. B., Trzesniewski, K. H., & Robins, R. W. (2009). An emerging epidemic of narcissism or much ado about nothing? *Journal of Research in Personality, 43(3),* 498-501.

11. DeWall, C. N., Pond, R. S., Campbell, W. K., & Twenge, J. M. (March 21, 2011). Tuning in to psychological change: Linguistic markers of psychological traits and emotions over time in popular U.S. songs. *Psychology of Aesthetics, Art, and Creativity.*

12. Buffardi, L. E., & Campbell, W. K. (2008). Narcissism and social networking web sites. *Personality and Social Psychology Bulletin, 34(10),* 1303-1314.

13. Mehdizadeh, S. (2010). Self-presentation 2.0: Narcissism and self-esteem on Facebook. *Cyberpsychology, Behavior, and Social Networking, 13(4),* 357-364.

14. Ryan, T., & Xenos, S. (2011). Who uses Facebook? An investigation into the relationship between the Big Five, shyness, narcissism, loneliness, and Facebook usage. *Computers in Human Behavior, 27(5),* 1658-1664.

15. Thomaes, S., Reigntjes, A., Orobio de Castro, B., Bushman, B. J., Poorthuis, A., & Telch, M. J. (2010). I like me if you like me: On the interpersonal modulation and regulation of preadolescents' state self-esteem. *Child Development, 81(3),* 811-825.

16. Lootens, C. M. (2010). *An examination of the relationships among personality traits, perceived parenting styles, and narcissism.* Doctoral dissertation. The University of North Carolina.

17. Bergman, S. M., Fearrington, M. E., Davenport, S. W., & Bergman, J. Z. (2011). Millennials, narcissism, and social networking: What narcissists do on social networking sites and why. *Personality and Individual Differences, 50(5),* 706-711.

18. Naaman, M., Boase, J., & Lai, C. H. (2010). Is it really about me? Message content in social awareness streams. In *Proceedings of Computer Supported Cooperative Work Conference,* pp. 189-192.

19. Goffman, E. (1959). *The Presentation of Self in Everyday Life.* New York: Doubleday.

20. Rosen, L. D. (2007). *Me, MySpace, and I: Parenting the Net Generation.* New York: Palgrave Macmillan.

21. Li, D. (2005). *Why do you blog: A Uses-and-Gratifications inquiry into bloggers' motivations.* Marquette University. Retrieved from http://citeseerx.ist.psu.edu/viewdoc/download?doi=10.1.1.91.6790&rep=rep1&type=pdf.

22. Bergman, S. M., Fearrington, M. E., Davenport, S. W., & Bergman, J. Z. (2011). Millennials, narcissism, and social networking: What narcissists do on social networking sites and why. *Personality and Individual Differences, 50(5),* 706-711.

23. Quan-Haase, A., & Young, A. L. (2010). Uses and gratifications of social media. A comparison of Facebook and instant messaging. *Bulletin of Science, Technology & Society, 30,* 309-315.

24. Raacke, J., & Bonds-Raacke, J. (2008). MySpace and Facebook: Applying the uses and gratifications theory to exploring friend-networking sites. *Cyberpsychology & Behavior, 11(2),* 169-174.

25. Chen, G. M. (2010). Tweet this: A uses and gratifications perspective on how active Twitter use gratifies a need to connect with others. *Computers in Human Behavior, 27(2),* 1-8.

26. Papacharissi, Z., & Mendelson, A. (2011). Toward a new(er) sociability: Uses, gratifications, and social capital on Facebook. In *Media Perspectives for the 21st Century,* Stelios Papathanassopoulos (Ed.). New York: Routledge.

27. Steinfield, C. E., Ellison, N., & Lampe, C. (May 21, 2008). *Net Worth: Facebook Use and Changes in Social Capital Over Time.* Paper presented at the annual meeting of the International Communication Association, Montreal, Quebec, Canada; Vitak, J., Ellison, N. B., & Steinfield, C. E. (2011). *Proceedings of the 44th Hawaii International Conference on System Sciences.* Retrieved from https://www.msu.edu/~nellison/VitakEllisonSteinfield2011.pdf.

28. Rosen, C. (Fall 2004/Winter 2005). The age of egocasting. *The New Atlantis,* 51-72.

29. DiSalvo, D. (2010). Are social networks messing with your head? *Scientific American Mind, 20(7),* 48-55.

30. Sheng, T., Gheytanchi, A., & Aziz-Zadeh, L. (2010). Default network deactivations are correlated with psychopathic personality traits. *PLoS ONE, 5(9).*

31. Amati, F., Oh, H., Kwan, V. S. Y., Jordan, K., & Keenan, J. P. (2010). Overclaiming and the medial prefrontal cortex: A transcranial magnetic stimulation study. *Cognitive Neuroscience, 1(4),* 268-276.

32. Kwan, V. S. Y., Barrios, V., Ganis, G., Gorman, J., Lange, C., Kumar, M., Shepard, A., & Keenan, J. P. (2007). Assessing the neural correlates of self-enhancement bias: A transcranial magnetic stimulation study. *Experimental Brain Research, 182(3),* 379-385.

33. Cacioppo, J. T., Norris, C. J, Decety, J., Monteleone, G., & Nusbaum, H. (2009). In the eye of the beholder: Individual differences in perceived social isolation predict regional brain activation to social stimuli. *Journal of Cognitive Neuroscience, 21(1),* 83-92.

34. Berman, M. G., Jonides, J., & Kaplan, S. (2008). The cognitive benefits of interacting with nature. *Psychological Science, 19(12),* 1207-1212.

CHAPTER 3

1. kmx (June 28, 2009). I've got more phones than fingers. Howard Forums, Mobile Community. http://www.howardforums.com/showthread.php/1534935-Why-are-some-people-so-attached-to-their-phones.

2. Hannaford, K. (May 16, 2011). Apparently one third of you open up apps before you even get out of bed. *Gizmodo, the Gadget Guide* (Gizmodo.com). Retrieved from http://

gizmodo.com/5802142/apparently-one-third-of-you-open-apps-before-you-even-get-out-of-bed.

3. Rosen, L. D. (2010). *Rewired: Understanding the iGeneration and the Way They Learn.* New York: Palgrave Macmillan.

4. Rosen, L. D., Carrier, L. M., Cheever, N. A., Rab, S., Arikan, M., & Whaling, K. (unpublished manuscript). *iDisorder: The Relationship between Media Use and Signs and Symptoms of Psychiatric Disorders.* Manuscript submitted for publication. .

5. Hannaford, K. (May 16, 2011). Apparently one third of you open up apps before you even get out of bed. *Gizmodo, the Gadget Guide* (Gizmodo.com). Retrieved from http://gizmodo.com/5802142/apparently-one-third-of-you-open-apps-before-you-even-get-out-of-bed.

6. Rosen, L. D. (October 11, 2010). Taking a (virtual) break: Can you survive without your technology for 24 hours? I doubt it! *Psychology Today* (PsychologyToday.com). Retrieved from http://www.psychologytoday.com/blog/rewired-the-psychology-technology/201010/taking-virtual-break-can-you-survive-without-your-tech.

7. Harris Interactive (July 28, 2011). *Americans work on their vacation: Half of those vacationing will work on their vacation, including checking emails, voicemails and taking calls.* Retrieved from http://www.harrisinteractive.com/NewsRoom/HarrisPolls/tabid/447/mid/1508/articleId/843/ctl/ReadCustom%20Default/Default.aspx.

8. Gump, B. B., & Matthew, K. A. (2000). Are vacations good for your health? The 9-year mortality experience after the multiple risk factor intervention trial. *Psychosomatic Medicine, 62(5),* 608-612.

9. Taylor, C. (April 29, 2011). For Millennials, social media is not all fun and games. *GigaOM.* Retrieved from http://gigaom.com/2011/04/29/millennial-mtv-study/.

10. James, D., & Drennan, J. (December, 2005). *Exploring addictive consumption of mobile phone technology.* Paper presented at ANZMAC 2005. Perth, Australia.

11. Panic Disorder. (July 11, 2011). *National Institute of Mental Health.* Retrieved from http://www.nimh.nih.gov/health/topics/panic-disorder/index.shtml; American Psychiatric Association. (2000). *Diagnostic and Statistical Manual of Mental Disorders* (Revised 4th ed., text revision). Washington, DC.

12. Obsessive compulsive disorder among adults. (2010). *National Institute of Mental Health.* Retrieved from http://www.nimh.nih.gov/statistics/1OCD_ADULT.shtml.

13. OCD Resource Center of Florida. (2008-2011). *About OCD and How It Is Diagnosed.* Retrieved from http://www.ocdhope.com/obsessive-compulsive-disorder.php.

14. What's the difference between an addiction and a compulsion? (2010). Go Ask Alice!, Alice! Health Promotion Program at Columbia University (www.goaskalice.columbia.edu). Retrieved from http://www.goaskalice.columbia.edu/2947.html.

15. Brian, M. (May 26, 2011). "Lost iPhone" vigilante attacks the wrong person after GPS error. *TNW: The Next Web* (thenextweb.com). Retrieved from http://thenextweb.com/apple/2011/05/26/lost-iphone-vigilante-attacks-the-wrong-person-after-gps-error/?awesm=tnw.to_18YL2.

16. Alpert, L. I. (May 26, 2011). Teen girl shoots dad with arrow because he took away her cell phone: Cops. *Daily News* (NYDailyNews.com). Retrieved from http://www.nydailynews.com/news/national/2011/05/26/2011-05-26_dad_shot_in_head_with_arrow_by_teen_daughter_over_cell_phone_dispute.html.

17. Taylor, J. (July 27, 2009). Technology: Disconnectivity Anxiety. *Psychology Today.* Retrieved from http://www.psychologytoday.com/em/31388.

18. Questionnaire items from Rosen, L. D., Carrier, L. M., Cheever, N. A., Rab, S., Arikan, M., & Whaling, K. (unpublished manuscript). *iDisorder: The relationship between media use and signs and symptoms of psychiatric disorders.*

19. Rosen, L. D. (2007). *Me, MySpace, and I: Parenting the Net Generation.* New York: Palgrave Macmillan; Rosen, L. D., Carrier, L. M., & Cheever, N. A. (2010). *Rewired: Understanding the iGeneration and the Way They Learn.* New York: Palgrave Macmillan.

20. Ericsson ConsumerLab. (2011). *From Apps to Everyday Situations.* Stockholm: Ericsson AB. Retrieved from http://www.ericsson.com/res/docs/2011/silicon_valley_brochure_letter.pdf.

21. kmx (June 28, 2009). I've got more phones than fingers. *Howard Forums, Mobile Community.* http://www.howardforums.com/showthread.php/1534935-Why-are-some-people-so-attached-to-their-phones.

22. Laramie, D. (2007). Emotional and behavioral aspects of mobile phone use. Doctoral dissertation. Alliant International University.

23. Rothberg, M. B., Arora, A., Hermann, J., St. Marie, P., & Visintainer, P. (2010). Phantom vibration syndrome among medical staff: A cross sectional survey. *British Medical Journal, 341(12)*, 6914.

24. Questionnaire items from Rosen, L. D., Carrier, L. M., Cheever, N. A., Rab, S., Arikan, M., & Whaling, K. (unpublished manuscript). *iDisorder: The relationship between media use and signs and symptoms of psychiatric disorders.*

25. Baron, N. (2008). Adjusting the Volume: Technology and Multitasking in Discourse Control. In *Handbook of Mobile Communication Studies*, J. E. Katz (Ed.). Cambridge, MA: MIT Press.

26. Fredricksen, C. (December 15, 2010). Time Spent Watching TV Still Tops Internet. *eMarketer: Digital Intelligence.* Retrieved from http://www.emarketer.com/blog/index.php/time-spent-watching-tv-tops-internet/.

27. Sieberg, D. (June 6, 2011). Detox your digital life and choose human connections instead. *The Sydney Morning Herald.* Retrieved from http://www.smh.com.au/opinion/society-and-culture/detox-your-digital-life-and-choose-human-connections-instead-20110605-1fn2w.html.

CHAPTER 4

1. Participant in a study in which students were asked to go a day without their technology-based devices; International Center for Media & the Public Agenda (n.d.). *The world UNPLUGGED: Going 24 Hours Without Media.* Retrieved at http://theworld unplugged.wordpress.com/.

2. Ulrich Weger, quoted in Tobin, L. (February 14, 2011). How to beat technology addiction. *The Guardian.* Retrieved from http://www.guardian.co.uk/education/2011/feb/14/information-overload-research.

3. American Psychiatric Association. (2000). *Diagnostic and Statistical Manual of Mental Disorders* (Revised 4th ed., text revision). Washington, DC; Goldberg, I. (1996). *Internet addiction disorder.* Retrieved from http://www.webs.ulpgc.es/aeps/JR/Documentos/ciberadictos.doc

4. Chen, S.-H., Weng, L.-C., Su, Y.-J., Wu, H.-M., & Yang, P.-F. (2003). Development of Chinese Internet Addiction Scale and its psychometric study. *Chinese Journal of Psychology, 45,* 279-294; Ko, C.-H., Yen, J.-Y., Chen, C.-C., Chen, S.-H., Wu, K., & Yen, C.-F. (2006). Tridimensional personality of adolescents with Internet addiction and substance use experience. *Canadian Journal of Psychiatry, 51(14),* 887-894.

5. Winn, M. (1977). *The Plug-in Drug.* New York: Viking Penguin, Inc.

6. Griffiths, M. (1991). Amusement machine playing in childhood and adolescence: A comparative analysis of video game and fruit machines. *Journal of Adolescence, 14,* 53-73; Griffiths, M. (1992). Pinball wizard: The case of a pinball machine addict. *Psychological Reports, 71,* 161-162; Keepers, C. A. (1990). Pathological preoccupation with video games. *Journal of the American Academy of Child and Adolescent Psychiatry, 29,* 49-50; Soper, B. W. (1983). Junk-time junkies: An emerging addiction among students. *School Counselor, 31,* 40-43.

7. Griffiths, M. (1995). Technological addictions. *Clinical Psychology Forum, 71,* 14-19.

8. Griffiths, M. (2000). Does Internet and computer "addiction" exist? Some case study evidence. *CyberPsychology & Behavior, 3(2),* 211-218.

9. Young, K. S. (1996). Psychology of computer use: XL. Addictive use of the Internet: A case that breaks the stereotype. *Psychological Reports, 79,* 899-902.

10. Griffiths, M. D. (1998). Internet addiction: Does it really exist? In *Psychology and the Internet: Intrapersonal, Interpersonal and Transpersonal Applications,* J. Gackenbach (Ed.). pp. 61-75. New York: Academic Press; Griffiths, M. (2000). Does Internet and computer "addiction" exist? Some case study evidence. *CyberPsychology & Behavior, 3(2),* 211-218.

11. Igarashi, T., Motoyoshi, T., Takai, J., & Toshida, T. (2008). No mobile, no life: Self-perception and text-message dependency among Japanese high school students. *Computers in Human Behavior, 24,* 2311-2324; Kamibeppu, K., & Sugiura, H. (2005). Impact of the

mobile phone on junior high-school students' friendships in the Tokyo metropolitan area. *CyberPsychology & Behavior, 8(2)*, 121-130.

12. Chen, S.-H., Weng, L.-C., Su, Y.-J., Wu, H.-M., & Yang, P.-F. (2003). Development of Chinese Internet Addiction Scale and its psychometric study. *Chinese Journal of Psychology, 45*, 279-294; Ko, C.-H., Yen, J.-Y., Chen, C.-C., Chen, S.-H., Wu, K., & Yen, C.-F. (2006). Tridimensional personality of adolescents with Internet addiction and substance use experience. *Canadian Journal of Psychiatry, 51(14)*, 887-894.

13. Young, K. S. (1999). Internet addiction: Symptoms, evaluation, and treatment. In *Innovations in Clinical Practice (Vol. 17)*, L. VandeCreek, & T. L. Jackson (Eds.). pp. 19-31. Sarasota, FL: Professional Resource Press. Used by permission.

14. Jenaro, C., Flores, N., Gómez-Vela, M., González-Gil, F., & Caballo, C. (2007). Problematic Internet and cell-phone use: Psychological, behavioral, and health correlates. *Addiction Research and Theory, 15(3)*, 309-320. Used by permission.

15. Igarashi, T., Motoyoshi, T., Takai, J., & Toshida, T. (2008). No mobile, no life: Self-perception and text-message dependency among Japanese high school students. *Computers in Human Behavior, 24*, 2311-2324; Kamibeppu, K., & Sugiura, H. (2005). Impact of the mobile phone on junior high-school students' friendships in the Tokyo metropolitan area. *CyberPsychology & Behavior, 8(2)*, 121-130.

16. Young, K. S. (1997). *Internet addiction: The emergence of a new clinical disorder.* Retrieved from http//:www.pitt.edu/~ksy/apa.html.

17. Young, K. S. (1996). Psychology of computer use: XL. Addictive use of the Internet: A case that breaks the stereotype. *Psychological Reports, 79*, 899-902.

18. Young, K. S. (1999). Internet addiction: Symptoms, evaluation, and treatment. In *Innovations in Clinical Practice (Vol. 17)*, L. VandeCreek & T. L. Jackson (Eds.). pp. 19-31. Sarasota, FL: Professional Resource Press.

19. Benesse Institute of Education, ed. (2002). Junior high school students' contact with media [in Japanese]. Monograph/Junior High School Students' World. 71. As reported by Kamibeppu, K., & Sugiura, H. (2005). Impact of the mobile phone on junior high-school students' friendships in the Tokyo metropolitan area. *CyberPsychology & Behavior, 8(2)*, 121-130.

20. Kamibeppu, K., & Sugiura, H. (2005). Impact of the mobile phone on junior high-school students' friendships in the Tokyo metropolitan area. *CyberPsychology & Behavior, 8(2)*, 121-130.

21. Ko, C.-H., Yen, J.-Y., Chen, C.-C., Chen, S.-H., Wu, K., & Yen, C.-F. (2006). Tridimensional personality of adolescents with Internet addiction and substance use experience. *Canadian Journal of Psychiatry, 51(14)*, 887-894.

22. Armstrong, L., Phillips, J. G., & Saling, L. L. (2000). Potential determinants of heavier Internet usage. *International Journal of Human-Computer Studies, 53*, 537-550.

23. Lavin, M., Marvin, K., McLarney, A., Nola, V., & Scott, L. (1999). Sensation seeking and collegiate vulnerability to Internet dependence. *CyberPsychology & Behavior, 2*, 425-430; Lin, S. S. J., & Tsai, C. C. (2002). Sensation seeking and Internet dependence of Taiwanese high school adolescents. *Computers in Human Behavior, 18*, 411-426.

24. Ko, C.-H., Yen, J.-Y., Chen, C.-C., Chen, S.-H., Wu, K., & Yen, C.-F. (2006). Tridimensional personality of adolescents with Internet addiction and substance use experience. *Canadian Journal of Psychiatry, 51(14)*, 887-894.

25. Suler, J. (2004). The online disinhibition effect. *CyberPsychology & Behavior, 7*, 321-326.

26. Ko, C.-H., Yen, J.-Y., Chen, C.-C., Chen, S.-H., Wu, K., & Yen, C.-F. (2006). Tridimensional personality of adolescents with Internet addiction and substance use experience. *Canadian Journal of Psychiatry, 51(14)*, 891.

27. Ko et al., 2006, Ibid.; Huang, X-q., Li, M-c., & Tao, R. (2010). Treatment of Internet addiction. *Current Psychiatry Reports, 12*, 462-470.

28. Frascella, J., Potenza, M. N., Brown, L. L., & Childress, A. R. (2010). Shared brain vulnerabilities open the way for nonsubstance addictions: Carving addiction at a new joint? *Annals of the New York Academy of Sciences, 1187*, 294-315; Holden, C. (November 6, 2001). Behavioral addictions: Do they exist? *Science, 294*, 980-982.

29. Grant, J. E., Brewer, J. A., & Potenza, M. N. (2006). The neurobiology of substance and behavioral addictions. CNS Spectrums: *The International Journal of Neuropsychiatric Medicine, 11(12)*, 924-930.

30. Yuan, K., Qin, W., Wang, G., Zeng, F., Zhao, L., Yang, X., Liu, P., Liu, J., Sun, J., von Deneen, K. M., Gong, Q., Liu, Y., & Tian, J. (2011). *PLoS ONE, 6(6)*. Retrieved from http://www.plosone.org/article/info:doi/10.1371/journal.pone.0020708.

31. Nagata, T. (October 7, 2010). Blizzard ready to talk numbers again, World of Warcraft tops 12 million subscribers. *Gamesradar*. Retrieved from http://www.gamesradar.com/pc/world-of-warcraft/news/blizzard-ready-to-talk-numbers-again-world-of-warcraft-tops-12-million-subscribers/a-2010100718521163062/g-2005120716480781115722.

32. Young, K. S. (1997). *Internet addiction: The emergence of a new clinical disorder.* Retrieved from http//:www.pitt.edu/~ksy/apa.html.

33. Griffiths, M. D. (1998). Internet addiction: Does it really exist? In *Psychology and the Internet: Intrapersonal, Interpersonal and Transpersonal Applications,* J. Gackenbach (Ed.). pp. 61-75. New York: Academic Press.

34. Hammersley, R. (1995). Cited in Griffiths, M. (2000). Does Internet and computer "addiction" exist? Some case study evidence. *CyberPsychology & Behavior, 3(2),* 211-218.

35. Griffiths, M. D. (April 7, 1995). Netties anonymous. *Times Higher Educational Supplement,* p. 18; Griffiths, M. (2000). Does Internet and computer "addiction" exist? Some case study evidence. *CyberPsychology & Behavior, 3(2),* 211-218.

36. Young, K. S. (1996). Psychology of computer use: XL. Addictive use of the Internet: A case that breaks the stereotype. *Psychological Reports, 79,* 899-902.

37. Igarashi, T., Motoyoshi, T., Takai, J., & Toshida, T. (2008). No mobile, no life: Self-perception and text-message dependency among Japanese high school students. *Computers in Human Behavior, 24,* 2311-2324.

38. Ajayi, A. (1995). Cited in Griffiths, M. (2000). Does Internet and computer "addiction" exist? Some case study evidence. *CyberPsychology & Behavior, 3(2),* 211-218.

39. Armstrong, L.; Phillips, J. G., & Saling, L. L. (2000). Potential determinants of heavier Internet usage. *International Journal of Human-Computer Studies, 53,* 537-550.

40. Davis, R. A. (2001). A cognitive-behavioral model of pathological Internet use. *Computers in Human Behavior, 17,* 187-195.

41. Igarashi, T., Motoyoshi, T., Takai, J., & Toshida, T. (2008). No mobile, no life: Self-perception and text-message dependency among Japanese high school students. *Computers in Human Behavior, 24,* 2311-2324.

42. Shotton, M. A. (1991). The costs and benefits of "computer addiction." *Behaviour Information and Technology, 10,* 219-230.

43. Young, K. S. (1999). Internet addiction: Symptoms, evaluation, and treatment. In *Innovations in Clinical Practice (Vol. 17),* L. VandeCreek & T. L. Jackson (Eds.). pp. 19-31. Sarasota, FL: Professional Resource Press.

44. Ibid.

45. Huang, X-q., Li, M-c., & Tao, R. (2010). Treatment of Internet addiction. *Current Psychiatry Reports, 12,* 462-470.

46. Ko, C.-H., Yen, J.-Y., Chen, C.-C., Chen, S.-H., Wu, K., & Yen, C.-F. (2006). Tridimensional personality of adolescents with Internet addiction and substance use experience. *Canadian Journal of Psychiatry, 51(14),* 887-894.

47. Young, K. S. (1999). Internet addiction: Symptoms, evaluation, and treatment. In *Innovations in Clinical Practice (Vol. 17),* L. VandeCreek & T. L. Jackson (Eds.). pp. 19-31. Sarasota, FL: Professional Resource Press.

CHAPTER 5

1. O'Keeffe, G. S., Clarke-Pearson, K., & Council on Communications and Media. (2011). Clinical Report: The impact of social media on children, adolescents, and families. *Pediatrics, 27(4),* 800-804.

2. A complete description of the HomeNet Project can be found at: http://homenet.hcii.cs.cmu.edu/progress/index.html.

3. http://homenet.hcii.cs.cmu.edu/progress/index.html.

4. Kraut, R., Kiesler, S., Boneva, B., Cummings, J., Helgeson, V., & Crawford, A. (2002). Internet paradox revisited. *Journal of Social Issues, 58(1),* 49-74.

5. http://www.nimh.nih.gov/statistics/1BIPOLAR ADULT.shtml.

6. O'Keeffe, G. S., Clarke-Pearson, K., & Council on Communications and Media. (2011). Clinical Report: The impact of social media on children, adolescents, and families. *Pediatrics, 27(4),* 800-804.

7. See this insightful report by technology journalist Larry Magid in the *Huffington Post* for more information about this controversy: http://www.huffingtonpost.com/larry-magid/facebook-depression-nonexistent_b_842733.html.

8. http://www.nimh.nih.gov/health/publications/bipolar-disorder/complete-index.shtml#pub1.

9. http://www.nimh.nih.gov/statistics/index.shtml.

10. http://www.nimh.nih.gov/statistics/1MDD_ADULT.shtml.

11. http://www.nimh.nih.gov/statistics/1DD_ADULT.shtml.

12. This study included people of all ages, and final relationships were calculated after controlling for age, gender, median income, children, and education, which were the only relevant (and statistically related) variables. Statistically controlling for these variables is a way of eliminating possible alternative explanations for results. For example, if girls are known to be more depressed than boys then controlling for gender essentially equalizes that issue and leaves you with room to find other explanations for your results.

13. The measure that was used in this study assessed both Axis I (clinical syndromes) and more serious Axis II personality disorders. This table presents the results for three Axis II diagnoses. The results for the depression Axis I scale were identical to these results and are not included in the table for simplicity.

14. Hancock, J. T., Gee, K., Ciaccio, K., & Mae-Hwah Lin, J. (November 8-12, 2008). I'm sad you're sad: Emotional contagion in CMC. Presentation at CSCW, San Diego, CA. Hancock used video clips from *Sophie's Choice* to provide the sad movie content and *Before Sunset* for the neutral movie. Music was manipulated by using a sad classical music piece (Alexander Nevsky, Opus 79) and a neutral classical piece (Brandenburg Concerto No. 3).

15. Primack, B. A., Swanier, B., Georgiopoulos, A. M., Land, S. R., & Fine, M. J. (2009). Association between media use in adolescence and depression in young adulthood: A longitudinal study. *Archives of General Psychiatry, 66(2),* 181-188.

16. See Chapter 9, which discusses body image issues for more on this form of iDisorder.

17. http://www.internetworldstats.com/facebook.htm.

18. http://www.asha.org/public/speech/development/pragmatics.htm; http://www.aligningaction.com/prgmodel.htm.

19. Goh, T. T., & Huang, Y. P. (2009). Monitoring youth depression in Web 2.0. *Vine: The Journal of Information and Knowledge Management Systems, 39(3),* 192-202.

20. Davila, J., Hershenberg, R., Feinstein, B. A., Gorman, K., Bhatia, V., & Starr, L. R. (2011). Frequency and quality of social networking: Associations with depressive symptoms, rumination, and co-rumination. Unpublished manuscript; Davila, J., Hershenberg, R., Feinstein, B., Starr, L. R., & Gorman, K. (November, 2010). Is use of social networking tools associated with depressive symptoms among youth? Paper presented at the 44th annual meeting of the Association for Behavioral and Cognitive Therapies, San Francisco, CA.

21. http://news.cnet.com/8301-19518_3-20048148-238.html.

22. Moreno, M. A., Jelenchick, L. A., Egan, K. G., Cox, E., Young, H., Gannon, K. E., & Becker, T. (2011). Feeling bad on Facebook: Depression disclosures by college students on a social networking site. *Depression and Anxiety, 28(6),* 447-455.

23. Valkenburg, P. M., Peter, J., & Schouten, A. P. (2006). Friend networking sites and their relationship to adolescents' well-being and social self-esteem. *Cyberpsychology & Behavior, 9,* 584-590.

24. Holleran, S. E. (2010). The Early Detection of Depression for Social Networking Sites. *Dissertation Abstracts International: Section B: The Sciences and Engineering, 71(5-B),* 3401.

25. http://www.huffingtonpost.com/larry-magid/facebook-depression-nonexistent_b_842733.html.

26. Primack, B. A., Swanier, B., Georgiopoulos, A. M., Land, S. R., & Fine, M. J. (2009). Association between media use in adolescence and depression in young adulthood: A longitudinal study. *Archives of General Psychiatry, 66(2),* 181-188.

27. Hyper-testing and hyper-networking pose new health risks for teens. (November 9, 2010). *Case Western News Release.* Retrieved from http://case.edu/medicus/breaking-news/scottfrankhypertextingandteenrisks.html.

28. Chen, S. Y., & Tzeng, J. Y. (2010). College female and male heavy Internet users' profiles of practices and their academic grades and psychosocial adjustment. *Cyberpsychology, Behavior, and Social Networking, 13(3),* 257-262.

29. Van der Aa, N., Overbeck, G., Engels, R. C. M. E., Scholte, R. H. J., Meerkerk, G. J., & Van den Eijnden, R. J. J. M. (2009). Daily and compulsive Internet use and well-being in adolescence: A diathesis-stress model based on Big Five Personality traits. *Journal of Youth Adolescence, 38,* 765-776; Selfhout, M. H. W., Branje, S. J. T., Delsing, M., ter Bogt, T. F. M., & Meeus, W. H. J. (2009). Different types of Internet use, depression, and social anxiety: The role of perceived friendship quality. *Journal of Adolescence, 32,* 819-833; Van den Eijnden, R. J. J. M., Meerkerk, G. J., Vermulst, A. A., Spijkerman, R., & Engels, R. C. M. E. (2008). Online communication, compulsive Internet use, and psychological well-being among adolescents. *Developmental Psychology, 44(3),* 655-665.

30. Huang, C. (2010). Internet use and psychological well-being: A meta-analysis. *Cyberpsychology, Behavior and Social Networks, 13(3),* 241-249; Subrahmanyam, K., & Smahel, D. (2011). *Digital Youth: The Role of Media in Development.* New York: Springer [NOTE: See Chapter 7 of this excellent volume, entitled "Internet Use and Well-Being: Physical and Psychological Effects]; Morrison, C. M., & Gore, H. (2010). The relationship between excessive Internet use and depression: A questionnaire-based study of 1,319 young people and adults. *Psychopathology, 43,* 121-126.

31. Starcevic, V., Berle, D., Porter, G., & French, P. (2010). Problem video game use and dimensions of psychopathology. *International Journal of Mental Health and Addiction, 8(2),* 248-256; Gentile, D. A., Choo, H., Liau, A., Sim, T., Li, D., Fung, D., & Khoo, A. (2011). Pathological video game use among youths: A two-year longitudinal study. *Pediatrics.* Retrieved from http://pediatrics.aappublications.org/content/127/2/e319.full.pdf+html.

32. http://www.thefreemanonline.org/featured/the-wild-west-meets-cyberspace; http://www.techdirt.com/articles/20110527/13281714462/can-we-kill-off-this-myth-that-internet-is-wild-west-that-needs-to-be-tamed.shtml; http://www.howtogeek.com/62135/geek-rants-why-the-internet-is-like-the-wild-west.

33. Santesso, D. L., Steele, K. T., Bogdan, R., Holmes, A. J., Deveney, C. M., Meites, T. M., & Pizzagalli, D. A. (2011). Enhanced negative feedback responses in remitted depression. *Neuroreport, 19(10),* 1045-1048.

34. Mathews, A., & MacLeod, C. (2005). Cognitive vulnerability to emotional disorders. *Annual Review of Clinical Psychology, 1,* 167-195.

35. http://www.cignabehavioral.com/web/basicsite/provider/treatingBehavioralConditions/PHQ9XscoringAndActionsv2.pdf.

36. The Goldberg Bipolar Screening Quiz can be found at http://psychcentral.com/quizzes/bipolarquiz.htm.

37. The following two articles provide a good summary of the drug vs. therapy controversy for treating depression and bipolar disorder: Cuijpers, P., van Straten, A., Warmerdam, L., & Andersson, G. (2009). Psychotherapy versus the combination of psychotherapy and pharmacotherapy in the treatment of depression: A meta-analysis. *Depression and Anxiety, 26(3),* 279-288; Dubicka, B., Wilkinson, P., Kelvin, R. G., & Goodyer, I. M. (2010). Pharmacological treatment of depression and bipolar disorder in children and adolescents. *Advances in Psychiatric Treatment, 16,* 402-412.

38. Selfhout, M. H. W., Branje, S. J. T., Delsing, M., ter Bogt, T. F. M., & Meeus, W. H. J. (2009). Different types of Internet use, depression, and social anxiety: The role of perceived friendship quality. *Journal of Adolescence, 32,* 819-833.

39. Hampton, K. N., Goulet, L. S., Rainie, L., & Purcell, K. (2011). *Social Networking Sites and Our Lives.* Washington, D.C.: Pew Internet & American Life Project. Retrieved from http://pewinternet.org/~/media//Files/Reports/2011/PIP%20-%20Social%20networking%20sites%20and%20our%20lives.pdf.

40. Spradlin, A., Bunce, J. P., Carrier, L. M., & Rosen, L. D. (2012). Virtual friendships: A study of digital media usage and empathy.

41. I describe co-viewing extensively as part of my TALK Model of Parenting in *Me, MySpace, and I: Parenting the Net Generation* (2007, Palgrave Macmillan). More details can be found in Chapter 10 of that book.

42. Hammons, A. J., & Fiese, B. H. (2011). Is frequency of shared family meals related to the nutritional health of children and adolescents? *Pediatrics, 127(6),* 1565-1574. Retrieved from http://pediatrics.aappublications.org/content/early/2011/04/27/peds.2010-1440; Neumark-Sztainer, D., Larson, N. I., Fulkerson, J. A., Eisenberg, M. E., & Story, M. (2010). Family meals and adolescents: What have we learned from Project EAT (Eating Among Teens)? *Public Health Nutrition, 13,* 1113-1121.

43. More on tech breaks can be found in a post that I wrote for *Psychology Today:* http://www.psychologytoday.com/blog/rewired-the-psychology-technology/201105/the-amazing-power-tech-breaks.

44. Lieverse, R., Van Someren, E. J. W., Marjan, N., Uitdehaag, B. M. J., Smit, J. H., & Hoogendijk, W. J. G. (2011). Bright light treatment in elderly patients with nonseasonal major depressive disorder: A randomized placebo-controlled trial. *Archives of General Psychiatry, 68,* 61-70. Retrieved from http://www.medscape.com/viewarticle/736105.

45. Even, C., Schroder, C. M., Friedman, S., & Rouillon, F. (2008). Efficacy of light therapy in nonseasonal depression: A systematic review. *Journal of Affective Disorders, 108(1-2),* 11-23. Retrieved from http://www.medscape.com/viewarticle/491504.

CHAPTER 6

1. Quote from Iowa State University Associate Professor of Psychology Douglas Gentile as told to *Science Daily.* (July 7, 2011). TV viewing, video game play contribute to kids' attention problems, study finds. *ScienceDaily.* Retrieved from http://www.sciencedaily.com/releases/2010/07/100706161759.htm. Gentile's research appears in Swing, E. L., Gentile, D. A., Anderson, C. A., & Walsh, D. A. (2010). Television and video game exposure and the development of attention problems. *Pediatrics, 126(2),* 214-221.

2. Retrieved from http://www.cdc.gov/nchs/fastats/adhd.htm.

3. *USA Today.* Retrieved from http://www.usatoday.com/news/health/2005-09-14-adhd-drugs-usage_x.htm.

4. Anxiety Disorders of America. (2011). Retrieved from http://www.adaa.org/understanding-anxiety/related-illnesses/other-related-conditions/adult-adhd.

5. Pal, S. (May 23, 2011). Reports of ADHD, autism on the rise. *MedPage Today.*

6. Report retrieved from http://www.webmd.com/add-adhd/news/20110818/adhd-in-children-is-on-the-rise?src=RSS_PUBLIC.

7. Christakis, D. A. (2009). The effects of infant media usage: What do we know and what should we learn? *ACTA Pediatrica, 98,* 8-16.

8. For more information about how multitasking is being blamed for the prevalence and rise of ADHD, take a look at the following articles from health websites:

   • http://health.msn.com/health-topics/adhd/
     multitasking-for-a-hyperactive-mind?wa=wsignin1.0
   • http://www.health.com/health/condition-article/0,20255244,00.html
   • http://www.webmd.com/mental-health/features/why-multitasking-isnt-efficient
   • http://www.emedicinehealth.com/script/main/art.asp?articlekey=115399
   • http://www.healthcentral.com/adhd/news-296432-98.html
   • http://www.psychologytoday.com/blog/
     rewired-the-psychology-technology/201102/multitasking-madness

9. Retrieved from http://www.dailymail.co.uk/news/article-1347989/Girl-falls-mall-fountain-texting-Why-walk-text.html.

10. Levine, L. E., Waite, B. M., & Bowman, L. L. (2007). Electronic media use, reading, and academic distractibility in college youth. *CyberPsychology & Behavior, 10(4),* 560-566.

11. See, for example, Wecker, C., Kohnlet, C., & Fischer, F. (2007). Computer literacy and inquiry learning: When geeks learn less. *Journal of Computer Assisted Learning, 23,* 133-144.

12. Carrier, L. M., Cheever, N. A., Rosen, L. D., Benitez, S., & Chang, J. (2009). Multitasking across generations: Multitasking choices and difficulty ratings in three generations of Americans. *Computers in Human Behavior, 25,* 483-489.

13. Nielsen Company (2011). *State of the media 2010. U.S. audiences & devices.* Retrieved from http://blog.nielsen.com/nielsenwire/wpcontent/uploads/2011/01/nielsen-media-fact sheet-jan-11.pdf.

14. Cherry, E. C. (1953). Some experiments on the recognition of speech, with one and with two ears. *The Journal of the Acoustical Society of America, 25(5),* 975-979.

15. Ophir, E., Nass, C., & Wagner, A. D. (2009). Cognitive control in media multitaskers. *Proceedings from the National Academy of Sciences.* Retrieved from http://www.pnas.org/content/early/2009/08/21/0903620106.full.pdf+html.

16. Ibid., p. 15585.

17. Gonzalez, V. M., & Mark, G. (2004). Constant, constant, multitasking craziness: Managing multiple working spheres. *Proceedings of CHI '04,* pp. 113-120.

18. Benbunan-Fich, R., & Truman, G. E. (2009). Multitasking with laptops during meetings. *Communications of the ACM, 52,* 139-141.

19. Judd, T., & Kennedy, G. (2011). Measurement and evidence of computer-based task switching and multitasking by "Net Generation" students. *Computers & Education, 56,* 625-631.

20. Jackson, T., Dawson, R., & Wilson, D. (2003). Reducing the effect of email interruption on employees. *International Journal of Information Management, 23,* 55-65.

21. Parnin, C., & Rugaber, S. (2009). Resumption strategies for interrupted programming tasks. *Software Quality Journal, 19,* 5-34.

22. Mark, G., Gudith, D., & Klocke, U. (2008). The cost of interrupted work: More speed and stress. In *Computer-Human Interactions (CHI),* Florence, Italy: ACM, 107-110.

23. U.S. Department of Transportation. (2011). *Statistics and facts about distracted driving.* Retrieved from http://www.distraction.gov/stats-and-facts/.

24. BBC News. (2008). L.A. rail driver was texting. *BBC News.* Retrieved from http://news.bbc.co.uk/2/hi/americas/7647567.stm.

25. Galvin, A. (January 27, 2010). Man convicted in texting-while-driving death. *Orange County Register.* Retrieved from http://articles.ocregister.com/2010-01-27/crime /24635615_1_texting-while-driving-text-messages-cell-phone.

26. Pines, M. (March 2, 2011). *Top 10 Worst Cell Phone-Related Injury Accidents of All Time: Prison Edition.* Retrieved from http://seriousaccidents.com/blog/accident-prevention/ten-worst-cell-phone-related-injuries-deaths/.

27. U.S. Department of Transportation. (2011). *Statistics and facts about distracted driving.* Retrieved from http://www.distraction.gov/stats and-facts/.

28. *Science Daily.* (2011, July 7). TV viewing, video game play contribute to kids' attention problems, study finds. *ScienceDaily.* Retrieved from http://www.sciencedaily.com/releases/2010/07/100706161759.htm.

29. Schmidt, S., & Petermann, F. (2009). Developmental psychopathology: Attention Deficit Hyperactivity Disorder (ADHD). *BMC Psychiatry, 9*(58), 1-10. Retrieved from http://www.biomedcentral.com/1471-244X/9/58.

30. Sanders, L. (May 3, 2011). Blame brain cells for lack of focus Scientists discover a neuronal network that may affect attention abilities. *ScienceNews.* Retrieved from http://www.sciencenews.org/view/generic/id/73838.

31. Hamzelou, J. (May 6, 2011). *Easily distracted people may have too much brain.* Retrieved from www.newscientist.com.

32. Georgetown University Press Release. (December 29, 2010). *Neuroscientists' Study Shows Kids are Naturally Egocentric.* Retrieved from http://www.georgetown.edu/story/1242667151985.html.

33. Klass, P. (May 9, 2011). Fixated by screens, but seemingly nothing else. *New York Times.* Retrieved from http://www.nytimes.com/2011/05/10/health/views/10klass.html.

34. Mozes, A. (May 29, 2011). Adults with ADHD lose 3 weeks' worth of work annually. *ABC News.* Retrieved from http://abcnews.go.com/Health/Healthday/story?id=49 43411&page=1

35. Anxiety Disorders of America. (2011). Retrieved from http://www.adaa.org/understanding-anxiety/related-illnesses/other-related-conditions/adult-adhd.

36. Benbunan-Fich, R., & Truman, G. E. (2009). Multitasking with laptops during meetings. *Communications of the Association for Computing Machinery, 52*(2), 139-141.

37. Ibid.

38. Mark, G., Gudith, D., & Klocke, U. (2008). The cost of interrupted work: More speed and stress. Proceedings of the twenty-sixth annual SIGCHI conference on Human factors in computing systems. New York, NY.

39. Rosen, L. D., Chang, J., Erwin, L., Carrier, L. M., & Cheever, N. A. (2009). The relationship between "texisms" and formal and informal writing among young adults. *Communication Research, 37*(3), 420-440.

40. Sisson, S. B., Broyles, S. T., Newton, R. L., Baker, B. L., & Chernausek, S. D. (2011). TVs in the bedrooms of children: Does it impact health and behavior? *Preventive Medicine, 52,* 104-108.

41. Barr-Anderson, D. J., van den Berg, P., Neumark-Sztainer, D., & Story, M. (2008). Characteristics associated with older adolescents who have a television in their bedrooms. *Pediatrics, 121(4),* 718-724.

42. Rosen, L. D., Cheever, N. A., & Carrier, L. M. (2008). The association of parenting style and child age with parental limit setting and adolescent MySpace behavior. *Journal of Applied Developmental Psychology, 29,* 459-471.

43. Carton, A. M., & Aiello, J. R. (2009). Control and Anticipation of Social Interruptions: Reduced Stress and Improved Task Performance. *Journal of Applied Social Psychology, 39(1),* 169-185.

CHAPTER 7

1. Burke, M., Kraut, R., & Williams, D. (2010). Social use of computer-mediated communication by adults on the autism spectrum. In *Proceedings of CHI 2010,* 1902-1912. Retrieved from http://citeseerx.ist.psu.edu/viewdoc/download?doi=10.1.1.155.1135&rep=rep1&type=pdf.

2. Weil, M. M., & Rosen, L. D. (1997). *TechnoStress: Coping with Technology @Work @Home @Play.* New York: John Wiley and Sons.

3. I discussed the penetration rate—the time it takes for a technology or website to reach 50 million people—in Rosen, L. D. (2010). *Rewired: Understanding the iGeneration and the Way They Learn.* New York: Palgrave Macmillan.

4. Moran, J. M., Young, L. L., Saxe, R., Lee, S. M., O'Young, D., Mavros, P. L., & Gabrieli, J. D. E. (2011). Impaired theory of mind for moral judgment in high_functioning autism. *Proceedings of the National Academy of Sciences, 108(7);* 2688-2692; Hood, B. M. (2010). Knowing me, knowing you: How social intuition goes awry in autism. *Scientific American Mind, 22(1),* 16-17.

5. Kapur, N. (2011). *The Paradoxical Brain.* Cambridge, UK: Cambridge University Press. NOTE: The chapter "The Paradoxical Self" by Ramachandran and Hirstein discusses these mirror neurons and their relationship to autism.

6. Baron-Cohen, S. (April 15, 2011). Lessons in empathy. *Financial Times.* Retrieved from http://www.ft.com/cms/s/2/6b3fd4c8-6570-11e0-b150-00144feab49a.html#axzz1SDHssTD3.

7. Konrath, S. H., O'Brien, E. H., & Hsing, C. (2011). Changes in dispositional empathy in American college students over time: A meta-analysis. *Personality and Social Psychology Review, 15(2),* 180-198.

8. Ibid., p. 188.

9. Kirsh, S. J., & Mounts, J. R. W. (2007). Violent video game play impacts facial emotion recognition. *Aggressive Behavior, 33,* 353-358.

10. Spradlin, A., Bunce, J. P., Carrier, L. M., & Rosen, L. D. (2012). Virtual friendships: A study of digital media usage and empathy.

11. In the same study we also examined the predictors of "real-world empathy," or that dispensed in person. Of course, the best predictor of this empathic responding was the amount of time spent with people face to face (rather than online). The only two technology-related variables that predicted real-world empathy were amount of hours playing video games alone and the amount of time sending and receiving e-mail daily. Both were negative predictors showing that the more time spent playing solo video games and the more time spent sending and receiving e-mail, the *less* real-world empathy.

12. This comic strip is from the July 5, 1993, issue of the *New Yorker* and has been posted on thousands of websites.

13. Brunet, P. M., & Schmidt, L. A. (2007). Is shyness context specific? Relation between shyness and online self-disclosure with and without a live webcam in young adults. *Journal of Research in Personality, 41(4),* 938-945.

14. Rubin, Z. (1975). Disclosing oneself to a stranger: Reciprocity and its limits. *Journal of Experimental Social Psychology, 11,* 233-260.

15. Joinson, A. N. (2001). Self-disclosure in computer-mediated communication: The role of self-awareness and visual anonymity. *European Journal of Social Psychology, 31,* 177-192.

16. Gonzales, A. L., & Hancock, J. T. (2008). Identity shift in computer-mediated environments. *Media Psychology, 11,* 167-185.

17. Orr, E. S., Sisic, M., Ross, C., Simmering, M. G., Arseneault, J. M., & Orr, R. R. (2009). The influence of shyness on the use of Facebook in an undergraduate sample. *CyberPsychology & Behavior, 12(3),* 337-340.

18. Ryan, T., & Xenos, S. (2011). Who uses Facebook? An investigation into the relationship between the Big Five, shyness, narcissism, loneliness, and Facebook usage. *Computers in Human Behavior, 27(5),* 1658-1664.

19. Blumer, T. (2010). Face-to-face or Facebook: Are shy people more outgoing on social networking sites? In *Media and Communication Studies Intersections and Interventions,* N. Carpertier et al. (Eds.). Ljubljana, Slovenia: ECREA and Fartu University Press. Reprinted by permission.

20. Baker, L. R., & Oswald, D. L. (2010). Shyness and online social networking services. *Journal of Social and Personal Relationships, 27(7),* 873-889.

21. Blumer, T. (2010). Face-to-face or Facebook: Are shy people more outgoing on social networking sites? In *Media and Communication Studies Intersections and Interventions,* N. Carpertier et al. (Eds.). Ljubljana, Slovenia: ECREA and Fartu University Press. Reprinted by permission.

22. Valkenburg, P. M., & Peter, J. (2007). Preadolescents' and adolescents' online communication and their closeness to friends. *Developmental Psychology, 43(2),* 267-277.

23. Valkenburg, P. M., & Peter, J. (2008). Adolescents' identity experiments on the Internet: Consequences for social competence and self-concept unity. *Communication Research, 35,* 208-231.

24. Barak, A., & Gluck-Ofri, O. (2007). Degree and reciprocity of self-disclosure in online forums. *CyberPsychology and Behavior, 10,* 407-417.

25. A complete description of the HomeNet Project can be found at: http://homenet.hcii. cs.cmu.edu/progress/index.html

26. Burke, M., Kraut, R., & Williams, D. (2010). Social use of computer-mediated communication by adults on the autism spectrum. In *Proceedings of CHI 2010,* 1902-1912. Retrieved from http://citeseerx.ist.psu.edu/viewdoc/download?doi=10.1.1.155.1135&rep=rcp1&type=pdf.

27. Kross, E., Berman, M. G., Mischel, W., Smith, E. E., & Wager, T. D. (2011). Social rejection shares somatosensory representations with physical pain. *Proceedings of the National Academy of Sciences, 108(15),* 6270-6275.

28. The long 25-item version of the Interpersonal Communication Test can be found at: http://testyourself.psychtests.com/testid/2151. The abridged ten-item version can be found at. http://cl1.psychtests.com/take_test.php?idRegTest=2967.

29. Berger, J. (2011). Arousal increases social transmission of information. *Psychological Science.* Retrieved from http://marketing.wharton.upenn.edu/documents/research/Arousal.pdf.

30. Khandaker, M. (2009). Designing affective video games to support the social-emotional development of teenagers with autism spectrum disorders. *Annual Review of Cybertherapy and Telemedicine, 7,* 37-39.

31. Hedman, E., Andersson, G., Ljotsson, B., Andersson, E., Ruck, C., Mortberg, E., & Lindfors, N. (2011). Internet-based cognitive behavior therapy vs. cognitive behavioral group therapy for social anxiety disorder: A randomized controlled non-inferiority trial. *PLoS One, 6(3),* e18001; Donoghue, K., Stallard, P., & Kucia, J. (2011). The clinical practice of cognitive behavioural therapy for children and young people with a diagnosis of Asperger's Syndrome. *Clinical Child Psychology and Psychiatry, 16(1),* 89-102; Wainer, A. L., & Ingersoll, B. R. (2011). The use of innovative computer technology for teaching social communication to individuals with autism spectrum disorders. *Research in Autism Spectrum Disorders, 5,* 96-107.

32. Trepagnier, C. Y., Olsen, D. E., Boteler, L., & Bell, C. A. (2011). Virtual conversation partner for adults with autism. *Cyberpsychology, Behavior, and Social Networking, 14(1-2),* 21-27.

33. Yee, N., & Bailenson, J. (2007). The Proteus Effect: The effect of transformed self-representation on behavior. *Human Communication Research, 33,* 271-290; Yee, N., Bailenson,

J. N., & Ducheneaut, N. (2009). The Proteus Effect: Implications of transformed digital self-representation on online and offline behavior. *Communication Research, 36(2),* 285-312.

CHAPTER 8

1. The Pew Internet and American Life project has estimated that 80 percent of adults have used online health websites. Studies from other countries have found similar results.
2. Fauman, M. A. (2002). *Study Guide to DSM-IV-TR.* Washington, D.C.: American Psychiatric Publishing.
3. Rief, W., Hiller, W., & Margraf, J. (1998). Cognitive aspects of hypochondriasis and the somatization syndrome. *Journal of Abnormal Psychology, 107(4),* 587-595.
4. Fauman, M. A. (2002). *Study Guide to DSM-IV-TR.* Washington, D.C.: American Psychiatric Publishing.
5. Walker, J. R., & Furer, P. (2008). Interoceptive exposure in the treatment of health anxiety and hypochondriasis. *Journal of Cognitive Psychotherapy: An International Quarterly, 22(4),* 366-378.
6. Bleichhardt, G., & Hiller, W. (2007). Hypochondriasis and health anxiety in the German population. *British Journal of Health Psychology, 12,* 511-523.
7. Walker, J. R., & Furer, P. (2008). Interoceptive exposure in the treatment of health anxiety and hypochondriasis. *Journal of Cognitive Psychotherapy: An International Quarterly, 22(4),* 366-378.
8. Rief, W., Hiller, W., & Margraf, J. (1998). Cognitive aspects of hypochondriasis and the somatization syndrome. *Journal of Abnormal Psychology, 107(4),* 587-595.
9. Fox, S. (August 2, 2011). Mind the Gap: Peer-to-peer healthcare. Pew Internet and American Life Project. Retrieved from http://pewinternet.org/topics/Health.aspx.
10. Retrieved April 18, 2011, from http://www.pewinternet.org/Commentary/2008/February/Health-InformationSeeking-on-a-Typical-Day.aspx.
11. Retrieved June 24, 2011, from http://www.drugs.com/news/still-trust-their-doctors-rather-than-internet-22990.html.
12. Ibid.
13. Retrieved April 18, 2011, from http://www.pewinternet.org/~/media//Files/Reports/2010/PIP-Better-off-households-final.pdf.
14. Van den Bulck, J. (2002). The impact of television fiction on public expectations of survival following in-hospital cardiopulmonary resuscitation by medical professionals. *European Journal of Emergency Medicine, 9(4),* 325-329.
15. A review of medical-related programming since the inception of television through the Academy of Television Arts and Sciences and other TV-related sources revealed that there were more of these programs in 2011 than ever before.
16. Retrieved June 26, 2011, from http://www.reuters.com/article/2010/10/19/us-doctors-influence-idUSTRE69I6DK20101019.
17. Cheever, N. A., Carrier, L. M., & Rosen, L. D. (2008). Wikipedia and weblogs: Assessing the credibility of unverified information on the Internet. Unpublished manuscript.
18. Carrier, L. M., Cheever, N. A., & Rosen, L. D. (2010). Preferences for expert versus peer reviews on the Internet. Unpublished manuscript.
19. Retrieved June 26, 2011, from http://www.ihealthbeat.org/articles/2011/5/3/webmd-more-popular-than-social-media-as-health-care-resource.aspx.
20. Li, D., Browne, G. J., & Chau, P. Y. K. (2006). An empirical investigation of website use using a commitment-based model. *Decision Sciences, 37(3),* 427-444.
21. Casalo, L. V., Flavia, N., & Guinali'u, M. (2007). The influence of satisfaction, perceived reputation and trust on a consumer's commitment to a website. *Journal of Marketing Communications, 13(1),* 1-17.
22. Ibid., p. 2.
23. Dutton, W. H., & Shepherd, A. (2006). Trust in the Internet as an experience technology. *Information, Communication & Society, 9(4),* 433-451.
24. Casalo, L. V., Flavia, N., & Guinali'u, M. (2007). The influence of satisfaction, perceived reputation and trust on a consumer's commitment to a website. *Journal of Marketing Communications, 13(1),* 1-17.

25. Dutton, W. H., & Shepherd, A. (2006). Trust in the Internet as an experience technology. *Information, Communication & Society, 9(4)*, 433-451.
26. Greer, J. D. (2003). Evaluating the credibility of online information: A test of source and advertising influence. *Mass Communication and Society, 6(1)*, 11-28.
27. Ibid., p. 13.
28. Choi, J. H., Watt, J. H., & Lynch, M. (2006). Perceptions of news credibility about the war in Iraq: Why war opponents perceived the internet as the most credible medium. *Journal of Computer-Mediated Communication, 12*, 209-229.
29. Tustin, N. (2010). The role of patient satisfaction in online health information seeking. *Journal of Health Communication, 15*, 3-17.
30. Feldman, M. D. (2000). Munchausen by Internet: Detecting factitious illness and crisis on the Internet. *Southern Medical Journal, 93(7)*, 669-672.
31. Body dysmorphic disorder is also a somatoform disorder that causes people to believe they have an overly exaggerated deficit in their appearance that is not recognized by others. See Chapter 9 for further information.
32. Taylor, S., Asmundson, G. J. G., & Coons, M. J. (2005). Current directions in the treatment of Hypochondriasis. *Journal of Cognitive Psychotherapy: An International Quarterly, 19(3)*, 285-304.
33. Ibid., p. 287.
34. Ibid.
35. A self-administered version of the Whiteley Test is available from http://www.thehypochondriac.com/hypochondria_diagnostic_test.htm.
36. For more information on how to assess the credibility of websites, see Chapter 7 of Rosen, L. D., Carrier, L. M., & Cheever, N. A. (2010). *Rewired: Understanding the Net Generation and How they Learn*. New York: Palgrave Macmillan.
37. Rosen, L. D., Carrier, L. M., Cheever, N. A., Rab, S., Arikan, M., & Whaling, K. (unpublished manuscript). *iDisorder: The relationship between media use and signs and symptoms of psychiatric disorders*.

CHAPTER 9

1. http://www.livereal.com/psychology_arena/whats_the_problem/anorexia_quotes.htm.
2. Anderson, L. H. (2009). *Wintergirls*. New York: Viking Juvenile.
3. The Renfrew Center Foundation for Eating Disorders. (2011). *Eating Disorders 101 Guide: A summary of issues, statistics and resources*. Retrieved May 21, 2011 from www.renfrewcenter.com/uploads/resources/1067338472_1.doc.
4. Polivy, J., Herman, C. P., & Boivin, M. (2005). Eating Disorders. In *Psychopathology: Foundations for a Contemporary Understanding*, J. E. Maddux & B. A. Winstead (Eds.). pp. 127-154. Mahwah, NJ: Lawrence Erlbaum Associates.
5. Ibid.
6. Strasburger, V. C., Wilson, B. J., & Jordan, A. B. (2009). *Children, Adolescents, and the Media*. Thousand Oaks, CA: Sage Publications.
7. Fauman, M. A. (2002). *Study Guide to DSM-IV-TR*. Washington, D.C.: American Psychiatric Publishing.
8. Ibid., 320.
9. National Institute of Mental Health. Retrieved from http://www.nimh.nih.gov/science-news/2011/most-teens-with-eating-disorders-go-without-treatment.shtml.
10. The Renfrew Center Foundation for Eating Disorders. (2011). *Eating Disorders 101 Guide: A summary of issues, statistics and resources*. Retrieved May 21, 2011 from www.renfrewcenter.com/uploads/resources/1067338472_1.doc.
11. Striegel-Moore, R. et al. (2000). One year use and cost of inpatient and outpatient services among female and male patients with an eating disorder: Evidence from a national database of insurance claims. *International Journal of Eating disorders, 27*.
12. Strasburger, V. C., Wilson, B. J., & Jordan, A. B. (2009). *Children, Adolescents, and the Media*. Thousand Oaks, CA: Sage Publications.
13. Ibid.
14. Ibid.
15. Becker, A. E. (2004). Television, disordered eating, and young women in Fiji: Negotiating body image and identity during rapid social change. *Culture, Medicine, and Society, 28*, 533-559.

16. Polivy, J., Herman, C. P., & Boivin, M. (2005). Eating disorders. In *Psychopathology: Foundations for a Contemporary Understanding*, J. E. Maddux & B. A. Winstead (Eds.). 127-154. Mahwah, NJ: Lawrence Erlbaum Associates.

17. Neziroglu, F., Khemlani-Patel, S., & Veale, D. (2008). Social learning theory and cognitive behavioral models of body dysmorphic disorder. *Body Image, 5,* 28-38.

18. Ibid.

19. http://www.facebook.com/press/info.php?statistics.

20. Ibid.

21. Ibid.

22. Ibid.

23. Polivy, J., Herman, C. P., & Boivin, M. (2005). Eating Disorders. In *Psychopathology: Foundations for a Contemporary Understanding*, J. E. Maddux & B. A. Winstead (Eds.). pp. 127-154. Mahwah, NJ: Lawrence Erlbaum Associates.

24. Abrams, D., & Hogg, M. A. (1999). *Social Identity and Social Cognition*. Malden, MA: Blackwell.

25. Berry, G. (2003). Developing children and multicultural attitudes: The systemic psychosocial influences of television portrayals in a multimedia society. *Cultural Diversity and Ethnic Minority Psychology, 9,* 360-366.

26. Neziroglu, F., Khemlani-Patel, S., & Veale, D. (2008). Social learning theory and cognitive behavioral models of body dysmorphic disorder. *Body Image, 5,* 28-38.

27. Berry, G. (2003). Developing children and multicultural attitudes: The systemic psychosocial influences of television portrayals in a multimedia society. *Cultural Diversity and Ethnic Minority Psychology, 9,* 360-366.

28. Marsh, R., Steinglass, J. E., Gerber, A. J., Graziano O'Leary, K., Wang, Z., Murphy, D., Walsh, B. T., & Peterson, B. S. (2009). Deficient activity in the neural systems that mediate self-regulatory control in Bulimia Nervosa. *Archives of General Psychiatry, 66*(1), 51-63.

29. Ibid.

30. Rosen, L. D. (2007). *Me, MySpace, and I: Parenting the Net Generation*. New York: Palgrave Macmillan. NOTE: I talk about co-viewing as part of my TALK Model for Parenting as a critical way of assessing what media your children are consuming.

31. Ibid.

32. Strasburger, V. C., Jordan, A. B., & Donnerstein, E. (2010). Health effects of media on children and adolescents. *Pediatrics, 125(4),* 756-767; Martins, N., Williams, D. C., Ratan, R. A., & Harrison, K. (2010). Virtual muscularity: A content analysis of male video game characters. *Body Image, 8(1),* 43-51.

33. Overbake, G. (2008). Pro-anorexia websites: Content, impact, and explanations of popularity. *Mind Matters: The Wesleyan Journal of Psychology, 3,* 49-62.

34. Retrieved from http://www.eating-disorder.com/treatments.php.

CHAPTER 10

1. Fauman, M. A. (2002). *Study Guide to DSM-IV-TR*. Washington, D.C.: American Psychiatric Publishing.

2. Ibid.

3. Ibid.

4. Bureau of Labor Studies. (2009). *Percent of employed persons who worked at home on an average workday*. Retrieved from http://www.bls.gov/tus/charts/chart12.pdf.

5. Amichai-Hamburger, Y., & Hayat, Z. (2011). The impact of the Internet on the social lives of users: A representative sample from 13 countries. *Computers in Human Behavior, 27,* 585-589.

6. Rosen, L. D., Carrier, L. M., Cheever, N. A., Rab, S., Arikan, M., & Whaling, K. (unpublished manuscript). *iDisorder: The relationship between media use and signs and symptoms of psychiatric disorders*.

7. Clark, K. R. (1996). The nowhere (wo)man: An example of the defensive use of emptiness in a patient with schizoid disorder of the self. *Clinical Social Work Journal, 24*(2), 153-166.

8. George Marsh Applied Cognition Laboratory, California State University, Dominguez Hills

9. Smith, A. (2006). Cognitive empathy and emotional empathy in human behavior and evolution. *The Psychological Record, 56,* 3-21.

10. Spradlin, A., Bunce, J., Rosen, L. D., Carrier, L. M., & Cheever, N. A. (2012). Virtual friendships: A study of digital media usage and empathy.

11. Fauman, M. A. (2002). *Study Guide to DSM-IV-TR.* Washington, D.C.: American Psychiatric Publishing.

12. Associated Press. (2011). *Police: Bad GPS directions led to Pa. crash.* Retrieved from http://abclocal.go.com/wpvi/story?section=news/local&id=8096736.

13. Zaremba, L. (May 10, 2011). GPS mishap results in wrong turn, crushed car. *The Review.* Retrieved June 15, 2011, from http://www.udreview.com/news/gps-mishap-results-in-wrong-turn-crushed-car-1.2225653.

14. Associated Press. (2011, June 15). *GPS blamed for wrong turn into Bellevue Slough.* Retrieved June 15, 2011 from http://seattletimes.nwsource.com/html/local news/2015325631_apwawrongturn.html.

15. Irvine, T. (July 2007). Cell phone phantom vibration. *Vibrationdata,* 8-12.

16. Bezuidenhout, C., & Collins, C. R. (2007). Implications of delusional disorders and criminal behavior. *Acta Criminologica, 20(3),* 87-99.

17. Ibid.

18. Duffy, J. (2011). Celebrity stalker cases. *The Boston Globe.* Retrieved June 15, 2011, from http://www.boston.com/ae/celebrity/gallery/celeb_stalkers?pg=19.

19. In our research on online dating, we found women tend to respond to men who use positive attributes to describe themselves and who portray a positive attitude. Rosen, L., Cheever, N., Felt, J., & Cummings, C. (2008). The impact of emotionality and self-disclosure on online dating versus traditional dating. *Computers in Human Behavior, 24(5),* 2124-2157.

20. Fauman, M. A. (2002). *Study Guide to DSM-IV-TR.* Washington, D.C.: American Psychiatric Publishing.

21. Muise, A., Christofides, E., & Desmarais, S. (2009). More information than you ever wanted: Does Facebook bring out the green-eyed monster of jealousy? *CyberPsychology & Behavior, 12(4),* 441-444.

22. Persch, J. A. (January 25, 2009). Jealous much? MySpace, Facebook can spark it. *MSNBC Online.* www.msnbc.msn.com=id=20431006=.

23. Sky News HD. (2009). *Facebook secrets led to woman's murder.* Retrieved June 18, 2011, from http://news.sky.com/skynews/Home/UK-News/Facebook-Murder-Brian-Lewis-Denies-Strangling-Girlfriend-Hayley-Jones-Over-Her-Online-activity/Article/200909115372746?lpos=UK_News_First_Home_Article_Teaser_Region_4&lid=ARTICLE_15372746_Facebook_Murder%3A_Brian_Le.

24. BBC News Online. (March 9, 2010). *Jealous lover jailed over London Facebook photo murder.* Retrieved June 18, 2011, from http://news.bbc.co.uk/2/hi/8557402.stm.

25. Rosen, L. D., Carrier, L. M., Cheever, N. A., Rab, S., Arikan, M., & Whaling, K. (unpublished manuscript). *iDisorder: The relationship between media use and signs and symptoms of psychiatric disorders.*

26. Generation Xers are not included in this; Only the iGeneration and NetGenerations showed these differences.

27. Mayo Clinic. (2011). *Signs and symptoms of schizoaffective disorder.* Retrieved April 3, 2011, from http://www.mayoclinic.com/health/schizoaffective-disorder/DS00866.

28. Compton, M. T., McGlashan, T. H., & McGorry, P. D. (2007, May). Prevention approaches for schizophrenia: An overview of prodromal states, the duration of untreated psychosis and early intervention paradigms. *Psychiatric Annals, 37(5),* 340-348.

29. Yung, A. R., Yuen, H. P., McGorry, P. D., Phillips, L. J., Kelly, D., Dell'Olio, M., Francey, S. M., Cosgrove, E. M., Killackey, E., Stanford, C., Godfrey, K., & Buckby, J. (2005). Mapping the onset of psychosis: The comprehensive assessment of at-risk mental states. *Australian and New Zealand Journal of Psychiatry, 39,* 964-971.

30. Olsen, K. A., & Rosenbaum, B. (2006). Prospective investigations of the prodromal state of schizophrenia: Assessment instruments. *Acta Psychiatrica Scandinavia, 113,* 273-282.

31. Yung, A. R., Yuen, H. P., McGorry, P. D., Phillips, L. J., Kelly, D., Dell'Olio, M., Francey, S. M., Cosgrove, E. M., Killackey, E., Stanford, C., Godfrey, K., & Buckby, J. (2005). Mapping the onset of psychosis: The comprehensive assessment of at-risk mental states. *Australian and New Zealand Journal of Psychiatry, 39,* 964-971.

32. The evolution of prodromal research has resulted in a small number of assessment tools that can identify symptoms associated with both early and later prodromal stages of schizophrenia; these include two basic approaches: the Attenuated Positive Symp-

toms (APS) approach, and the Basic Symptoms (BS) approach. These assessment instruments—developed in the mid-1990s—are helpful in identifying individuals who are at risk for developing psychosis in clinical populations. However, measurements of reliability are limited and the negative symptoms "and other symptoms not directly related to full-blown psychosis are underestimated in the most commonly used instruments" (Olsen, K. A., & Rosenbaum, B. [2006]. Prospective investigations of the prodromal state of schizophrenia: Assessment instruments. *Acta Psychiatrica Scandinavia, 113,* 273). Instruments that measure the intensity of a psychotic experience include the Brief Psychiatric Rating Scale (BPRS), the Comprehensive Assessment of Symptoms and History (CASH), and psychotic subscales that measure suspiciousness, hallucinations, unusual thought content, and conceptual disorganization. Researchers out of the University of Melbourne developed the Comprehensive Assessment of At-Risk Mental States (CAARMS) instrument to determine whether certain people meet the criteria for being at high risk for the onset of a psychotic disorder. The CAARMS measures the duration, frequency, and intensity of the episodes.

CHAPTER 11

1. John O'Neill, director of addiction services at the Menninger Clinic in Houston, in Wetzstein, C. (August 18, 2009). Expert: Technology fosters voyeurism. *The Washington Times.* Retrieved from http://www.washingtontimes.com/news/2009/aug/18/therise-of-a-paraphilia/?page=1.
2. Leveille, D. (April 7, 2011). *What is social voyeurism? Quora: A continually improving collection of questions and answers created, edited, and organized by everyone who uses it.* Retrieved from http://www.quora.com/What-is-social-voyeurism.
3. Lenhart, A. (2009). *Teens and Sexting: How and why minor teens are sending sexually suggestive nude or nearly nude images via text messaging.* Washington, D.C.: Pew Internet & American Life Project. Retrieved from http://www.pewinternet.org/Reports/2009/Teens-and-Sexting.aspx.
4. For example, two teenage boys in Arizona were arrested; one boy was the recipient of a nude photo of a 13-year-old girl, the other boy, having received the photo from the original recipient, shared it with others. Francis, C. (September 10, 2009). Two boys arrested on "sexting' charges. *KOLD News 13.* Retrieved from http://www.kold.com/story/10999418/two-boys-arrested-on-sexting-charges?redirected=true. In another example, six teens were arrested on child pornography charges in Greensburg, Pennsylvania, three of the teens being girls who sent nude photos of themselves. High schoolers accused of sending naked pictures to each other (January 13, 2009). *WPXI* (Pittsburgh). Retrieved from http://www.wpxi.com/news/18469160/detail.html.
5. Shafron-Perez, S. (2009). Average teenager or sex offender? Solutions to the legal dilemma caused by sexting. *The John Marshall Journal of Computer & Information Law, 26(3),* 431.
6. Slater, P. (1970). *The Pursuit of Loneliness: American Culture at the Breaking Point.* Boston: Beacon Press.
7. Herbert, W. A. (2010). Workplace consequences of electronic exhibitionism and voyeurism. 2010 IEEE International Symposium on Technology and Society.
8. Holmes, R. M., Tewksbury, R., & Holmes, S. T. (1998). Hidden JPGs: A functional alternative to voyeurism. *Journal of Popular Culture, 32(3),* 17-29.
9. American Psychiatric Association. (2000). *Diagnostic and Statistical Manual of Mental Disorders* (Revised 4th ed., text revision). Washington, DC. Although it is easy to feel disturbed by the variety of images that are available online, you shouldn't jump quickly to the conclusion that online voyeuristic content is altogether bad. Ronald Holmes and colleagues raised two alternatives with respect to the impact of online voyeuristic images. The first possibility—the harmful one—is that the availability of an online source of voyeuristic images increases the total exposure to this type of content. But another possibility is that, according to the researchers, " . . . these images serve the important societal function of providing users with a means for satisfying needs, desires, and appetites that, if not satisfied this way, would be pursued in less socially acceptable (and in this case more socially harmful) ways." Ybarra and Mitchell raised an analogous set of possibilities when they asked whether exposure to pornography online replaces offline exposure or increases the total exposure to pornography.

10. Långström, N., & Seto, M. C. (2006). Exhibitionistic and voyeuristic behavior in a Swedish national population survey. *Archives of Sexual Behavior, 35,* 427-435.

11. Marsh, P. J., Odlaug, B. L., Thomarios, N., Davis, A. A., Buchanan, S. N., Meyer, C. S., & Grant, J. E. (2010). Paraphilias in adult psychiatric inpatients. *Annals of Clinical Psychiatry, 22(2),* 129-134.

12. Ybarra, M. L., & Mitchell, K. J. (2005). Exposure to Internet pornography among children and adolescents: A national survey. *CyberPsychology & Behavior, 8(5),* 473-486.

13. Chung, M-Y., & Kim, H. S. (2009). It looks so cool to use podcast!: Exploring motivations, gratifications and attitudes toward using podcasts among college students. Paper presented at the Annual Conference of the International Communication Association.

14. Jung, Y., Vorderer, P., & Song. H. (2007). Motivation and consequences of blogging in social life. Paper presented at the Annual Conference of the International Communication Association.

15. Baruh, L. (2009). Publicized intimacies on reality television: An analysis of voyeuristic content and its contribution to the appeal of reality programming. *Journal of Broadcasting & Electronic Media, 53(2),* 190-210. Tables 11.1 and 11.2 used by permission.

16. Bagdasarov, Z., Greene, K., Banerjee, S. C., Krcmar, M., Yanovitzky, I., & Ruginyte, D. (2010). I am what I watch: Voyeurism, sensation seeking, and television viewing patterns. *Journal of Broadcasting & Electronic Media, 54(2),* 299-315.

17. Papacharissi, Z., & Mendelson, A. (2007). An exploratory study of reality appeal: Uses and gratifications of reality TV shows. *Journal of Broadcasting & Electronic Media, 51(2),* 355-370.

18. Baruh, L. (2009). Publicized intimacies on reality television: An analysis of voyeuristic content and its contribution to the appeal of reality programming. *Journal of Broadcasting & Electronic Media, 53(2),* 190-210.

19. Ybarra, M. L., & Mitchell, K. J. (2005). Exposure to Internet pornography among children and adolescents: A national survey. *CyberPsychology & Behavior, 8(5),* 473-486.

20. Rosen, L. R., Cheever, N. A., & Carrier, L. M. (2008). The impact of parental attachment style, limit setting and monitoring on teen MySpace behavior. *Journal of Applied Developmental Psychology, 29,* 459-471.

21. Sontag, S. (October 1, 2010). TV voyeurism '50s style. *Electronic Media, 20(40).*

22. Montemurro, B. (2007). Surveillance and power: The impact of new technologies on reality television audiences. Paper presented at the Annual Conference of the American Sociological Association.

23. Hughes, D. M. (2004). Prostitution online. *Journal of Trauma Practice, 2(3&4),* 115-131.

CHAPTER 12

1. Maynard, A. (August 15, 2011). *Is the Internet dangerous? Taking a closer look at Baroness Greenfield's concerns.* Risk Science Blog, University of Michigan Risk Science Center. Retrieved from http://umrscblogs.org/2011/08/15/is-the-internet-dangerous-taking-a-closer-look-at-baroness-greenfields-concerns/.

2. Baroness Susan Greenfield. (September 15, 2010.) Society should wake up to harmful effects of Internet. *The Telegraph.* Retrieved from http://www.telegraph.co.uk/technology/internet/8002921/Baroness-Susan-Greenfield-society-should-wake-up-to-harmful-effects-of-internet.html.

3. Chopra, D. (April 7, 2011). Mind, games, genes, neuroplasticity and enlightenment. *Huffington Post.* Retrieved from http://www.huffingtonpost.com/deepak-chopra/mind-brain-genes-and-neur_b_846198.html.

4. Blake, H. (May 4, 2010). Digital universe to smash "zettabyte" barrier for first time. *The Telegraph.* Retrieved from http://www.telegraph.co.uk/technology/news/7675214/Digital-universe-to-smash-zettabyte-barrier-for-first-time.html.

5. Sparrow, B., Liu, J., & Wegner, D. M. (2011). Google effects on memory: Cognitive consequences of having information at our fingertips. *Science, 333(6043),* 776-778.

6. If you would like to see the brain scan, it is from an article on the National Institute of Mental Health website and was retrieved from http://www.nimh.nih.gov/science-news/2009/impaired-brain-activity-underlies-impulsive-behaviors-in-women-with-bulimia.shtml. The original journal article: Marsh, R., Steinglass, J. E., Gerber, A. J., Graziano O'Leary, K., Wang, Z., Murphy, D., Walsh, B. T., & Peterson, B. S. (2009). Deficient activ-

ity in the neural systems that mediate self-regulatory control in bulimia nervosa. *Archives of General Psychiatry, 66(1),* 51-63.

7.   Dong, G., Huang, J., & Du, X. (2011). Enhanced reward sensitivity and decreased loss sensitivity in Internet addicts: An fMRI study during a guessing task. *Journal of Psychiatric Research.* Published online July 16, 2011.

8.   Han, D. H., Bolo, N., Daniels, M. A., Arehella, L., Lyoo, I. K., & Renshaw, P. F. (2011). Brain activity and desire for Internet video game play. *Comprehensive Psychiatry, 52(1),* 88-95.

9.   Lahnakoski, J. (2010). Functional magnetic resonance imaging of human brain during rest and viewing movies. Unpublished master's thesis. Aalto University, Helsinki, Finland. Retrieved from http://lib.tkk.fi/Dipl/2010/urn100264.pdf.

10.   Frings, L., Mader, I., & Hull, M. (2010). Watching TV news as a memory task—Brain activation and age effects. *BMC Neuroscience, 11,* 1-7.

11.   Small, G. W., Moody, T. D., Siddarth, P., & Bookheimer, S. Y. (2009). Your brain on Google: Patterns of cerebral activation during Internet searching. *American Journal of Geriatric Psychology, 17(2),* 116-126.

12.   Hummer, T. A., Wang, Y., Kronenberger, W. G., Mosier, K. M., Kalnin, A. J., Dunn, D. W., & Mathews, V. P. (2010). Short-term violent video game play by adolescents alters prefrontal activity during cognitive inhibition. *Media Psychology, 13(2),* 136-154.

13.   Kaplan, S. (1995). The restorative benefits of nature: Toward an integrative framework. *Journal of Environmental Psychology, 15,* 169-182.

14.   Valtchanov, D., Barton, K. R., & Ellard, C. (2010). Restorative effects of virtual nature settings. *Cyberpsychology, Behavior, and Social Networking, 13(5),* 503-512.

15.   Berman, M. G., Jonides, J., & Kaplan, S. (2008). The cognitive benefits of interacting with nature. *Psychological Science, 19(2),* 1207-1212.

16.   Ishizu, T., & Zeki, S. (2011). Toward a brain-based theory of beauty. *PLoS ONE, 6(7),* 1-10.

17.   Ross, V. (June 28, 2011). Music makes a brain happy—and hungry for more music. *Discover.* Retrieved from http://discovermagazine.com/2011/may/05-music-makes-brain-happy-hungry.

18.   Salas, C., Minakata, K., & Kelemen, W. (2011). Walking before study enhances free recall but not judgment-of-learning magnitude. *Journal of Cognitive Psychology, 23(4),* 507-513.

19.   Nicholson, C. (July 2, 2011). Hot baths may cure loneliness. *Scientific American.* Retrieved from http://www.scientificamerican.com/podcast/episode.cfm?id=hot-baths-may-cure-loneliness-11-07-02.

20.   Wang, M., Gamo, N. J., Yang, Y., Jin, L. E., Want, X. J., Laubach, M., Mazer, J. A., Lee, D., & Arnsten, A. F. T. (2011). Neuronal basis of age-related working memory decline. *Nature, 476,* 210-213.

21.   Bekinschtein, T. A., Davis, M. H., Rodd, J. M., & Owen, A. M. (2011). Why clowns taste funny: The relationship between humor and semantic ambiguity. *Journal of Neuroscience, 31(26),* 9665-9671.

22.   Pulakkat, H. (August 14, 2011). *Physical exercise, social life and arts can keep your brain young.* Retrieved from http://articles.economictimes.indiatimes.com/2011-08-14/news/29884510_1_human-brain-mind-training-posit-science.

23.   Fields, R. D. (2011, August 20). Genius across cultures and the "Google Brain." *Scientific American Blogs.* Retrieved from http://blogs.scientificamerican.com/guest-blog/2011/08/20/genius-across-cultures-and-the-google-brain

24.   Cohen, E. (June 23, 2011). Does life online give you "popcorn brain"? *CNNHealth.* Retrieved from http://blogs.scientificamerican.com/guest-blog/2011/08/20/genius-across-cultures-and-the-google-brain/ http://www.cnn.com/2011/HEALTH/06/23/tech.popcorn.brain.ep/index.html.

25.   Sieberg, D. (2011). *The Digital Diet: The 4-Step Plan to Break Your Tech Addiction and Regain Balance in Your Life.* New York: Three Rivers Press.

26.   Nuttal, I. (2011). *How to remove distractions with information fasting.* Retrieved from http://www.blogussion.com/expansion/remove-distractions-information-fasting.

27.   Carrier, L. M., Cheever, N. A., Rosen, L. D., Benitez, S., & Chang, J. (2009). Multitasking across generations: Multitasking choices and difficulty ratings in three generations of Americans. *Computers in Human Behavior, 25,* 483-489.

28. Wijekumar, K., & Meidinger, P. (2005). Interrupted cognition in an undergraduate programming course. *Proceedings of the American Society for Information Science and Technology, 42(1).*

29. Rosen, L. D., Lim. A. F., Carrier, L. M., & Cheever, N. A. (2011). An empirical examination of the educational impact of text message–induced task switching in the classroom: Educational implications and strategies to enhance learning. *Psicologia Educativa.* Retrieved from http://www.copmadrid.org/webcopm/publicaciones/educativa/ed2011v17n2a4.pdf.

30. Dumontheir, I., Gilbert, S. J., Burgess, P. W., & Otten, L. J. (2010). Neural correlates of task and source switching: Similar or different? *Biological Psychology, 83,* 239-249.

31. Bucciol, A., Houser, D., & Piovesan, M. (2011). Temptation and productivity: A field experiment with children. *Journal of Economic Behavior & Organization, 78,* 126-136.

32. Bucciol, A., Houser, D., & Piovesan, M. (2011). *Temptation at Work.* Harvard Business School Working Paper 11-090. Harvard University.

33. More information on this process can be found in an article that I wrote for my *Psychology Today* blog at http://www.psychologytoday.com/blog/rewired-the-psychology-technology/201105/the-amazing-power-tech-breaks.

34. De Baene W., Kuhn, S., & Brass, M. (2011). Challenging a decade of brain research on task switching: Brain activation in the task-switching paradigm reflects adaptation rather than reconfiguration of task sets. *Human Brain Mapping.* Retrieved from http://www.ncbi.nlm.nih.gov/pubmed/21391280.

35. Goffman, E. (1959). *The Presentation of Self in Everyday Life.* New York: Doubleday.

36. Valenzuela, S., Park, N., & Kee, K. F. (2009). Is there social capital in a social network site? Facebook use and college students' life satisfaction, trust, and participation. *Journal of Computer-Mediated Communication, 14,* 875-901.

37. Donath, J., & boyd, d. (2004). Public displays of connection. *BT Technology Journal, 22(4),* 71-82.

38. Ellison, N. B., Steinfield, C., & Lampe, C. (2007). The benefits of Facebook "friends": Social capital and college students use of online social network sites. *Journal of Computer-Mediated Communication, 12,* 1143-1168.

39. Goncalves, B., Perra, N., & Vespignani, A. (2011). Validation of Dunbar's number in Twitter conversations. *PLoS ONE, 6(8).*

40. Wang, J., & Wang, H. (2011). The predictive effects of online communication on well-being among Chinese adolescents. *Psychology, 2(4),* 359 362; Valkenburg, P. M., & Peter, J. (2009). Social consequences of the Internet for adolescents: A decade of research. *Current Directions in Psychological Science, 18,* 1-5.

41. Ling, R., & McEwen, R. (2010) Mobile communication and ethics: Implications of everyday actions on social order. *Nordic Journal of Applied Ethics—Special Issue on Mobile/Ubiquitous Computing, 4(2).*

42. National Sleep Foundation. (2011). *2011 Sleep in America Poll.* Crofton, MD: National Sleep Foundation.

43. CTV News Staff. (August 25, 2011). *Sleep-deprived advised to turn off the technology.* Retrieved from http://www.ctv.ca/CTVNews/Health/20110307/american-sleep-habits-electronics-in-bed-110307/.

44. Ibid.

45. Ibid.

46. Goleman, D. (June 28, 2011). Retrain your stressed-out brain. *Psychology Today.* Retrieved from http://www.psychologytoday.com/blog/the-brain-and-emotional-intelligence/201106/retrain-your-stressed-out-brain.

47. Ibid.

48. One study asked elderly people to reminisce often about their twenties and thirties. In just a week they all had a stronger range of motion. This was from an online blog by Mark Flanagan entitled "Mindfulness and Stress" and was retrieved from http://blogs.plos.org/neuroanthropology/2011/08/06/mindfulness-and-stress/.

49. Brynie, F. (July 19, 2011). Does meditation change the brain? Can it slow aging? *Psychology Today* blogs. Retrieved from http://www.psychologytoday.com/blog/brain-sense/201107/does-meditation-change-the-brain-can-it-slow-aging; *ScienceDaily.* (2011, July 21). Mindfulness meditation training changes brain structure in eight weeks. Retrieved from http://www.sciencedaily.com/releases/2011/01/110121144007.htm.

50. Harris, D., & Brady, E. (July 28, 2011). *Re-wiring your brain for happiness: Research shows how meditation can physically change the brain.* Retrieved from http://abcnews.go.com/US/meditation-wiring-brain-happiness/story?id=14180253.

51. Visit the Positive Psychology Center at http://www.ppc.sas.upenn.edu.

52. CBSNews. (September 22, 2011). *Survey: Family meals have big benefits for kids.* Retrieved from http://www.cbsnews.com/stories/2010/09/22/earlyshow/living/parenting/main6890613.shtml; Eisenberg, M. E., Olson, R. E., Neumark-Szainer, D., Story, M., & Bearinger, L. H. (2004). Correlations between family meals and psychosocial well-being among adolescents. *Archives of Pediatric Adolescent Medicine, 158,* 792-796; Fulkerson, J. A., Pasch, K. E., Stigler, M. H., Farbakhsh, K., Perry, C. L., & Komro, K. A. (2010). Longitudinal associations between family dinner and adolescent perceptions of parent-child communication among racially diverse urban youth. *Journal of Family Psychology, 24(3),* 261-270; Davis, J. L. (2007). Family dinners are important: 10 reasons why, and 10 shortcuts to help get the family to the table. *WebMD.* Retrieved from http://children.webmd.com/guide/family-dinners-are-important?

Index